# Marketing in Manageable Bites

# Marketing in Manageable Bites
## for busy managers and
## overworked students

Mike Meldrum
and
Malcolm McDonald

First edition 1995
Reprinted 1998
Second edition 2000

Published by
MACMILLAN PRESS LTD
Houndmills, Basingstoke, Hampshire RG21 6XS
and London
Companies and representatives
throughout the world

ISBN 0–333–76443–9

A catalogue record for this book is available from the British Library.

10   9   8   7   6   5   4   3   2   1
09  08  07  06  05  04  03  02  01  00

Copy-edited and typeset by Povey–Edmondson
Tavistock and Rochdale, England

Printed in Great Britain by
Creative Print & Design (Wales) Ebbw Vale

# Contents

**Group D   Understanding Product Management**

**Group E   Understanding Positioning**

**Group F   Understanding Marketing
               Relationships**

**Group G   Understanding Marketing Planning
               and Control**

# List of Tables

# List of Figures

# Foreword

This book was produced to meet a clear need expressed by many people for a series of concise summaries or overviews of marketing principles, concepts, tools and techniques. It is not a textbook or reader which needs to be studied cover to cover, but a work of reference for those wishing to familiarise or refamiliarise themselves with the essence of a particular aspect of marketing.

Each piece is a stand-alone coverage of an important concept in marketing which presents the essential features of that concept in a straightforward manner. It assumes some previous exposure to marketing, either from practical experience of working in an organisation or from some past or present study. It does not, however, assume any expertise on the part of the reader.

The book is, therefore, a quick and efficient reference for busy practising managers who do not have the time to go through a whole book to find the concept they need. It can also be used as a revision text for those studying marketing in some form or another. It is an excellent accompaniment to short courses on marketing.

To review a particular area in marketing, the reader simply refers to that group and selects the concept or concepts in which they are most interested. As an example, anyone wishing to get to the heart of **pricing strategies** will be able to find it either by looking at the alphabetical checklist of concepts (pp. xii–xiii) or by referring to Group E, on Understanding Positioning.

The book has been made easier to write as a result of the help and advice given by our colleagues at Cranfield. In particular, we should like to pay tribute to Professor Martin Christopher, who provided the inspiration for a number of the ideas included in the book. Without his support, this book would not have been possible.

Our students at Cranfield School of Management and other practising managers have found this approach to understanding marketing invaluable and we are pleased to be able to share it with a much wider audience.

*Cranfield School of Management*　　　　MIKE MELDRUM
*2000*　　　　MALCOLM McDONALD

xi

# Checklist of Topics

**Section A**

# UNDERSTANDING THE BASICS OF MARKETING

# TOPIC 1

# Understanding Marketing

Good marketing has long been recognised as an important contributor to the long-term survival and success of organisations, be they commercial or non-profit-making. Indeed, any analysis of the more success-ful companies in the world usually confirms their continued use of sound marketing principles. In other organisations, it is also accepted that marketing is something that is often not done particularly well.

Organisations can survive without marketing. This will be because they have, for example, some natural advantage over competitors such as a patent or a monopoly, or they are operating under conditions of excess demand. In the long run, however, these advan-tages are rarely sustainable and continued success will require the management of a large number of other activities such as operating efficiency, financial matters and the effectiveness of its logistics. Many of these will have an impact on an organisation's relationship with its customers and this makes practical marketing difficult because it implies keeping a large number of 'balls in the air' at once. Underlying this, however, is a set of ideas, principles and concepts which are relatively simple to understand, but which (like most simple things) are quite deep in their meaning. Getting to grips with marketing is thus a two-stage process: first, the devel-opment of an understanding of these principles and second, the application of them to individual circum-stances.

*Organisations can survive without marketing, but seldom for long*

There are many definitions around which try to provide a clear insight into what marketing is all about. One of the best describes marketing as 'the way in which an organisation matches its human, financial and physi-cal resources with the wants and needs of its customers'. This is a bit of a mouthful and, on the surface, does not mention any of the things we usually associate with marketing, i.e., the high-profile activities such as

3

advertising, mail shots, give-aways and so on. This definition, however, does focus attention on the crucial elements which the whole organisation has to manage correctly – the mechanisms by which a relationship is developed between that organisation and its customers so that mutually beneficial exchanges will take place.

*The substance of marketing is a matching relationship*

At the heart of the relationship is what is offered by an organisation, which must match the wants and needs of its target customers. If one company offers a closer match, this will be to the disadvantage of their competitors. The process of creating this match, however, is quite complex. The substance of a matching relationship and the factors which will affect it are at the heart of any understanding of marketing.

The key question to which this approach leads is thus: 'What will make a potential customer want to enter into an exchange with our organisation as opposed to another?' In other words: 'Why will they buy our product, give to our charity or cooperate with our service, given that they have plenty of choice?'

The answer to this question is a long list of different factors, all of which will affect the possibility of achieving such an exchange. Some of these will be under the control of the supplying organisation, while others will be beyond their control but can still fundamentally affect their chances of completing the exchange. No matter how good our product is, interest rates, new laws, fashion, etc., can affect its attractiveness to customers. In order to make sense of these factors and to put them into an understandable form, they are usually classified as the marketing mix and the marketing environment. The marketing mix is the offering we control; the environment is the set of uncontrollable variables within which the marketing process takes place.

The marketing mix is usually classified as aspects of either product, price, promotion, or place – the four Ps. *Products* can be varied in terms of quality, size, functionality, range and so on. *Price* can be high or low, can involve a discount or can be affected by credit terms. *Promotion* can utilise television advertising, can concentrate on using sales people or can involve branding. *Place* includes the channels through which we choose to make a product available plus the service elements involved in delivering the offering, such as after-sales service or delivery lead times.

The importance of the marketing mix is that successful matching depends on customers being aware of the products or services on offer, finding them available and favourably judging the attractiveness of the offering in terms of both price and performance. If one of these is missing or wrong from the customer's point of view, a long-term relationship will be difficult to sustain. Effective marketing management welds these variables into a coordinated whole in the market place in exactly the right combination for the targeted customer.

*Effective marketing welds the four Ps into a coordinated whole*

The marketing environment is a similarly complex set of factors that can be considered under five distinct headings:

- *Social or cultural factors* These can include fashion, religious preferences, population trends and other developments such as more working women and an increasing awareness of green issues, all of which will affect people's perception of the appropriateness and value of a product or service.
- *Competition* Whatever an organisation is offering in the market place, there will be some form of substitute somewhere. This may be direct, such as a Ford Mondeo versus an equivalent Citroën, or it may be indirect such as a holiday versus a home extension. Organisations should never underestimate the power of different sources of competition.
- *Technological change* The pace of change in technology appears to be increasing at an ever-faster rate. It is therefore dangerous to assume that existing products will continue to be demanded by customers. There are many examples of organisations' products being significantly affected by advances in technology elsewhere, for example, slide rules, mechanical watches, copper pipes, vinyl records and fax machines. Technological developments will determine what is both possible and attractive in all markets.
- *Government activities* These include political, fiscal, environmental, economic and legal activities. All of them will affect what can be done in a particular market. Interest rates will affect the willingness to purchase on credit, deregulation will alter entry barriers to a market and the nature of competition, exhaust emissions requirements will affect the saleability of motor vehicles, and so on. Governments, even

if they do nothing, will still be a significant influence on an organisation's marketing environment.

- *Institutional changes*   All markets contain a number of institutions which have developed over the years and which impact on marketing activities. It is important to understand the effect of these institutions and to predict the consequences of any change. Important examples include the changes that have occurred in food distribution, from small local outlets to large out-of-town supermarkets, the role of the Standards Institutes, the influence of the press, the rise of consumer associations and the advances in telecommunications networks.

Both consciously and unconsciously, customers are constantly performing a matching exercise between their needs and wants, and the products and services they see in the market place. When the match is sufficiently good they will purchase. Both customers and suppliers are affected by the environment within which they operate. Marketing is therefore that part of an organisation's activities which seeks to create the best match with its targeted customers within the constraints and opportunities created by the environment, thereby developing a long-term relationship with them. The methodology for this is the manipulation and management of the marketing mix, and the monitoring and evaluation of the environment.

*Marketing operates at three levels: the philosophical, strategic and tactical*

To clarify what marketing is, however, it is necessary to understand that it operates at three levels.

The first is what might be termed the 'philosophical' level. If the people who control an organisation do not believe that in the long run it is by providing superior customer value that the long-term interests of all stakeholders are both served, marketing will never be anything other than a trivial functional department.

The second level is what is often called the 'strategic' level. Here, market analysis and understanding, market segmentation, product development, branding, positioning and pricing become major determinants of success, and are clearly essential ingredients in corporate strategy.

Finally, there is the 'tactical' or implementation level of marketing, of which more detailed issues relating to the offer and customer satisfaction are considered.

These points are explained in more detail in Topic 2.

# TOPIC 2

# A Market Orientation

Many organisations have experienced the introduction of a rallying cry from their senior management to the effect that '. . we will now become a marketing-led organisation . . '. In effect, what they really mean is that they wish to become a *market-driven* organisation, as marketing is generally perceived to be another function, alongside finance, personnel, etc. Turning this statement into reality requires more than just the pronouncement of the principle and the employment of a few people with marketing titles. It requires something much more difficult; the creation of a customer orientation throughout the whole organisation. It does not mean being literally 'led' by the marketing department, but rather that its operations should be guided and influenced by customer-driven principles.

*A market-driven organisation operates on customer-driven principles*

To gain a better understanding of the difference between marketing and a market orientation, it is sometimes helpful to think of marketing as occurring in three distinct forms. These can be characterised as: **marketing tasks**; **marketing management**; and in addition, **a market orientation**.

The first form, *marketing tasks*, will involve a number of specialised activities requiring a degree of experience and expertise to be performed well. Some of these will be tasks that are normally associated with successful marketing, such as designing brochures, selling, commissioning market research and brand management. Other tasks will often still affect marketing success, but will often be the responsibility of managers in other functional areas. These can include calculating volume discounts, stock control, after-sales service activities and product development. Each area will often be the responsibility of different parts of an organisation, but each will affect the nature of relationships with customers and therefore, the possibility of new and continued sales.

7

The second form, *marketing management*, is thus the management of these tasks. If there are a multitude of activities, each of which can affect an organisation's success in the market place, then it follows that a degree of management has to be applied to them. In the absence of any management, these tasks will be performed according to the beliefs and preferences of the individuals involved. It does not stretch the imagination to foresee the problems that this might cause. In Topic 1, we referred to this as the 'strategic' level of marketing.

The function of marketing management is to provide coordination by whatever mechanism is appropriate to an organisation. The job is to ensure a common direction; an agreement between the various activity centres on what the organisation is trying to achieve. The usual outcome of such management would be a set of policies or guidelines for the individuals engaged in performing the various tasks which affect the marketing mix. The overall outcome would be a better degree of organisational integration in relation to its markets.

Such management will occur at different levels within an organisation. It will range from the strategic positions adopted or defined by the leaders of any organisation, through the specific responsibilities of a marketing director, to the various operational activities of the managers and section heads of functional units. At whatever level this management occurs, however, it will still have the same purpose: coordinating and integrating activities to achieve a good match with customer requirements.

*A market orientation is reflected in organisational culture*

*A market orientation* is, then, the third form of marketing found within organisations. It is something which goes beyond marketing tasks and management and is the most intangible aspect of marketing. Orientations are to do with the values, attitudes and beliefs of the people working within an organisation. In this, they are an aspect of an organisation's culture. Orientations are very powerful influences since they will determine what are considered to be legitimate concerns in management action.

The phrase 'we are a market-driven organisation' should therefore be a reflection of the organisation's culture. It encompasses the way in which priorities are determined and what sort of questions managers and operatives feel they should be asking each other. It also includes the type of management information readily available, the ease with which budgets are obtained for various types of expenditure and the processes by which decisions are made.

The focus of a market orientation is, of course, the customer. More important, however, is a focus on an organisation's *relationships* with its customers. Since marketing is about matching resources with the wants and needs of customers, a market orientation exists when all personnel view activities in terms of their likely impact on relationships with customers. Important questions include:

• Why will these customers want to obtain this product from us?
• What impact will this action have on our customers?
• What is happening out there in our markets which will affect our activities?

A market orientation exists when people make sense of their business, justify actions and authorise spending by reference to customers.

Instilling a market orientation within an organisation is a difficult job. It is easy to accept that long-term survival depends on creating and keeping customers, whether they are paying customers or otherwise, but it is quite another matter to introduce this philosophy into managerial processes. This is because people are subject to a large number of influences and pressures in their work which will tend to counter the pursuit of marketing principles.

As an example, pressures will derive from people's professional backgrounds where problems are often tackled using different methodologies from those involved in marketing. As an art, rather than a science, marketing is sometimes difficult for people from engineering and scientific backgrounds since there are few constant input/output relationships. In addition, most people's work is performed away from the customer interface. When people go to work their direct concerns are with their jobs and their in-trays, not with matching customer needs.

*Marketing is an art rather than a science*

Other orientations which can exist side by side with marketing include: production, design, technology, financial, sales, and social orientations. These are not 'wrong' and are all needed at certain times to a greater or lesser extent. If, for example, a company has profitability problems, it will be important that a financial orientation should emerge as a priority to enable the short-term survival of the business. Alternatively, an organisation which relies on product innovation and development for its success in the market place should encourage a technology orientation within its ranks.

The problem with these various types of orientation is obtaining the right balance between them to match the environmental conditions within which the organisation operates. Successful organisations are good at matching, not only in terms of the four Ps, but also in terms of the ways in which they manage and set priorities for themselves. In good times, marketing tends to be forgotten and other priorities dominate. Marketing then becomes the way forward in bad times, but by that point is often perceived as a threat to the other traditional values already well-embedded in the organisation.

*A market orientation need not stem from a marketing department*

As with other disciplines, a market orientation needs to exist in an organisation. It does not have to stem from a marketing department. Indeed, many successful marketing organisations do not have a formal marketing department. It is therefore important that general management are aware of the need for, and are active in the promotion of, a marketing philosophy alongside the other orientations necessary for continued success.

# TOPIC 3

# The Marketing Mix

The marketing mix is the name given to the main *demand-influencing variables* that are available to an organisation. This is because, when a customer makes a purchase or engages in an exchange, what they are responding to is not just the product, but a whole range of variables which constitute the offer. The classic description of the marketing mix, although something of a simplification, is 'the four Ps'. The four Ps and the fundamental questions associated with them are:

*The marketing mix comprises the key demand-influencing variables*

- *Product*
  What type and range of product or service should we provide?
- *Price*
  What price should be set for each product or service?
- *Promotion*
  How do we best communicate with our target customers and persuade them to buy our offer?
- *Place*
  What channels of distribution and what levels of service are appropriate?

Each of these elements is capable of influencing demand either separately or together with the other marketing mix elements. When considering the marketing mix, it is important to look at some of the general principles underlying decisions about the actual mix that an organisation might choose to implement.

## Product (Including Service Products)

Although customers and their needs are the focal point of the marketing process, few organisations started with this in mind. Invariably somebody had a good idea for a product and this became the germ of the business idea.

11

**Table 3.1**  Product variables

| | |
|---|---|
| • Technical features | • Packaging |
| • Design | • Compatibility with |
| • Durability | existing equipment/ |
| • Robustness | services |
| • Innovativeness | • Degree of customisation |
| • Functional performance | • Flexibility |
| • Noise control | • Upgrading |
| • Range of sizes, colours, | • Quality |
| etc. | • Volumes available |
| • Ease of maintenance | • Safety |
| • Pollution hazard reduction | • Ease of use |

Not surprisingly, then, many enterprises see the product to be at the heart of their firm's marketing efforts. There may be nothing intrinsically wrong with this attitude as long as managers can see that their product does not have to remain as a fixed, unchanging entity: a sort of organisational straitjacket. Instead, the company must learn to see its output as flexible, being subject to development and adaptation, just like any other component of the marketing mix. Because the world is never static, an organisation should keep asking itself the question: 'Does each product we offer provide relevant and desired benefits for today's customers' needs?'

Some of these benefits can be provided by other elements of the marketing mix, such as availability, after-sales service, and value for money. Aspects of the product which can provide appropriate benefits are shown in Table 3.1.

### Price

*Pricing is both an art and a science*

Pricing is an area of marketing with a tremendous potential for increasing short-term profits, but unfortunately, if managed badly, can equally quickly bring a business to its knees. Pricing is both an art and a science. The options open to an organisation for using pricing as a flexible 'connector' which helps to match efforts to the needs of the customer, are many as shown in Table 3.2.

There is a fear amongst many managers that unless they offer the lowest possible price they will not win the order. Whilst this can be true for some businesses, it is

**Table 3.2** Pricing variables

| | |
|---|---|
| • Price point adopted | • Credit terms |
| • Discount structure | • Stage payments |
| • Discount amounts | • Residual value |
| • Special offers | • Leasing arrangements |
| • Sales (end of season, etc.) | • Financial deals |
| • Cost of ownership | • Psychological elements |

rarely the case with market leaders. Take the case of the really successful builder who has developed a reputation based on quality workmanship. The business continues to thrive and prosper, whilst many other builders without the same quality reputation have gone bankrupt through quoting low prices to get a job and then doing poor quality work to make it pay.

Also, take the example of a shopper who prefers to buy goods from a local shop rather than a supermarket or hypermarket where cheaper prices can be obtained. Why? Quite apart from the convenience factor, the shopper knows and values the personal service from a local shop, and is prepared to pay for this.

When a customer buys, he or she purchases a 'package' of benefits and the price ought to reflect the value of the *total package*. Clearly, price is an important element of the business transaction and, appropriately chosen, it can not only have a big impact on a company's marketing strategy in the long term, but can also help to differentiate the product or service from those of competitors.

*Price should reflect a 'package' of benefits*

## Promotion

The promotional element of the marketing mix is concerned with ways of communicating with customers and potential customers. In practice the promotional element of the marketing mix falls into two broad categories: personal promotion and impersonal promotion.

### Personal Promotion

This is the role of selling, which is usually accomplished through a sales force or sales assistants. Face-to-face selling has a number of advantages over impersonal methods:

- It is a two-way process which gives the prospective purchaser the opportunity to ask questions about the product.
- The sales message can be tailored to the needs of individual customers.
- The sales person can use in-depth knowledge about the product to identify new customer needs and overcome objections.
- The customer can be prompted to buy by being asked for an order.
- The sales person can negotiate on price, delivery or special requirements.
- Personal relationships with customers can be developed and thereby lay the foundations for longer-term business.

However, selling also involves a lot of 'dead' time such as preparing sales aids, telephoning for appointments, travelling, failing to win an order, administration and research. Therefore it is a costly business, and needs to be regularly monitored to ensure that it provides a good return for the cost and effort that goes into it.

## Impersonal Promotion

Typically, this area of promotion takes the form of advertising and sales promotion. Let us take advertising first. It is often felt that this is the province of only the very large organisations and that it is something best left to the 'experts'. In fact, advertising can be addressed by any competent manager, and can encompass: slots on television; billboards throughout the country; local radio; leaflets; brochures; stories in the papers and trade journals; cards on newspaper display boards; advertisements in the local paper, in the Yellow Pages and on local buses; plus gifts such as calendars and pens.

*Advertising should be regarded as an investment rather than a cost*

Thus, advertising can be appropriate for any organisation. To be managed well, however, it needs to be looked upon as an investment, rather than a cost, and like any other investment, it is only going to be any good if it achieves a return. To obtain this, it is important to address the following questions:

- At whom is it aimed? (target customers)
- What is it trying to achieve? (objectives)
- What should it say? (message)
- How should the message be communicated? (medium)
- How will the result be measured? (monitoring)

These questions can only be answered if an organisation has a good understanding of its customers and potential customers, what interests them, what motivates them to buy and how messages can reach them.

Although the various advertising media mentioned above vary in terms of their costs and potential for reaching customers, different combinations of message and media will provide a very flexible advertising repertoire that can be tailored to fit most budgets.

*Sales Promotions*

Sales promotions are essentially short-term campaigns to influence customers (perhaps a competitor's customers, or even intermediaries) to buy more of a product or to use it faster. Some companies use promotions to encourage their own sales force to sell more. Generally, promotions take the form of offering a **money** incentive, such as a price reduction or a coupon against the next purchase, **goods** such as two for the price of one, or **services** such as free estimates and holidays.

**Place**

If a market gardener started a business farming organically-grown vegetables, he or she would immediately be faced with several different routes for getting them to the consumer, some direct, some through intermediaries, as illustrated in Figure 3.1.

This example provides a good illustration of the 'place' element of the marketing mix and how this needs to be integrated with delivery, consignment 'packaging' and the service elements associated with delivery.

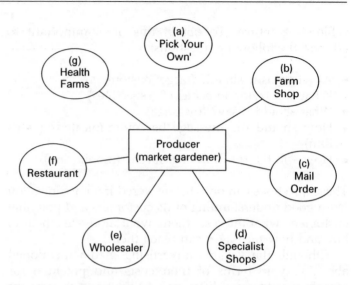

**Figure 3.1**    Channel possibilities for the produce of a market gardener

Clearly, the cheapest channel is option (a), where getting the consumer to come along to bear the harvesting costs while receiving no customer service, will save the farmer money. But suppose that does not appeal to people in the catchment area, or suppose the farm is in a sparsely populated area? A farm shop (b) would have the advantage of appealing to passing trade as well as to regular customers, but distribution costs are already escalating.

On analysis, each option offers commercial possibilities; equally, each one involves costs. Indeed, within any particular channel, there are areas for cost management. For example, with option (f), the farmer could deliver to the restaurants or could demand that the restaurants arrange collection. In the same way, the essential decision for any supplying organisation is to choose those distribution channels which provide a sizeable element of control at a reasonable cost. A supplier might also want to safeguard its interests by using more than one channel to reach different customer segments.

*The choice of channel can enhance differentiation*

The choice of channel can also help enterprises to differentiate their product. A classic UK example of this was when Avon Cosmetics took their products into the home of the consumer, while the competition continued to trade in department stores and chemists' shops.

When developing policies for the various elements of the marketing mix, it is important to be comprehensive, but also to identify those areas which are significant in the markets in which an organisation operates. Thus, some organisations use an expanded marketing mix for managerial and planning purposes. This can involve isolating sales plans, processes, people or customer service for special attention. Whatever the case, the key task of the marketing manager is to ensure that the mix presented to the market place is internally consistent and provides a set of benefits which target-customers will find preferable to the offerings of other organisations.

*The key task of the marketing manager is to ensure the marketing mix is internally consistent and offers superior customer value*

## TOPIC 4

# International Marketing

International marketing, at its simplest, is the performance of the marketing task across national boundaries. The basic approach, therefore, is no different from domestic marketing and the principles involved remain the same. Thus, a supplier organisation has to perform market research, identify a target market, develop appropriate products, adopt a pricing policy, promote sales and so on. In spite of this, whenever organisations begin to operate outside their domestic markets, many otherwise successful enterprises seem to suffer setbacks to their marketing efforts.

*The focus of international marketing is differences rather than similarities*

Observation of this phenomena has led both academics and practitioners to pay increasing attention to the subject of international marketing in an attempt to reduce the problems which seem to arise. When this is done, what emerges is the significance of the *differences* rather than the *similarities* involved when marketing abroad. Within this, it becomes important to recognise that:

- The environment in which international marketing takes place is significantly different in certain areas.
- There is a different dimension of complexity involved in planning the marketing function.
- The control it is possible to exercise over the marketing mix is reduced.

### Environment and Complexity

It is obvious that there are likely to be major differences in the way that customers behave between different countries. For many organisations, however, although these differences are acknowledged, they are not always investigated or consciously included in the planning processes. There are many examples of simple mistakes

18

**Table 4.1** Environment differences when marketing overseas

| | |
|---|---|
| • Language | • Business hours |
| • Tastes and fashions | • What is polite and impolite |
| • Religion | • Social priorities |
| • Physical environment | • Literacy levels |
| (temperature, humidity) | • Communications |
| • Power sources | infrastructure |
| • Security arrangements | • Distribution facilities |
| • Family structure and size | • Methods of transaction |

which have cost organisations millions of dollars through lost sales, and which have occurred as a result of a lack of rigour in investigating such differences. Some are amusing, such as Toyota's launch of the MR2 in France, not realising that, when spoken in French, the letters and numbers made a rude word. Others are just silly, such as the poor translations often found in technical instructions. Some of these areas of difference are shown in Table 4.1.

In addition, organisations seeking to market internationally also face political, legal and regulatory differences. Thus, they may find that they are required to use a local partner as a distributor or that prices are controlled by the government. There may also be different technical standards operating in the country and taxation may be applied in a completely different way. The economic situation is also likely to involve complications including: tariffs; quotas; exchange controls; non-tariff barriers; customs; unions; and so on. Together with such factors as volatility, an additional element of complexity and uncertainty is added to the marketing task.

## International Control

The degrees of freedom an organisation has when operating abroad, and the consequent control they can exert over their marketing activities, will be mostly determined by the method chosen for entering a foreign market. The two main forms can be described as simply exporting or alternatively, actually producing, abroad.

Straightforward *exporting* can be either indirect or direct. Indirect exporting is when a third party arranges the documentation, shipping and selling of an organisation's goods abroad, and this usually represents the lowest level of commitment to international marketing. As foreign sales grow, however, an organisation often begins to make a limited commitment, frequently in the form of taking on the documentation task for itself. It is usually at this stage that overseas agents or distributors are appointed to carry out the selling task abroad, with the result that the business is now a direct exporter, although it is likely that the commitment is still limited to marginal production capacity, with no additional fixed investment.

*The importance of overseas trading is acknowledged by having a marketing subsidiary abroad*

Recognition of the importance of overseas trading really happens when a limited fixed investment occurs, not just in the form of production capacity, but often also in the form of a marketing subsidiary abroad in recognition of the need for a more aggressive marketing approach.

*Foreign production* can take the form of licensing, contract manufacturing, local assembly or full manufacture, either by joint ventures or wholly-owned subsidiaries. With licensing, the company is hiring out its brand name, technical expertise, patents, trademark, or process rights. The licensee manufactures and markets abroad for the licensor. Whilst this avoids the need for a heavy investment, it can lead to an over-dependence on the licensee, who quickly builds up both manufacturing and marketing expertise. Associated Engineering, the largest engine components manufacturer in the world, and Pilkington Glass are just two examples of organisations with a successful record of licensing abroad.

Contract manufacturing is merely using someone else's production capacity and is usually only possible for technically simple products like some basic foods. It is a useful way of getting round tariff barriers, as well as of gaining experience of a foreign market, without the need for investment in capital and labour. Similar advantages apply to local assembly, which is also a learning device, as well as enabling a company to avoid paying the higher tariffs on assembled products, since bringing in unassembled goods helps local employment.

Sometimes, laws forbid 100 per cent foreign ownership of assets, especially in less-developed countries. Many companies, therefore, set up joint ventures, either with a foreign government, or with local partners. This is certainly a good way of sharing risk and of gaining experience using local expertise. Its major disadvantage lies in the loss of complete control, and hence freedom of action, especially in the field of marketing.

One-hundred per cent ownership of foreign production plants represents a major commitment to international marketing and should only be done after much research. Most overseas manufacturing occurs as a result of some factor associated with that market. As an example, Nissan and Toyota have both built manufacturing plants in the USA and Western Europe because this was the best way to overcome barriers to entry. Likewise, GKN's big stake in the German components industry gave them a market share which could not have been achieved by direct export from the UK as a result of the German need for short delivery lead times.

From this, it will be clear that there is a big difference between the marketing task of a company selling to an intermediary as a final customer, and the task facing the organisation that assumes full responsibility for all stages of marketing right through to final user satisfaction. The important point is that each of the options should not be considered as a series of steps to be followed *en route* to becoming a multinational company (in which all opportunities are assessed from the world-wide viewpoint, and in which the terms 'home' and 'foreign' are meaningless), but more as strategic

**Table 4.2** Key questions in international marketing

- *Whether* to sell abroad. Geographical diversification may be more desirable than product diversification, depending of course on circumstances. However, the decision to sell abroad should not be taken lightly.
- *Where* to sell abroad. This is one of the major decisions for international marketing. Choosing foreign markets on the basis of proximity and similarity is not necessarily the most potentially profitable option to go for.
- *What* to sell abroad and the degree to which products should be altered to suit foreign needs is also one of the major problems of international marketing.
- *How* to sell abroad is concerned, not just with the issue of how to enter a foreign market, but also with the management of 'the four Ps' once a company arrives. It also involves the difficult question of how to coordinate the marketing effort across a number of foreign countries.

*Overseas*
*options*
*represent*
*strategic*
*alternatives*

alternatives. And since the method of market entry is the major determinant of the degree of control a company has over its marketing, each of the different options should be carefully considered before a decision is made.

Overall, then, international marketing can be seen to involve a number of issues which make decision-making a difficult task. Merely recognising the differences and the complexities, however, is not enough. Policies must be debated in the context of the critical questions which need to be addressed when considering marketing internationally (see Table 4.2).

# Relationship Marketing

The concept of relationship marketing has evolved as a consequence of some of the limitations traditional approaches to marketing are perceived to foster. In terms of relationships, the most important one for marketing purposes is that between the supplying organisation and its customers. This relationship is managed through the activities involved in delivering the marketing mix. In this, the four Ps are probably the most universally accepted method for structuring the marketing mix. Since the late 1980s, however, both the ideas of a four Ps mix, and customers being the only markets requiring attention, have been questioned. This has led to the propositions contained within the relationship marketing approach.

## An Expanded Marketing Mix

The four Ps of product, price, promotion and place constitute the 'offer' which an organisation presents to the market place. If the offer is sufficiently well-matched to customers' needs, it should lead to sales. In addition, if it is sufficiently well-managed, these sales should be profitable to the organisation. The potential down-side to this is that an organisation's attention becomes too focused on a 'profitable sale', leading to a *transaction* approach to marketing (see Table 5.1). The danger is that interactions based on transactions can ignore other aspects of supplier/buyer relationships which can provide something of greater substance for longer-term marketing success. The manifestation of this is the development of customer loyalty and commitment which will survive the attempts of competitors to lure away customers.

*A transaction approach to marketing can be dangerously limiting*

**Table 5.1** Tendencies inherent in a transaction approach to marketing

- Priority is achieving a sale
- Focus on margins rather than profitability
- Meeting short-term sales targets overrides other priorities
- Product is 'pushed' at customer
- Limited commitment to customer
- Acceptance of unrealistic terms of sale
- Responsibility passed to customer at earliest opportunity

*Volatile environments have led to the need to change*

The need for such relationships as a means of retaining customers has, in reality, long been recognised. Fast-moving consumer goods organisations have become very sophisticated in developing brands which act as surrogates for personal relationships, and business-to-business selling has traditionally utilised both corporate image and sales teams to keep customers loyal. In general terms, however, growth and the winning of new customers have tended to attract the greater amount of managerial attention. The increasingly volatile competitive environment in which organisations operate, however, has required this approach to change. From a marketing perspective, the attitudes towards managing existing relationships have, therefore, had to adopt a higher profile.

The key attitude shifts involved are:

- A recognition of the value of retaining customers *as well as* attracting new ones.
- An acceptance that there are elements within the existing components of the marketing mix which, perhaps, have special significance in terms of managing relationships.
- An acknowledgement of the influence that people and institutions outside of the customers can have in developing and maintaining relationships.

An examination of the offer presented to the market place in terms of its impact on customer relationships reveals certain elements which are probably worthy of being separated and treated as distinct elements of the marketing mix (see Figure 5.1). The first of these, *customer service*, is normally included as part of the 'P' of place and consists of the activities which support the

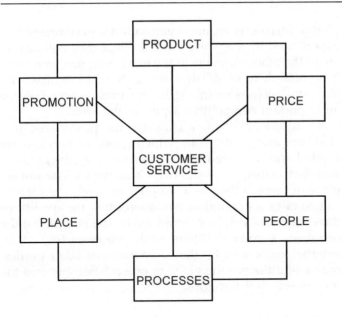

**Figure 5.1**   Expanded marketing mix

*Source:* Adapted from M. Christopher, A. Payne and D. Ballantine, *Relationship Marketing* (Butterworth-Heinemann, 1993), reproduced with kind permission.

placement of orders, the delivery of goods or services, either directly or via third party channels, and any post-purchase assistance required. Such support is obviously an important aspect of an organisation's relationships with customers and will help to determine customers' experience of a purchase and product utilisation. Indeed, in many service businesses, mature markets or markets where the products are technically complex, customer service is seen as a significant vehicle for competitive differentiation.

These factors help to argue the case for isolating customer service as a separate element of an organisation's marketing plans.

The recognition that an organisation's employees will have a significant impact on the way that customers and other interested parties perceive that organisation means that *people* can also be regarded as an extra element of the marketing mix. Whenever a person is identified as a member of a particular establishment, he or she will perform an ambassadorial role, whether they like it or not. Similarly, people will be responsible for the majority

*Employees often perform an ambassadorial role*

of the variations in an organisation's performance as experienced by the world outside. Since they will impact on all the other elements to the marketing mix, and since it is difficult to establish sustainable relationships with inanimate objects or intangible features, people become an important competitive aspect of the offer.

An additional element concerns the procedures, mechanisms and routines by which goods or services are created and delivered to the customer, i.e., the *processes* which structure an organisation's activities. The importance of these is that, as a supplier unravels the various elements of its significant relationships, the quality of these elements will be determined by the integrity of the processes involved. Where such processes impact on external audiences, be they customers or other parties, they will influence the viability of a relationship and the way in which it develops.

## The Six Markets Model

*Relationship marketing recognises that customer markets do not exist in isolation*

Relationship marketing also recognises that customer markets do not exist in isolation, but are surrounded by other markets for which organisations may need to develop marketing plans. These have been termed:

- **Influencer** markets.
- **Referral** markets.
- **Supplier** markets.
- **Recruitment** markets.
- **Internal** markets.

This provides a *six markets* model, as shown in Figure 5.2. Customers, of course, remain the prime focus. The success of an organisation in its customer markets, however, can be affected to quite a high degree by these 'other' markets and an organisation's strength within them.

Influencer markets are important because customers are affected as much by independent third parties as they are by the direct activities of supplier organisations. These may be simple media channels, or they may consist of regulatory bodies who set standards, or decide on what can, or cannot, be done and to what extent resources will be available for an organisation's activities. Thus, influencer markets such as banks and

**Figure 5.2** The relationship marketing six markets model

government bodies, plus pressure groups which can legitimise activities or organisations, will influence the scope and perception of a supplier just as much as the media activities.

People who will refer potential customers to a supplier, such as existing customers or professional advisers, are also an important market. They are particularly significant for the generation of new business, but also for the reinforcement of existing relationships. They can include consultants, other professionals, intermediaries, suppliers and so on.

Suppliers can also be a critical, separate, market for an organisation, not just because they are a source of referral, but because their performance can help or hinder a business to fulfil its promises. Thus, many businesses are interested in better relations with their suppliers, particularly following the example set by the Japanese. In some quarters, this is described as 'reverse marketing'.

*Better supplier relations can enhance business performance*

As well as capital and other physical resources, organisations need to recruit skilled people. The scarcity of skilled people is a consequence of the changing demographics in many developed nations, plus the increased specialisation required for people to be able to work with many of the advanced technologies which are so important to organisational efficiency and effectiveness.

As skills become more specialised and less available,
and as people themselves become a more significant
element of the marketing mix, internal marketing must
also be addressed both to retain scarce skills and opti-
mise employees' interactions with external markets.

*Relationship*
*marketing*
*recognises the*
*value of*
*internal as*
*well as*
*external*
*marketing*

Traditional marketing is usually outwardly focused and
has for too long ignored the people within the organisation who have to turn a market promise into a reality. In
this way, the concept of relationship marketing brings
up to date the efforts of many organisations who have
tried to take a broader view of the markets of which they
are part and to develop a more sophisticated approach to
profitable marketing.

# TOPIC 6

# Marketing and Ethics

In recent years, dissatisfaction has been expressed by increasingly large numbers of people about a society which seems to have consumption as both its means and its end. In the late 1960s and early 1970s, there was a growing consciousness of the problems that the age of mass consumption brought with it. A new awareness of the alternatives that might be possible, indeed necessary, became apparent. Such moves were supported by books like Charles Reich's *The Greening of America*, Alvin Toffler's *Future Shock* and Theodore Roszak's *The Making of a Counter Culture*. The message articulated by these and other writers of the movement was basically a simple one: that people could no longer be thought of as 'consumers', as some aggregate variable in the grand design of market planning. They were individuals intent on doing their own bidding.

Feelings such as these led to critical examinations of commercial activity of all kinds. As one of the more visible manifestations of such activity, marketing has been singled out for special attention. One criticism frequently brought against marketing is that it plays on people's weaknesses. By insidious means, it is claimed, marketing attempts to persuade consumers that they must smoke this brand of cigarette or use this brand of deodorant; that without them their lives are somehow incomplete. This argument involves the notion of the defenceless consumer.

*Marketing is criticised for playing on people's weaknesses*

Viewing marketing in this way tends to exaggerate the influence that the marketer can bring to bear on the market place. It implies that consumers' powers of perception are limited and that their intelligence is minimal. It further suggests that skilful marketing can create needs.

The argument to support this would be that 'Nobody wanted television before it was invented; now it is a highly competitive market. That market must have been created.' This, however, confuses needs and wants. Clearly, nobody wanted television before it was invented; but there has always been a need for home entertainment. Previously, that need had been met by a piano, a book, parlour games, or something of that kind. Now technology has made available a further means of satisfying that basic need for domestic entertainment – television. Many consumers find that television better satisfies their need for home entertainment than did the piano. The arrival of digital television will bring even more changes in home entertainment.

In this example, the contribution of marketing was to identify in as much detail as possible what a customer needed and then to persuade him or her that a specific product or brand would provide the most effective means of satisfying the expressed need. Underlying this view of marketing is the belief that consumers seek satisfactory solutions to their buying problems; first, by acquiring information about available goods and services and their attributes and, eventually, by choosing that product which comes closest to solving their problem.

*Marketing offers the choices; consumers do the choosing*

No matter what 'marketing' is performed, the consumer is still sovereign as long as he or she is free to make choices – either choices between competing products, or the choice not to buy at all. Indeed, it could be argued that by extending the range of choices that the consumer has available, marketing is enhancing consumer sovereignty rather than eroding it. It should be noted, too, that although promotional activity may persuade an individual to buy a product or service for the first time, promotion is unlikely to be the persuasive factor in subsequent purchases, when the consumer is acting from first-hand experience of the product.

## Some Ethical Concerns

Several specific issues have formed the focus of the debate on the ethics of marketing. The main concerns include:

- Marketing's contribution to materialism.
- Rising consumer expectations as a result of marketing pressure.
- The use of advertising to mislead or distort.

It is, therefore, important to consider the arguments involved in these discussions.

Marketing, it has been suggested, helps to feed, and in turn feeds on, the materialistic and acquisitive urges of society. Implicit in such criticism is the value judgement that materialism and acquisitiveness are in themselves undesirable. Supporters would argue that marketing contributes to a general raising of the level of consumer expectations. These expectations are more than simple aspirations: they represent a desire to acquire a specific set of gratifications through the purchase of goods and services. The desire for these gratifications is fuelled by marketing's insistent messages. Further, if the individual lacks the financial resources with which to fulfil these expectations, then this inevitably adds to a greater awareness of differences in society and to dissatisfaction and unrest among those in this situation.

The counter-argument here is that marketing itself does not contribute to rising expectations and thus to differences in society; it merely makes people aware of, and better informed about, the differences that already exist in society. In this respect, it can be claimed that its effects are beneficial, since it supports, even hastens, pressures for redistribution. It can also be argued that materialism is not a recent phenomenon correlated with the advent of mass marketing.

Much of the criticism levelled at marketing is in fact directed at one aspect of it: advertising. Advertising practitioners themselves are fully conscious of these criticisms. These include the ideas that advertising:

*Most criticism is levelled at advertising*

- Makes misleading claims about product or services.
- Uses hidden, dangerously powerful techniques of persuasion.
- By encouraging undesirable attitudes, has adverse social effects.
- Works through the exploitation of human inadequacy.

Advertisers themselves would point to the fact that advertising in all its forms is heavily controlled in most Western societies, either by self-imposed codes (such as the British Code of Advertising Practice) or by legislation (such as the Trade Description Acts) and that it cannot by itself achieve sustained patterns of repeat purchase.

The debate about the ethics of marketing also often confuses marketing institutions with the people who work in them. Clearly, there are dishonest business people who engage in activities that are detrimental to their fellow-citizens. However, it seems a grave error to criticise marketing institutions because of the practices of a small number of unethical marketers. It is clear, for example, that there are advertisers who engage in deceptive practices designed to mislead and possibly defraud consumers. Nevertheless, the institution of advertising can be used not only to inform consumers about potentially beneficial new products, such as new energy-saving technologies, but also to promote non-profit community services, such as theatres and state education. This argument can, of course, be applied to all marketing activities.

## Consumerism and Marketing

*Ironically, consumerism is pro-marketing*

Closely connected with the issue of the ethics of marketing is the issue of consumerism. Ironically, consumerism is pro-marketing; it wants the marketing approach to business implemented in a sincere rather than cynical spirit. The cynical implementation, which consumerists claim has been all too widely practised, is no better than high-pressure salesmanship or misleading puffery. The sincere implementation of the marketing approach entails respect for each individual customer served. An interpretation of the consumerist desire is that the sort of relationship found between a manufacturer and a customer in, say, a capital goods market, should be created in consumer markets. In so far as that is both economically feasible and what the consumer

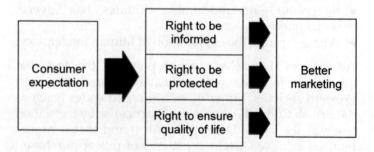

**Figure 6.1**    Consumerism's way to better marketing

really wants, marketers should also want a more satisfactory relationship between organisation and customer (see Figure 6.1).

The marketing of children's toys provides an example of how customers, consumers and company objectives can all be satisfied by careful business practice. The successful toy companies of today are those which inform parents that their products are not potentially dangerous, not coated with lead paint, and not destroyed the hour after they are first pressed into active service. Fisher-Price is one of the most successful toy manufacturers. Since 1968 it has eschewed child-manipulative promotion, carefully tested its products with children for durability, safety and purposeful play, and charged the prices necessary to make and market 'good' toys. The consequent sales and profit margins have been impressive and the US giant Toys-Я-Us, are also now trying to follow this approach.

*Customers, consumers and company objectives can all be satisfied by careful business practice*

**Section B**

# UNDERSTANDING DIFFERENT FORMS OF MARKETING

# TOPIC 7

# Marketing Consumer Products

Consumer products are those which are sold to individuals and which are then consumed by them, or someone they pass them on to, for the satisfaction they provide. This distinguishes them from industrial products which are purchased for their ability to help make another product. Consumer products are therefore at the head of the value chain and rely on the whole chain performing well for their success. At the same time, those in charge of marketing the final output also determine the survival of that value chain. Effective marketing in consumer markets therefore requires not only that products find favour with consumers but that all parts of the value chain work well in the provision of that product.

*Consumer products both head the value chain and rely on it*

## Consumer Markets

The key marketing issue for manufacturers or retailers of consumer goods, or providers of consumer services, is that they are usually faced with large numbers of potential customers. This applies equally to organisations which supply consumer durables such as refrigerators and consumables such as grocery products. The main differences between these two categories tend to be:

- Frequency of purchase.
- Absolute cost.
- Degree of involvement.

For these reasons, consumables are often referred to as 'fast moving consumer goods' (FMCGs) where acceptance or rejection occurs in a relatively short space of time. Consumer durables, such as 'white goods' (freezers, cookers, etc.) or 'brown goods' (furniture, etc.), on the other hand, tend to be infrequent purchases of some significance to a household. Their purchase therefore tends to be a much longer and more considered process, requiring a supplier to adapt their marketing accordingly.

Whatever their category, the fact of very large numbers of potential purchasers presents the purveyors of these products with a significant problem: how to persuade so many people to buy their products in preference to a competitor's? This is, of course, compounded when those potential consumers are geographically dispersed or where they represent a small proportion of each community.

## Main Methods for Marketing Consumer Products

Over the years, this difficulty has been addressed in a number of different ways and is an area in which significant innovations have taken place at various times.

### Personal Selling

The most effective way to develop a sales relationship with a potential customer is for a person to meet with that customer to explore his or her needs and to explain the virtues of the offer to him or her. In most consumer markets, this would involve a sales person calling on individuals and engaging them in the sales process either over the phone or in person. Traditionally, this is known as door-to-door selling. However, employing sales people in this way is a very expensive means of making a sale and, where the value of each sale is relatively small, not very profitable. For this reason, consumer goods sold in this manner tend to be those which are:

- Difficult to sell (the benefits are hard to explain, e.g., insurance or double glazing).
- Highly profitable (margin per sale is large, e.g., some vacuum cleaners).
- Commodity items (where the only differentiating aspect is the sales process).

*Direct Mail*

In parallel with the sophistication of information technology and databases has come a significant increase in the use of direct mail. This is a cheaper means of placing a product in front of a consumer but enables a direct contact to be made. The increasing ability to target particular types of customer has encouraged many consumer products organisations to explore this route, and in the late 1990s there has been a proliferation of letters and catalogues arriving through consumers' doors.

The downsides of this method are: a relatively low response rate, progressive disillusionment on the part of consumers who begin to feel deluged with offers, and a loss of any personal contact with suppliers.

*Retailers*

Given the number and dispersal of potential customers, suppliers of many consumer products rely on retailers to distribute and sell their goods and services. This emphasises the need to select appropriate retail organisations and the requirement for maintaining good relations with them. Indeed, in some FMCG areas, simply being on the right shelf in the right part of the right chain of shops is almost enough to guarantee success for a product line. The power of such retailers has also given rise to a particular type of marketing in the form of trade marketing and a supplier industry providing retail 'own label' products.

*Brands*

Creating and maintaining a brand for a product or set of products is essentially a way of developing and keeping a relationship with a consumer without the need for personal contact. Strong brands are those that have a personality with which consumers can identify or that evoke a feeling within a consumer which matches their personal values and lifestyle. Consumers are therefore attracted to brands of this nature and will buy them in preference to lesser (commodity) brands or brands that are targeted at a different segment of the market.

*Strong brands elicit customer identification*

Figure 7.1    Priorities for a consumer brand manager

Possessing a strong product or company brand name provides their owners with a lot of power in the market place. Manufacturers and service suppliers who own such brands are able to exert considerable influence on retailers in terms of price, shelf location, competitor positioning, merchandising, promotions policy, acceptance of new products and many other areas. Distinct retail brands are similarly able to influence lesser branded suppliers and to gain favourable locations and terms for their outlets.

*Brands are often central to consumer marketing strategy*

For these reasons, brands and brand strategy are often at the heart of a supplier of consumer products' marketing strategy. The priorities or focus of attention for marketing managers of such supplier and retail brands are depicted in Figure 7.1.

## Value Chain Management

The highly competitive world of consumer marketing has led many suppliers and retailers to pay closer attention to the value chain at whose head they sit. These organisations have recognised that advantage can be gained by exerting influence across all those who affect their products and their ability to supply. These advantages include: lower cost, higher quality, better availability, product innovation, speed to market, and a host of other important competitive factors.

In some industries, such as automotive manufacture, this management is sometimes delegated to a small group of key suppliers who are expected to influence and coordinate the other suppliers in the chain. In others, such as the computer supply industry, many businesses are working directly with suppliers right down to component level and beyond in seeking efficiency and innovation for competitive advantage.

## Micro Marketing

Large numbers of potential consumers with similar needs leads many consumer marketing organisations to a mass marketing approach which tries to satisfy the majority of the market with an undiscriminating product, brand or approach as classically practised by Ford, Coca-Cola or McDonald's. Modern consumer marketers are, however, increasingly finding that markets are fragmenting as consumers become more sophisticated, individualistic and demanding.

The result has been a proliferation of new brands, or an existing brand 'stretched' across a number of product variations, and efforts to provide 'mass customisation'. This last involves consumers being able to configure their own product from a series of modular offerings added on to the core product or service. Finding ways of keeping the cost of such practices down, and utilising the growth of new direct consumer channels to provide such customisation in innovative and consumer-friendly ways remain important challenges for future consumer marketers.

*The fragmentation of consumer markets has led to a growth in brands*

# TOPIC 8

# Marketing Industrial Products

Whenever an organisation consciously applies marketing to the management of its products, be they services, fast-moving consumer goods or industrial products, the fundamental principles of marketing always apply. Any market-orientated organisation will seek an understanding of its customers, the markets of which they are a part, the opportunities which exist within that market, the best ways to compete with its rivals and so on.

In spite of these similarities, most organisations in industrial markets instinctively know that the marketing of their products requires a different set of approaches from those appropriate to the marketing of consumer goods. To operate effectively in industrial markets, it is important to understand what these differences are since they will highlight those areas on which the organisation must focus within the basic tenets of marketing.

*Industrial marketing is different from consumer marketing, but the divide is not easily drawn*

Having accepted this, it is also important to note that there is no simple or clear divide between industrial and consumer products and markets. On the product side, some products are sold in the same form to both industrial and consumer markets. Examples of this include bank accounts, motor cars, personal computers and parts for washing machines. In terms of markets, some consumer-goods manufacturers will only sell directly to other businesses, i.e., retail organisations. As a consequence, industrial marketing cannot be defined simply by the products involved or by the fact that it involves business-to-business selling.

## Conceptualising Industrial Marketing

The best way to conceptualise industrial marketing is to look at it as a continuum with obvious slow-moving industrial products at one end and fast-moving consumer products at the other (see Figure 8.1). In the

42

| Industrial Markets | | | Consumer Markets |
|---|---|---|---|
| Machine tools | Ball bearings | Furniture | Soap powder |
| Complex software | Printed circuit boards | Domestic appliances | Canned food |

**Figure 8.1** Continuum of industrial marketing

middle of the continuum are faster moving industrial products and slower moving consumer products.

The existence of this continuum also illustrates the possibility of the transfer of marketing approaches between these different markets. Whilst the context of their usage and the way in which they are applied may vary, no idea should be ignored because it is thought to be more appropriate to the realm of one market or product than another. A good example would be efforts by industrial businesses to develop brand names for their products. The transfer cannot be made, however, unless the dynamics of the different contexts are well understood.

*No idea should be ignored*

## Issues in Industrial Marketing

The first issue concerns the way in which an industrial purchaser views a product it is considering purchasing. Industrial products are often thought of as being more **complex** than the equivalent consumer products, which is obviously not always the case. What is different is the attention paid to the details of a product. Even a commodity product, such as sheet steel or a simple component, will be considered in much greater detail by an industrial purchaser. This is because it will be used in more complex ways, or that small variations will have potentially harmful consequences. As an example, the wrong grade of steel will not machine properly and may put cost up and quality down. Similarly, a personal computer with a slightly wrong specification may make previous software purchases obsolete or networking with existing machines impossible.

The implications of such detailed product evaluations are that industrial purchasers have greater **information needs** than consumer purchasers both before and after a purchase is made. In turn, this implies larger numbers of people being involved in the purchase decision. Consequently, organisations marketing industrial products have to cope with a larger and more diverse **decision-making unit** and a greater degree of **formalisation** in the procedures applied to a purchase.

It also implies that a greater degree of **personal contact** between the supplier and buyer will be necessary, since this is the best way of providing complete information. Personal contact is necessary to isolate *who needs to know what* and *at what point in the decision-making process*, in order to improve the chances of a sale, or continued sales.

Apart from costly and infrequently purchased capital goods, the **volumes** bought by an industrial purchaser are also likely to be higher than by individuals or families in a consumer market. The significance of this is the importance of the loss of these volumes to *both* the supplier and the purchaser. If a supplier fails to deliver the right quantity, the purchaser will find it difficult to continue their business. On the other hand, if a purchaser stops buying, this will have a significant impact on the supplier's income. In industrial markets, therefore, there is often a high degree of **interdependence**. Both supplier and purchaser will rely on each other for their continued existence. The loss of one purchaser in a consumer market is not nearly so significant.

*Industrial markets exhibit a high degree of interdependence between buyer and supplier*

This situation is further complicated by the fact that it is difficult in the industrial context to find mass markets. Apart from there being **smaller numbers of customers**, one buying organisation is likely to differ significantly from the next in their buying requirements. This means that **segmentation** in industrial markets has to be conducted on a different basis.

A further implication is that the degree of **product variability** required can also be greater. In some cases, a single customer can form an entire segment and consequently can demand a high degree of customisation. In others, the consumer variables for segmentation such as demography, life stage and life style need to be replaced by alternatives such as size, applications and competitive positioning. Such **heterogeneity** is an important factor for the organisation marketing industrial products.

In trying to understand, and give some structure to, the markets which industrial suppliers face, it must be recognised that their customers also have customers of their own, who may in turn have customers! Unless the customer is the Ministry of Defence or some similar body, all industrial products will eventually translate into a consumer purchase. This means that the structure of the market in which an industrial organisation operates can be complex, with a whole series of intermediaries or 'value adders' between them and the final consumer. Industrial suppliers are thus faced with a situation of **derived demand** for their goods and services. The way they perceive their market and the way in which opportunities are identified and defined can therefore become a very complicated process.

Paradoxically, these factors combine to make **market research** in industrial markets sometimes more problematic, and sometimes easier, than consumer market research. Because of their low numbers, potential customers are likely to be difficult to find, extract information from, and generalise about. One cannot simply stand in shopping centres and stop passers-by or ring at random from the telephone directory. In addition, the influences on demand are likely to be more complex and remote from each organisation, making them difficult to interpret. Where an organisation has existing customers, however, market research is often easier since the people who hold valuable information and opinions should already be known and are usually quite willing to be approached.

## Industrial Marketing and General Management

One of the consequences of the complexities which exist in the buyer/seller relationship in industrial markets is that many different functions within the selling organisation are required to interact with various aspects of the customer organisation. This can include service or maintenance sections, the design team, installation group, training, delivery and finance as well as senior directors and the sales people. While many of these are also points of contact in consumer marketing, these contacts tend to be extensive and of greater significance in industrial markets.

*Industrial marketing requires involvement across the management functions*

*Key account
management
is often a
feature of
industrial
marketing*

Such complexity has also given rise to a need for Key
Account Management. Supply relationships which are
significant for both parties can easily falter if left on a
simple transactional basis. Key Account Managers who
take a relationship perspective on an organisation-wide
basis are more likely to ensure that potential problems
are avoided.

The management of marketing in industrial organisations, therefore, tends towards a **general management**
function with small decisions in one area having a
greater impact on the customer and business success.
This is not to say that such coordination is inappropriate
for consumer markets, but that closer attention to building a marketing approach across the management functions has a higher profile.

In general, then, marketing industrial products is a
diverse area which can utilise a number of the approaches developed by consumer marketing organisations. What is important is a recognition of the
differences which exist in industrial markets and the
implications these hold for the supplying organisation.
In particular, the way that the relationship between
supplier and customer is managed takes on a different
perspective, but one which must be well understood and
nurtured over time for the achievement of continuing
and successful business.

# TOPIC 9

# Marketing Service Products

Service businesses were an increasingly significant sector of most advanced economies throughout the 1980s and 1990s, and will continue to be a dynamic sector into the millennium and beyond. It currently provides around 70 per cent of civilian employment in the USA and the UK. Table 9.1 illustrates the potential range of service activities. At the same time, there has been an accelerating trend to differentiate what were once considered to be simply 'goods' by highlighting the service elements of the offer. Together with the deregulation experienced by many professional and government services, these factors have forced organisations to consider whether any differences will be required when marketing services.

*Service is an important differentiation factor*

At one level, a negative answer can be justified, since the theory of marketing has universal application. At another, the nature of many types of service dictate that more emphasis is placed on certain elements of marketing. It is, therefore, crucial that marketing organisations understand what these elements are and how they will affect the marketing tasks they face.

**Table 9.1**  Major examples of service industries

- Retailing, wholesaling and distribution
- Banking, insurance and other financial institutions
- Real estate
- Communications, information and multimedia services
- Health services
- Business, professional and personal services
- Leisure and entertainment
- Education
- Public utilities
- Government services and non-profit service organisations

### Defining a Service

Defining a service for marketing purposes, however, is not easy. The diversity of organisations involved in services and the tendency to highlight the service elements of an 'offer' for competitive advantage, means that they are sometimes hard to classify. One important element, however, is the degree of tangibility involved. Table 9.2, for example, identifies four categories, varying from a 'pure' product to a 'pure' service.

**Table 9.2**  Variations in product tangibility

| | |
|---|---|
| • A pure tangible product | A tangible offer, such as sugar, coal, or tea. No services are bought with the product |
| • A tangible product with accompanying services such as commissioning, training, maintenance, etc. | The offer has built-in services to enhance its customer appeal, e.g. computers, machine tools |
| • An intangible product with accompanying minor goods | The offer is basically a service, but has a physical element, e.g., property surveyors, whose expert inspection is encapsulated in a report. Similarly, airlines offer in-flight meals or entertainment |
| • A pure intangible product, where one buys expertise | The offer is a stand-alone service such as psychoanalysis or ski-instruction |

Such a categorisation leads to the notion of a continuum of tangible-intangible products as illustrated in Figure 9.1. Point 'a' on the left-hand side of this figure illustrates an offer where there is no service element and the product is highly tangible. At the other end of the spectrum, point 'd' illustrates a product which is entirely a service and is therefore highly intangible. Points 'b' and 'c' show varying mixes. For example, point 'b' illustrates the mix of tangibility for a computer company.

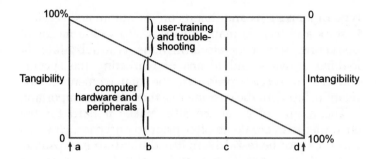

**Figure 9.1** Continuum of tangible–intangible products

Computer hardware and peripherals are highly tangible and can be regarded as commodities, whereas the service elements of user-training and trouble-shooting are largely intangible.

The intangible nature of a service leads to a number of other differences of significance for marketing. These include the implications that:

- Services can be easily copied by competitors, since they cannot be patented and specified with drawings.
- Quality cannot be guaranteed since services are not previously produced or 'manufactured' under controlled conditions. Instead, they are produced and delivered at the time of consumption.
- A service cannot be stored on a shelf or taken down and used at a later time. Services are therefore highly perishable.
- People are an intrinsic part of most services and are difficult to separate from the product.
- The true value of a service can only be assessed on consumption. Thus, the purchase of a service involves a high component of trust.
- Services are often very personal in their nature and can involve the customer in their delivery and consumption, as in the case of a golf lesson or IKEA.

An important area in marketing services is, therefore, the **relationship** between the customer and the supplier. The close link between production and consumption, and the personal nature of many service products, have served to emphasise this aspect. Where no personal relationship exists, the contrast between membership-

*The relationship between customer and supplier is an important aspect of marketing services*

type organisations and 'hands off' or automated services is stark and has led many businesses to seek a means of marketing more concrete affiliations as a substitute. In looking at ways and means of marketing the specific features of service products, the management of the relationship with the customer is, thus, always important.

The nature of a service also makes it hard for the customer to **evaluate** an offer prior to purchase. Unlike a car, it cannot be test-driven; it is difficult to encapsulate in a technical specification and quality is uncertain. As examples, it is hard for a potential customer to assess a bank before opening an account with them and a stay in a hotel can only be judged after one has checked out.

*Demonstrating product quality and integrity is crucial to marketing services*

Thus, a crucial aspect of marketing services is to provide, as far as is possible, tangible evidence of the product quality. This highlights the need for careful attention to the 'product promise', such as the initial points of contact, descriptive literature and the peripherals which provide clues to the product's integrity. It is no coincidence that professional services often have plush reception areas, holiday brochures are a masterpiece of presentation, and aqua-based health clubs make a big show of testing the water. The problems associated with service evaluation can also be addressed by focusing on reputation, or by enhancing the value of a service through the provision of extra benefits such as free offers. Here, word of mouth or third-party endorsement become particularly influential. These can come from existing customers, referral markets and media institutions, all of whom can provide powerful testimony to the quality or value of an organisation's offering.

Since many services rely heavily on a personal interaction between the service provider and the customer, or depend on individuals exercising judgement when creating the service, considerable **heterogeneity** between purchases becomes possible, so that customer-experiences of the product may vary enormously. Thus, the performance of a waiter or a shop assistant will have a great impact on the way a customer experiences the core benefit they are seeking. Similarly, two customers in the same hotel can have completely different opinions of their visit if one found their towels unlaundered, or had their breakfast delivered late. Since the quality of such elements is in the hands of the people performing the service, employees become a vital concern for marketing services effectively. This requires attention to service-modelling to identify people-related 'fail points', as well as taking an interest in internal and recruitment markets to ensure the right calibre of person. The process of **service delivery** thus needs careful specification which should include an identification of the skills necessary to reduce the likelihood of product heterogeneity as a consequence of 'people problems'.

At this point, it should also be noted that both the intangibility and heterogeneity of services mean that **attention to detail** becomes central to marketing effectiveness. This is, first, because details, as mentioned, provide clues for the consumer about quality and, second, because details can be a major cause of customers perceiving the same service product in different ways. Details, however, are also that part of the process of delivering the service most influenced by individual employees, thereby giving further weight to the focus on process design and human resource management.

The fact that a service will require the customer's involvement in its creation and delivery enhances the need for efficient management of this customer/provider **interaction**. Since manufacturers are able to check quality prior to delivery, service providers have to find substitutes for this. One solution has been to utilise technology to enhance consistency and improve accessibility, as was achieved by banks when they introduced automated tills or 'banking through the wall'. Another approach has been to focus attention on front line staff and to 'empower' them to negotiate service delivery to prevent excessive disappointment. Such a situation has worked with in-store supervisory staff, receptionists and service engineers. A further method has involved better customer management to ensure satisfactory service delivery. Customer management can cover a number of different aspects, from setting appropriate expectations and encouraging customers to signify their satisfaction levels whilst utilising a service, to getting them to behave in a way which enhances the service. A good example of the latter is the widespread improvement in the queueing technology which now ensures nobody waits longer than necessary in many banks, post offices and railway stations.

*Customer management is important in service delivery*

*Interest in relationship marketing probably stems from the problems of marketing services*

For marketing managers the perishability of a service places extra emphasis on understanding demand patterns and why such fluctuations exist. However, **matching demand** at all times is rarely possible or, indeed, cost-effective. In the end, the only alternatives are to try to change patterns of demand or to generate increased capacity at peak times. The techniques for managing demand revolve around incentives, such as offering better value and other sales promotion activities, or using pricing mechanisms, such as premiums or discounts. Capacity can be enhanced by using part-time staff, subcontractors and shared facilities, or by carrying overheads in the form of staff, or assets, which are redundant at certain times. Marketing, therefore, has to ensure careful coordination to balance the overall offer with the market's preferred pattern of utilisation.

Services are sold to industrial, government and consumer markets. Whilst each market creates its own unique marketing scenarios, for services it is the distinct characteristics of the product which provide the major marketing challenges. In particular, it would seem to demand an expanded marketing mix beyond the four Ps of product, price, place and promotion, to include **people**, **processes** and **customer service**. These three additional elements appear to have a significant impact on the strategic success of an organisation and benefit from discrete programmes and action plans being developed for them. The features of service products also underline the importance of third-party markets such as recruitment, referral, influencer and internal markets, plus the overall concept of relationship marketing. Indeed, it has been argued that the current interest in relationship marketing first grew from developments initiated within service businesses.

# Marketing High-tech Products

Technology is becoming an important competitive tool for many organisations as a means of differentiating themselves from other businesses in the market place. Where such technology is a significant part of the overall market offering, organisations must consider whether its inclusion requires a particular approach or whether the nature of the technology will have little impact on the way in which the product is marketed.

For marketing management, then, the key distinction is between products which are high-tech for marketing purposes and products which involve advanced technology, but which do not require specific attention to that aspect of the offer. If the situation is the former, then there are a number of marketing issues which should occupy a significant proportion of managerial attention. If it is the latter, then other product and market issues are likely to be more important.

*Marketing high-tech products involves identifying whether a product is high-tech for marketing purposes*

### Distinguishing High-tech Products

In trying to identify whether or not a product is high-tech for marketing purposes, it must be recognised that few products consist of a single technology. They are more usually a mixture of advanced, new and old technologies which, together, create the substantive product. Thus, automobiles, copiers and cameras utilise a whole range of technologies, but will only be high-tech for marketing purposes if the new or advanced technology they incorporate acts as a focus for customers' evaluation of the product. The first criteria for identifying a product as high-tech is, therefore, how the customer views the product.

Whatever the product, purchases involve a risk for the buyer. For high-tech products, marketing has the

*High-tech
products
involve
greater risk
for buyer and
supplier alike*

problem that the **risk** for the purchaser is increased as a result of the uncertainties associated with a new or advanced technology. However, risk does not only exist for the buyer – the supplier will also experience a higher than usual element of risk. This is because both the supplier and the buyer, be they end-users or supply-chain intermediaries, will lack experience of applying, maintaining and using the technology. In turn, this will increase the chances of unforeseen problems arising, such as further cost, interruptions to supply continuity, side effects, or quality problems.

The newness of a technology forming the key feature of a high-tech product will also contribute to marketing issues since the product is unlikely to be an accepted solution, yet, for the problem(s) it has been designed to solve. As such, there is unlikely to be widespread under-standing of how a high-tech product can provide bene-fits for both customer, and potential customer, organisations. In addition, it is doubtful if there will be support structures in the market which supplying orga-nisations can utilise to assist them in their marketing efforts.

A further implication of high-tech or 'state-of-the-art' technology is that supplying organisations will have to employ comparatively large proportions of highly skilled specialists in scientific and technical activities. These will be necessary to obtain the developments needed to create devices which can be turned into products and to provide the know-how required for manufacture, sales and post-purchase support. This will be particularly important given the absence of external expertise, but can lead to a strong technological orienta-tion within the organisation, which may be at odds with the development of a market orientation.

The key description of high-tech products which generate the management issues of particular signifi-cance for marketing can thus be identified as products:

- For which the advanced technology they incorporate acts as the focus for product evaluation.
- About which there is a high degree of uncertainty on the part of both the supplier and the customer.
- Which are not yet accepted as a natural solution for the problems they have been designed to address.

- For which an associated external infrastructure does not yet exist.
- Which have been developed in a highly technical environment.

These do not negate the fundamentals of marketing management such as benefit analysis, segmentation and careful targeting via the marketing mix. They do, however, raise the critical issues which marketing managers of high-tech products must address.

## Critical Marketing Issues

### Technology Seduction

Since high-tech products tend to be derived in a technologically orientated organisation peopled by large numbers of technical specialists, marketing managers must first be aware of the potential for **technology seduction**. Seduction will involve the internal promotion of a technology which is unwarranted by the market(s) which a business can realistically address. This can lead to either products whose performance exceeds market needs, or investment based on gaining technical improvements rather than market potential. The role of marketing managers is to recognise a case of technology seduction and to avoid becoming seduced, themselves, by the enthusiasm of others.

### Credibility

As a second issue, if high-tech products are not yet accepted solutions and tend to generate a high level of uncertainty, customers will need to develop a greater degree of trust than might otherwise be the case. An important ingredient for the creation of trust is **credibility**. This can involve both the credibility of the supplying organisation and the technology itself. Establishing credibility may require: high-profile demonstrations; the offer of substantial guarantees; wooing 'lead users'; fostering excellent media relations; and so on. Creating or changing people's perceptions, however, can take a long time. This means that high-tech marketing

*Creating or changing people's perceptions can take a long time*

managers need to foresee the potential for credibility problems well in advance to avoid them becoming barriers to entry into new markets or establishing new products in existing ones.

### Standards

In technology-based markets, **standards** have always had a significant impact on marketing strategy, but for high technology they can be very important. As an example, conforming to standards can enhance credibility while the absence of standards can increase the uncertainty felt by customers and can leave a supplier without frameworks within which to work. In addition, the creation of a standard which is based on an alternative interpretation of a technology can make an organisation's products obsolete. When marketing high-tech products, attention must therefore be paid to:

- Influencing the creation of standards.
- The possibility of becoming 'the standard'.
- Conforming to standards.
- Gaining approval or being certified as meeting a standard, and so on.

Unfortunately, this usually requires a lot of time, money and effort, and will demand careful coordination to gain the maximum marketing benefits.

### Technology Life-Cycles

*Marketing decisions should be placed in the context of the technology's life-cycle*

The 'newness' of a high-tech product and the uncertainty associated with it implies that managers should also place their marketing decisions in the context of the technology's life-cycle (see Figure 10.1). By definition, a high-tech product is at the early stages of its technological (as opposed to market) life. This means that marketing managers have to prepare for the transition from a situation where performance improvements have been hard to achieve to one where improvements become relatively easy to obtain. At the same time, the marketing task will change as risk and uncertainty reduce as technologies move through their life-cycles. This also suggests that marketing should

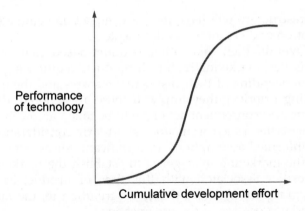

**Figure 10.1**  The technology life-cycle

contribute to decisions about which element of performance should be prioritised for development, and how sufficient flexibility can be maintained for future product development.

## Positioning

A further contributor to overcoming the problems associated with high-tech products is good **positioning**. Favourable product evaluation, reduced uncertainty and broadened supplier acceptance can be enhanced by positioning which implies leadership (to support credibility), customer service (to compensate for the lack of general knowledge about the technology), and a clear performance benefit (to make the risk of purchase worthwhile). This could involve positioning the supplier as the technology innovator and service leader, and the product's benefits as improved quality, cost savings, or performance levels which were previously impossible.

## Infrastructure

Finally, since a critical feature of high-tech products is the lack of associated market and technological **infrastructures**, marketing managers must also find a means of redressing this problem. Where they cannot be redressed externally, a business must seek an in-house solution and bear the associated costs. Alternatively, it will require an enterprise to select markets, and, therefore, product development priorities, where limited

*The role of the marketing manager is to establish marketing priorities*

infrastructure will have the least impact on commercialisation and business development.

Overall, then, like other product-based marketing activities, marketing high-tech products requires a good understanding of their distinctive features and the marketing priorities they imply. If these are ignored, decisions and consequent actions will be taken according to other criteria such as: instinct; short-term considerations; ill-informed assumptions; or significant voices. The role of the marketing manager is to establish the marketing priorities associated with this type of product as an integral part of, and a timely contribution to, the managerial processes of the organisation.

In addition, and unlike products in established and growing markets, high-tech products require a more proactive approach to the establishment of demand. The sheer newness of the product or its position will necessitate a 'supply-push' approach as opposed to the product being able to ride on the back of 'demand-pull' conditions. Latent demand will need to be sought and activated into purchasing activity.

# TOPIC 11

# Trade Marketing

In the marketing of consumer products and 'fast-moving' industrial goods, much effort is applied to 'pull' activities (i.e., creating demand amongst large numbers of users which will 'pull' products through the supply chain). This is the logic behind most branding strategies and promotional activities such as couponing or distributing free samples through the door. An alternative or complementary approach is to apply marketing effort to a 'push' strategy focusing on intermediaries (the trade) and 'pushing' products through the supply chain to the consumer.

*A 'push' strategy focuses on intermediaries*

The power and influence of these trade intermediaries in western economies has grown significantly over the last 30 years. Indeed, the ability to have your product on the shelves or in the catalogues of these prominent intermediaries is often a key factor to gaining position and advantage in many end-use markets. Focusing marketing effort on these intermediaries, termed trade marketing, has therefore increased in importance for many organisations and has required the development of new approaches to relationship management.

## The Rise of Intermediaries

Factors which have contributed to the increasing importance of trade intermediaries for suppliers of mass market goods and services can be identified as follows.

### Retail Power

As has already happened in North America and much of Western Europe, retailing and some aspects of industrial distribution have become dominated by a small number of large organisations. Suppliers relying on these intermediaries for sales to end users can easily be denied access to such markets if even one intermediary decides not to stock their products. Effective marketing to these intermediaries therefore takes on much greater significance. The strategy can no longer be a reliance on large sales forces placing their products in a wide range of different retailers or distributors in a 'hit or miss' fashion but one which sustains effective presence in these outlets.

### Brand Differentiation

In some markets, consumers are finding it increasingly difficult to differentiate between leading brands or suppliers. This is particularly true in markets such as mobile telephony or personal computing, but it is also observable in traditional fast-moving consumer areas such as washing powders or tinned foods. The result of this growing brand parity is that consumers more frequently purchase on the basis of availability and price within their chosen 'retail set'.

### Market Fragmentation

As markets become more competitive and customers grow in sophistication, demands for individualised supply similarly increase. Demand consequently fragments making it less effective to adopt mass marketing techniques. While this has encouraged organisations such as Heinz to transfer its marketing budgets to more direct and individualised marketing methods, it has also emphasised the value of reaching out to customers at the point of purchase. This requires trade promotions to encourage preferential stocking and point-of-sale support.

### E-commerce

Advances in information technology have meant that suppliers can be in direct contact with an intermediary on a real-time basis. This has enabled retailers and other intermediaries to reduce cost and increase efficiency by effectively delegating inventory responsibilities to a small number of key suppliers. Establishing oneself as one of these key suppliers in the eyes of intermediaries therefore becomes a priority for many manufacturers.

*Brand Management Deficiencies*

Brand managers in many organisations are often young and ambitious people trying to leave their mark on a brand's performance. The most effective way of achieving short-term position is often through trade promotions since brand value enhancement in the eyes of the consumer is more difficult and inevitably a longer-term proposition. Trade marketing therefore becomes more valuable to a brand manager's career than brand development.

## Trade Marketing Tactics

Traditionally, the tactics for trade marketing have centred on the marketing mix elements of promotion and price. These have taken the form of:

*Promotion*
- Incentives to staff of intermediaries
- Point-of-sale material
- Merchandising support
- Cooperative advertising
- Joint trade fair representation

*Price*
- Additional discounts
- Supplying to retailer price points
- Supporting buyer margin targets
- Price promotions such as 'buy two and get a third free'

## Trade Marketing Strategies

As intermediaries have become an increasing focus for marketing activities, so approaches based on simple tactics have given way to a more strategic view. The heart of this is an understanding of how both supplier and intermediary can mutually benefit from a well managed long-term relationship.

One manifestation of this is product profitability studies which analyse in great detail the way that cost attaches itself to a product both during manufacture and in its distribution and handling within the retail environment. Another is the development of category management whereby a single supplier takes responsibility

*Effective trade marketing strategies deliver a mutually-beneficial, long-term supplier–intermediary relationship*

for a product category such as hair care or chocolate bar confectionery.

Where category management has become widespread, as in the case of the USA, Germany and the UK, suppliers vie with each other to become 'category leaders', leading to significant adjustments in the structure of many suppliers' brand portfolios.

The strategic importance of trade marketing has also led to heavy investment in information technology by many suppliers to enable logistics and communications to proceed as smoothly as possible. Other aspects of the relationship will be enshrined in joint product development plans, the sharing of 'best-practice' information and a long-term view of category development such as the introduction of more organic produce.

### The Future

*Trade marketing has seen an upsurge in 'direct' provision and self-service*

The factors which have led to the expansion of trade marketing have also stimulated many suppliers to reassess their relationship with end users. Whilst some suppliers have concentrated on better marketing relationships with intermediaries, others have sought to strengthen their brand franchise so that retail or product categories will be weakened without the inclusion of their brand. This is quite apparent in a number of areas such as fashionable sports wear, pet foods and some aspects of the soft drinks market. It is also a major part of Intel's long-term strategy and the global 'Intel Inside' campaign.

At the same time, there has been an upsurge of 'direct' provision in many areas, particularly in the financial services arena. The advent of the Internet is dramatically fuelling this trend. Whilst some retailers are also beginning to add this to the range of services they offer, the possibility of direct provision for manufacturers is an attractive proposition. Not only does it imply higher margins but it also reduces their reliance on retailers who may not always approach supply relationships in the true 'spirit of partnership'.

The increase in global retailing and the emergence of 'category killers' are also good and bad news for suppliers. The global expansion of stores such as Toys-Я-Us, K-Mart and Carrefour means access to much expanded markets and growth in line with the retailers. However, such stores are usually situated out of town and offer focused category goods at heavily discounted prices. Their predatory nature often decimates local retail competition, reducing suppliers' routes to a market, and putting them in a stronger position to demand lower prices from suppliers.

Managing the conflicting demands of these powerful intermediaries, including the need for independence and long-term profitability on the part of a supplier and the continuing possibility for creating a consumer or brand franchise, will be an important determinant of the way trade marketing develops in the future.

*The future of trade marketing lies in how the conflicting demands of powerful intermediaries are managed*

# TOPIC 12

# Marketing Capital Goods

*The purchase of capital goods involves high cost and high risk*

As with any product-based approach to marketing, the marketing of capital goods presents suppliers with some special concerns. These are generated by the nature of the products and the circumstances under which they are bought and sold. Capital goods can be pieces of plant and equipment, such as large machines, boilers or storage facilities, or complete systems such as refineries, telecommunications networks or civil engineering projects.

Customers will similarly be large organisations and may be either private or public sector. Whichever the case, the purchase will be a significant event for the customer in terms of both the amounts of money involved and the benefits which the products will be required to deliver. At the same time, purchaser and supplier risk are also high, requiring a systematic approach to marketing which takes all these factors into consideration.

## Consequences for Marketing

By their nature, orders for capital goods tend to be few in number, even for the 'faster-moving' capital goods such as machine tools. In addition, their cost makes them very prone to economic fluctuations. Suppliers are thus often faced with a 'feast or famine' situation whereby they either have no orders and are standing around idle or they are overwhelmed with enquiries and find it difficult to meet delivery or completion schedules.

This is further exacerbated by the fact that each purchase is usually supplied against a different specification since it is unlikely that such large and complex products will be used in the same way, or serve exactly the same purpose, from one customer to another. Such a

64

situation prohibits the creation of finished stock except at a very early stage in the manufacture or construction process.

The risk associated with the supply and purchase of capital goods also creates pressures which mitigate against the use of innovative technologies or concepts. On the supplier side, the consequence of product failure in terms of financial penalties or loss of reputation can be very high. Similarly, from the customer's point of view, a capital purchase will often have strategic, or at least operational, significance and buyers are likely to be anxious to reduce the chances of something going wrong by sticking to proven technologies or methodologies. Where innovation does occur, its adoption is therefore likely to be a slow process and the recovery of development costs a long-term activity.

The consequences that such product features will have for marketing cover a number of areas. High levels of customisation plus the complexity of (particularly) larger products will mean that a product specification will take time to evolve and will typically be the result of much negotiation between supplier and customer. This will require suppliers to resource such negotiations and to maintain the ability to understand a customer's perspectives so that they can translate the benefits which customers seek into a product specification. Protracted negotiations and the absence of finished goods stock will create long order lead times which will also require suppliers to maintain sales relationships over time. Without this, suppliers may risk losing an order through: changes in personnel; loss of interest; situational changes which will alter the product specification; and the activities of competitors.

The size of an order may also require suppliers to join together, sometimes as international consortia, to be able to fulfil the requirements of a customer. Managing such relationships in a way which presents customers with a unified face is a distinct skill, but one which is important for the maintenance of relationships with customers. Such relationships, however, will also need to be continued after a sale has been made since capital goods usually involve lengthy installation or construction. Although repeat business is not as significant a feature of capital goods marketing as it is for other types of industrial products, client or customer referrals and

*Repeat business is not a significant feature of capital goods marketing*

references *are* an important aspect of selling and good relationships will be needed to ensure that these are forthcoming.

## Capital Goods Pricing

Since each product is unique, the price of a particular sale will also vary. In addition, since there is much negotiation about each specification, price is often one of the last factors to be considered. The complexity of supply also means that competing bids for a contract often vary significantly between competitors as a result of the way prices are calculated and the different methodologies which can be applied to the fulfilment of a specification.

At the same time, the variations in demand mean that organisations may sometimes adopt a pricing strategy which is closer to marginal cost pricing. This may be done to maintain capacity during times of 'famine' in order to prevent the loss of resources which would make them uncompetitive when business becomes more buoyant. Alternatively, during periods of growth, organisations will often seek to recover cost and limit demand, which will tempt them to quote much higher prices.

*The price of capital goods tends to fluctuate wildly*

Prices in capital goods markets, then, have a tendency to fluctuate quite wildly, both between time periods and between different forms of the same product, which makes it difficult to decide how to use price as a competitive weapon. On the other hand, the amounts of money involved and the complexity of the product provide more scope than in other areas for variations on the pricing mix. This can involve:

- Payment terms.
- Payment penalties and bonuses.
- Leasing arrangements.
- Modular pricing.
- The way a price is presented.
- Technology transfer agreements.

## Decision-making in the Purchase of Capital Goods

The size and significance of a capital purchase will mean that large numbers of people are likely to combine to form the decision-making unit. Since relationships are an important factor in capital goods sales, contacts, and the ability to keep and develop such relationships, is a critical factor for success, as is the flexibility to have different types of relationships with different people. The significance of capital purchases, however, can mean that governments can also have an interest in the product. Indeed, for some products, governments may even be *the* customer. Thus, there can be a political, as well as a commercial, influence in the decision to buy.

In some instances, such as a defence project, high levels of secrecy may also be required. In others, such as a large infrastructural civil engineering project, awareness of a country's development plans, the involvement of national suppliers or some 'tit-for-tat' investment by the supplier or the supplier's government may be a prerequisite for a successful sale. This political aspect, plus the complex nature of the 'buy-centre', may require a lot of 'politics' and building of credibility along a number of different dimensions for an organisation to be a viable contender for a piece of business.

*Capital goods marketing demands that suppliers are flexible*

Marketing capital goods is, therefore, conducted in a complex market environment. Marketers are faced with long product life-cycles and circumstances which make it difficult to innovate. In contrast, they are also faced with volatile demand and large variations between one purchase and the next. This is further complicated by the need to develop good relationships with customers, but with the likelihood that any relationship will only be temporary since any one customer is only likely to purchase once or, at best, infrequently. This demands that suppliers are able to be flexible in terms of relationships, capacity and the product they supply. It also demands that they take a long-term perspective on several counts including sales negotiations, product design and development, relationship management, profit planning and funding issues.

# TOPIC 13

# Internet Marketing

The term 'Internet marketing' can best be summarised as:

'The effective promotion of goods and services through the medium of an interactive, computerised information channel and the enhancement of existing customer information for the purpose of refining an integrated marketing strategy.'

The two most important Internet applications are the World Wide Web and electronic mail, or e-mail. These provide the vehicles for the most extreme example of Internet marketing, 'electronic commerce': the sale and purchase of goods and services over the Internet. The idea is a new communication channel in the form of electronic interaction via computer networks which have quite different advantages and disadvantages from the alternatives. The long-term future of the Internet is difficult to predict with some commentators forecasting that it will be replaced by media such as interactive digital television. However, as a prototype, it demonstrates the potential for expanding interactive communication of electronic information.

*Internet marketing presents unique marketing challenges*

The challenge for suppliers is that many web sites attract a continuum of visitors. At one end are passive users seeking a reference site. The challenge is to satisfy these 'browsers' while finding innovative ways of attracting active users to visit the site and get involved in *your* product rather than a competitor's.

As an example, *The Economist* relies on weekly subscriber e-mails to keep their publication in front of Web site visitors on a regular basis. Internet Florist use 'Virtual Bouquets' to encourage visitors and to generate 'pick-ups' from their Web site by providing users with the opportunity to send a real bouquet as an alternative. The 'AIDA' standard applies to the Internet as much as any other advertising media. In order to attract and involve users, providers must generate awareness, interest and desire, culminating in action, as a result of effective marketing communications.

## Internet Marketing: Principles and Considerations

The Internet is an important new way of interacting with customers, but as just one of the channels for interaction, it cannot be considered in isolation. Its potential contribution can be assessed through a model of the role of IT in marketing generally. This can be summarised under the following headings.

### Integration: Know Your Customer

In order to manage customer relationships, organisations need systems which can manage data throughout the customer purchase-cycle, from initial contact through sales to delivery and post-sales service. Customer data must also be integrated across communication mechanisms to ensure coordination across the multiple channels by which consumer demands can reach the supplier (e.g., by telephone, through a sales person, via written communication and so on).

Many organisations fail to integrate their web sites in this way, simply advertising their products on the Web and making no attempt to gather vital customer information in the form of customer feedback. Web sites are frequently wasted as an opportunity to obtain, utilise and enhance existing knowledge about customers, and fail to exploit the Web's own interactive nature to add value through product configuration, online pricing, information on availability, decision trees and other sales support activities.

### Interactivity: Beyond Addressability to Dialogue

Truly knowing your customers means effectively closing the loop between the messages sent to them and the messages they send back. In the age of 'addressability', where organisations try to communicate with individual customers through carefully targeted direct mail, 'interactivity' goes one step further. The Web's interactive

*Good customer communications requires a 'closed-loop' relationship*

nature can be used by retailers like Waitrose to provide
customer services such as 'Recipe Search', which allows
users to search for a recipe by type (i.e., vegetarian,
month, cooking and preparation time and even including or excluding specified ingredients). The Web site
builds up its customer knowledge, enabling it, for
example, to offer personalised promotions as a by-
product of the service.

### Individualisation: Mass Marketing and Micro-Segmentation

*Internet
marketing
enables
personal
service
through mass
customisation*

The ability to deal directly with individual members of a
mass market from one central source enables personal
service through mass customisation. Amazon.com, for
instance, provide a simple book retail service, but over
time begin to offer customers information about other
books that other readers of similar purchasing patterns
have found interesting. Leveraging their data on
customers and the interactive potential of the Web, the
company can move beyond personalised promotions to
the provision of information and product configurations
unique to each of their individual customers. Once this is
combined with a pricing and delivery/customer service
package similarly uniquely configured, the age of mass
customisation is truly upon us.

### Independence of Location: The Death of Distance

A bedroom made to order by an Internet design service
achieves the individualisation of a men's tailors, combined with post-industrial revolution economies of scale.
The independence of location allows individualisation to
be achieved economically on a grand scale. Niche
products can serve their target markets even if spread
globally.

Being able to reach customers wherever they are
may have the effect of widening consumer choice and
extending consumer power. The growth of software
'agents' (who search the Web for specific items at the
lowest price) effectively outsources a time-consuming
activity whilst levelling prices. One survey found that 22
per cent of US car buyers paid the asking price, against
only 9.3 per cent of online buyers. Computer support in
the areas of pricing individually tailored services or

providing information services has the added benefit of freeing up the expensive individual sales person for the tasks that they are good at: building up individual relationships with key accounts at senior levels.

### Intelligence: Informed Strategy

Better customer data can also improve decisions on marketing strategy. In some cases, segments may also be derived from the data gathered. This again illustrates the importance of data integration, enabling more effective planning and initiatives to serve particular target segments more effectively.

### Industry Restructuring: Redrawing the Market Map

As organisations redefine themselves to take advantage of IT-enabled marketing, or are replaced by newcomers who operate according to the new rules, some industries are restructuring. In the financial services sector, the Internet is replacing human advice in product specification, as well as basic transactions. As an example, new electronic intermediaries will search for the best live quote from a range of life insurance companies.

*IT-enabled marketing is causing some industries to restructure*

## Top Six Considerations

The appropriateness of the Internet for a particular customer interaction will vary according to the characteristics of the market segment. It can be used to advantage where its features match the needs of the customer interaction.

- As long as the Internet is only accessible by a proportion of the population, it is necessary to establish what proportion of the target segment of the market will have access.
- The accessibility provided by the Internet means that those communicating do not need to do so at the same time. Information can be accessed across time-zones without the restrictions of contact in respective national business hours only. It is therefore particularly relevant to geographically dispersed markets and those where the cost of sales visits is prohibitive.

- The Internet offers the benefits of being more interactive than direct mail or broadcast media. Since interaction is with a computer rather than a person, the interactivity is different from that of a telephone or sales visit, making it appropriate for pre-programmed, high-volume, repetitive tasks.
- The Web is mainly a medium of two-dimensional static words and graphics, although use of sound and video is expanding. This has enabled, for example, hotels and conferences to make use of virtual reality technology to demonstrate their services and facilities to Internet browsers. The Internet restrictions still make certain products such as clothes less appropriate for sale over the Web since, as part of the purchase, the customer may wish to feel the fabric or try an item on.
- The marginal cost of the Internet as a communication tool can be low. It is generally false that the cost of advertising is saved, however, since the size of the Internet still poses the problem of how to get people to the Web site in the first place. This can be done using online search engines such as Yahoo and Excite, or service providers such as America Online.

*Issues of security and privacy still plague the Internet*

- User concerns about security and privacy can impede the placement of orders over the Internet. This is likely to bias Internet sales in the direction of relatively low-value items such as books or CDs, and in favour of suppliers with strong, trusted brands. Market research suggests that the dominant factors affecting Internet use remain the traditional concerns: price, convenience, service levels, product availability and so on. Internet speed and the quality of Web sites will therefore be just as important as addressing security issues for the growth of the Internet over the coming years.

## Future Challenges

With the advent of digital and WebTV, one of the major challenges for advertisers is determining how products are going to be promoted most effectively in five years' time. In the 1940s, Procter & Gamble spent more than half its advertising dollars on radio. From 1950 to 1955, the new medium of television went from taking nearly nothing to 80 per cent of the advertising budget. In contrast, only 0.4 per cent of its 1998 $3 billion-a-year advertising budget was spent on the Internet. Unilever, meanwhile, have agreed to invest $20 million in partnerships with America Online and Microsoft to explore ways of Internet advertising.

Part of the problem is that while, in the USA, radio and television developed as a form of mass-market entertainment with advertising slots incorporated from the start, the Internet evolved mainly as an information resource used by individuals. Advertisements only started to appear on the Internet in the mid-1990s and generally rely on the user to click on the rectangular 'banner' to be taken to the advertiser's Web site.

Digital television and WebTV challenge the Internet's big advantage over traditional television in their potential for interaction, transforming a passive viewer into an active participant, more likely to absorb and respond to the advertiser's message. The question for advertisers is, will any of these new media replace television as the main form of home entertainment?

*The advent of digital and WebTV raises significant issues for advertisers*

**Section C**

# UNDERSTANDING MARKETS AND COMPETITORS

# TOPIC 14

# Marketing Information and Research

Decision-making in organisations requires relevant information to be available if the outcomes are not to be based on those often-used management support tools – 'gut feel' or rationalised personal preference. Within this, marketing information is of vital importance. Indeed, one of the key roles of marketing professionals should be the supply of market and marketing-performance information, which will enable the rest of the organisation to make decisions about the market-related areas of their responsibilities. As examples, corporate or strategic managers need good market environment and competitor information to be able to set the overall strategic direction of the organisation, and operations managers need to understand the critical success factors associated with the delivery of their product or service, since these should form the basis for the design of their operating systems.

These examples illustrate that marketing research is not an activity which is performed in isolation, but is one where the results will contribute to many managerial or policy decisions. The implication of this is that the collection, collation and reporting of marketing information needs to be structured in ways appropriate to the decisions it will support. Managers requesting marketing information and research must, therefore, have a clear understanding of exactly what they need to know in order to make the judgements for which they are responsible. This is often one of the biggest problems in drafting a market research brief or in specifying a marketing information system: distinguishing between what it would be 'nice to know' and what is actually needed for management purposes. Tables 14.1 and 14.2 illustrate the areas which commonly form the focus of marketing research.

*It is important to distinguish between 'nice to know' and 'need to know'*

**Table 14.1**  Main areas of market research

| | |
|---|---|
| • *Customers* | Behaviour |
| | Needs |
| | Responses |
| | Beliefs |
| | Characteristics |
| • *Markets* | Size |
| | Structure |
| | Dynamics |
| | Relationships |
| | Trends |
| • *Competition* | Share |
| | Positioning |
| | Aims |
| | Strengths/weaknesses |
| • *Environment* | PEST* |
| | Institutions |
| | Trends |
| • *Our impact* | Share |
| | Penetration |
| | Coverage |
| | Image |
| | Service levels |

*PEST = Political, Economic, Social and Technological factors of the environment.

**Table 14.2**  Top ten marketing research topics*

- Market-share analysis
- Market potential
- Market characteristics
- Sales performance
- Business trends
- Economic forecasting
- Competitor products
- Pricing studies
- Product testing
- Information systems

*Note that these cover both internal and external topics investigated to enhance marketing performance.

The activities involved in marketing research can be described in a number of different ways, but together indicate the major issues in conducting marketing research or creating marketing information systems.

*Marketing research involves a combination of research techniques and activities*

## Reactive versus Passive Research

This is sometimes used to distinguish between the different forms or styles of research and is a useful way of classifying the various types of marketing research activities. Reactive research implies an interaction between the researcher and the subject(s). It can, therefore, take the form of asking questions as part of a postal survey, an interview, or a group discussion. In each case, the researcher will be prompting the subject(s) to provide their views, state their intentions, or recall their experiences. Reactive research can also take the form of experiments, such as test-marketing a product, altering an aspect of the marketing mix to establish variations in response, or 'laboratory' studies such as simulated shopping environments.

Passive research concerns the pure observation of subjects, or the collection of data. These could include: consumer panels who simply report their activities on a regular basis in order to establish patterns of behaviour; retail audits, where stock levels and shelf-space allocations are observed on a sample basis to ascertain market share, market penetration, etc.; surveys of publicly available reports for the development of overviews and general impressions; or internally generated data which will provide indications of organisational performance. Passive research limits the researcher's understanding to his or her own interpretations of observed phenomena or data. Reactive research provides more scope for prompting subjects or for seeking clarification.

## Primary versus Secondary Research

These distinguish between the various sources of data available to the researcher. Secondary sources refer to data already available in some form or another and may include the results of previously performed research or other publicly available material such as newspaper reports or government statistics. Primary research involves gathering data directly from the market through the collection of opinions, the observation of behaviour, or through tapping into sources within the organisation. The advantage of primary research is that it will probably provide information which is unique, whereas secondary sources are likely to be available to everyone else in a market.

## Desk versus Field Research

These are another way of describing the sources which can be used to provide marketing information. **Desk research** usually involves a search of existing data sources, whereas **field research** involves going 'out into the field' or market place to collect, usually primary, data. It is normal to engage in desk research first to establish what information needs to be obtained from field research because it is unavailable elsewhere.

## Internal versus External Research

*A wealth of internal information sources is often overlooked*

This distinction draws attention to the range of information sources which often exist within an organisation without having to look outside or commission specific market research projects. Internal sources can include sales records, shipping documentation and invoices, as well as reports generated by sales people, service engineers or delivery and installation personnel. Customer correspondence can also be a useful source of data on the way that the market is responding to an organisation's offering. Sadly, it is not unusual for organisations to commission, for example, competitor-analysis market research when they themselves employ people who previously worked for those competitors and whom their current employers had ignored in their search for information.

When considering marketing research, it is also useful to distinguish between marketing data, information and intelligence when discussing any activity or system. In this context, data can best be thought of as the raw facts, figures or descriptions of the topic being researched. Information is ordered data, or data which has been selected to describe a particular market or performance feature. Intelligence can best be regarded as information from which conclusions have been drawn. As an example, an 80:20, or **Pareto analysis** of an industrial company's customers based on sales invoices (the data) would yield information (a list of their best customers in revenue terms) which could then be interpreted and/or explained to provide intelligence. Thus, an organisation might conclude that its best customers were financial services companies from the northern regions of the country.

## Marketing Information Systems

A comprehensive marketing information system re-quires attention to four main areas of activity. The first area concerns **performance monitoring over time** and relies heavily on information drawn from internal sources. Such information can include profitability analyses, which can cover customer, segment and product profitability. Also important are sales volumes across different sectors, product mixes and the effective-ness of discount structures. Other points of interest might be trends pertaining to delivery performance, complaints and product returns. The widespread use of computer systems for many of the administrative routines of organisations provide a good opportunity for the regular generation of timely reports on these critical aspects of an organisation's performance effec-tiveness.

The second area, **market monitoring**, refers to the regular collection of externally generated material which provide insights into developments in the marketing environment. This activity could be performed by an organisation's library, if they have one, an outside agency, or by individuals in marketing or marketing associated roles. Whatever the mechanism used, it should be able to deliver steady flows of newspaper, journal and other published matter which will alert managers to changes in their areas of interest. It should also act as a repository from which information required on an occasional basis can be drawn. Market monitoring could also involve the generation of information from employees who operate in the field, from regular sur-veys, or from panel reports generated at specific inter-vals. Topics for market monitoring might embrace: competitor reconnaissance; standards bodies; legislative activities; technological advances; pressure group cam-paigns; fashion trends; and so on.

The third aspect of an integrated marketing information system is a **market investigation facility** for specific questions or *ad hoc* projects. This would involve expert researchers administering questionnaires (postal or telephone), conducting interviews, or engaging in desk research of some form or another. The popular conception of market research usually focuses on this type of activity, but requires careful management if it is to be useful. Critical is the process of problem definition, from which a research plan is developed. The plan will focus on two main elements: the population to be researched; and the methodology to be employed. Such projects, however, are very expensive and need to be used carefully for the best effect.

The fourth feature of a system would be a mechanism for a **decision support** system, so that marketing personnel can manipulate information and intelligence using the analytical tools of marketing. These may be various statistical techniques such as: correlation; cluster or conjoint analysis; or may be based on analytical models of different kinds. Such models could include: 'What if' facilities; portfolio modelling; or complete planning systems. Just as the increased use of computers for administrative systems has enabled much more data to become available for analysis, so the leaps made in information technology towards expert systems and virtual reality will provide ever-increasing sophistication in this type of activity.

*Marketing information is a source of competitive power*

Marketing information is now recognised as a source of competitive power and increasing amounts of effort are being spent on the development of marketing information systems. Systems, however, cannot substitute for personal judgement and the creativity required to develop innovative marketing strategies. Such attributes are needed to identify the 'golden nuggets' often hidden by systematic approaches, and to generate the unique positioning or segmentation programmes essential for competitive advantage. In addition, it must be remembered that data, information or intelligence is only ever as good as the specifications from which it was produced, and much information is either too general, or the result of poorly conducted research, to be relied upon. Finally, it must also be remembered that any market research or marketing information systems invariably throw up more questions than they answer. There is no such phenomenon as perfect information.

## TOPIC 15

# Preparing the Marketing Research Brief and Proposal

Regardless of who carries out the work involved in a market research project, it is important that a clear brief is produced against which the subsequent work will be undertaken and judged. The research brief, which should be produced in both written and verbal form, is a key document and the starting point. In its preparation it is important that the following questions are to the fore:

- What do we want to know?
- What will we do with the information when we get it?

In this way clearly defined objectives can be set and adhered to.

### Contents of a Brief

First, the commissioning organisation should think very carefully about what, and how much, it wishes to reveal in the brief. Ideally, the brief should be open, precise and factual, but there may be particular points, such as the exact budget, which are best omitted. A good briefing document, preferably accompanied by product litera-ture, may span 1–5 pages. Its elaboration/discussion at a briefing meeting should clarify points, confirm contents and remove any written ambiguities. At the end of the meeting, if a quotation is to be submitted, the con-sultant/agency should try to find ways of demonstrating both competence and a firm commitment to the project.

*The brief should be open, precise and factual*

A good research brief should contain the following:

- Background information: on the market; the company; its products/services; market standing; and so on.
- Research objectives: perhaps both primary and sec-ondary; in this section it may be useful to define precise question areas to be covered by the research.

- Desired time scale: overall project completion date, together with any interim report times or key decision dates such as product development stages or interfaces with other departments.
- Report format and presentation requirements: this is a good opportunity, if the commissioning organisation wishes, to indicate preferences.
- Company liaison/contact: this should also include the information to be made available in support of the research.
- Market-place confidentiality or openness required from the research.

It is not suggested that the briefing document be seen as a 'straitjacket' but as a series of well-thought-out guidelines. As such, the expertise of the agency/ consultancy should be sought in the briefing meeting, both with regard to the information and requirements of the brief, as well as in discussion of the subsequent best methods for achievement of the brief's objectives.

Whilst it is not suggested that the brief should define exactly all aspects of the project, such as research methodology or specific budget allocation, it can be helpful if some verbal discussion on these points has *It is fair to* taken place during the briefing meeting. Given the *ask for a* expected expertise of the agency/consultancy, it is a *written* very fair approach to provide a comprehensive briefing *proposal* and to ask for a written proposal offering best solutions. *offering best* This should include the recommended methodologies, *solutions* the expected time frames and the costs involved.

Some commissioning organisations set a proposal deadline or tender submission date. At the briefing stage, it may be best to indicate the competitive quoting levels involved without necessarily defining or naming these precisely. Normally, the costs involved in the briefing meeting and preparation of the research proposal are seen by consultants/agencies as part of their prospecting and business development costs, and involve no client charges (whether the proposal is accepted or not) unless specifically previously agreed (and then, best in writing).

## The Research Proposal

Basically the proposal, which is often both a written document and personal presentation, is a 'best response' to the marketing research brief. As such, it represents an ability to communicate and this should be a selection factor given that the organisation subsequently commissioned to carry out the research is providing an indication or preview of its listening, communication and presentation skills. The proposal is therefore an opportunity to provide additional clues as to the likely quality of the final product. This assessment opportunity for the client should not be overlooked!

*The proposal is an opportunity to provide clues to the likely quality of the final product*

The research proposal also needs to provide a specification of what the research organisation will do, how it will carry out the work and what it will cost. It is important that it conveys its understanding of what is expected and its competence to provide the work most efficiently. A good research proposal should, therefore, include:

- Background information, to convey a clear understanding of the project and the issues involved.
- Objectives, which should be clearly listed and very precisely defined against the specification of the problem.
- Work programme and methodology, covering both the way that the objectives will be achieved and the way that the work programme would be completed; it should detail sample size, research stages and questionnaire methods.
- Fees/payment terms and time scales, which should be clearly stated and classified showing expenses, tax and so on, set against the work schedule.
- Company details and research personnel involved, including research company competence and brief biographies of personnel, plus, if relevant, any business terms.
- Summary of research project benefits and agency's confidence in its competence to 'deliver' what is required.

## The Sponsoring Organisation's Response

Acceptance of the proposal should be in writing. It should authorise the work and confirm the points of agreement and costs involved. This should provide a binding agreement as to what is to be done and at what cost, so as to eliminate any subsequent disagreement between the sponsoring organisation and the agency/consultancy.

# TOPIC 16

# Auditing a Market

Basically, a marketing audit is the means by which a company can understand how it relates to the environment in which it operates. It is also the means by which a company can identify its own strengths and weaknesses as they relate to external opportunities and threats. It is thus a way of helping management to select a position in that environment based on known factors.

Expressed in its simplest form, the purpose of a marketing plan is to answer three central questions:

- Where is the company now?
- Where does the company want to go?
- How should the company organise its resources to get there?

*A marketing audit answers the question: 'Where is the company now?'*

The audit provides the information from which the first of these questions is answered. An audit, then, is a systematic, critical and unbiased appraisal of an organisation's market environment and of its operations. A marketing audit is also part of the larger management audit and is often undertaken as part of a wider business planning process.

Often the need for an audit does not manifest itself until things start to go wrong, such as declining sales, falling margins, lost market share, under-utilised production capacity, and so on. At this point the marketing audit becomes a last-ditch, end-of-the-road attempt to define a company's marketing problem. An equally problematic approach is that an audit is something done by an independent body, from time to time, to ensure that a company is on the right lines. However, since marketing is such a complex function, it seems illogical not to carry out a thorough situation analysis at least once a year at the beginning of the planning cycle.

There is much evidence to show that many highly successful companies, as well as using normal information and control procedures and marketing research throughout the year, also start their planning cycle each year with a formal review, through an audit-type process, of everything that has had an important influence on marketing activities. Certainly, in many leading consumer goods companies, the annual self-audit approach is a tried and tested discipline integrated into the management process, which, like other managerial processes, becomes easier to perform the more regularly it is conducted.

*An audit is a structured approach to collecting and analysing information*

The audit, then, is a structured approach to the collection and analysis of information and data in the complex business environment, and is an essential prerequisite to problem-solving.

## Marketing Audit Variables

Any company carrying out a marketing audit will be faced with two kinds of variables. First, there are variables over which the company has no direct control. These usually take the form of what can be described as environmental, market and competitive variables. Second, there are variables over which the company has complete control. These can be called operational variables. This gives a clue as to how to structure an audit in two parts:

- External audit.
- Internal audit.

The external audit is concerned with the uncontrollable variables, whilst the internal audit is concerned with the controllable variables. It, therefore, starts with an examination of information on the general economy and then moves on to the outlook for the health and growth of the markets served by the company. The purpose of the internal audit is to assess the organisation's resources as they relate to the environment and *vis-à-vis* the resources of competitors. Table 16.1 contains a checklist of areas that should be investigated as part of both the internal and external marketing audit.

Each of the headings shown in Table 16.1 should be examined with a view to isolating those factors that are considered critical to the company's performance. Initially, the auditor's task is to screen the enormous amount

**Table 16.1** The marketing audit checklist

---

**EXTERNAL AUDIT**

| | |
|---|---|
| Business and economic environment | Economic<br>Political/Fiscal/Legal<br>Social/Cultural<br>Technological<br>Inter-company |
| The market | Total market, size, growth and trends (value/volume)<br>Market characteristics<br>Developments and trends in marketing mix variables as follows: |

- products
- prices
- physical distribution
- channels
- customers/consumers
- communication
- industry practices

| | |
|---|---|
| Competition | Major competitors<br>Size<br>Market shares/coverage<br>Market standing/reputation<br>Production capabilities<br>Distribution policies<br>Marketing methods<br>Extent of diversification<br>Personnel issues<br>International links<br>Profitability<br>Key strengths and weaknesses |

**INTERNAL AUDIT**

Marketing operational variables

Sales (by geographical location, industrial type, customer, and product)
Market shares
Profit margins/costs
Marketing information/research
Marketing mix variables as follows:

- product management
- price
- distribution
- promotion
- operations and resources

---

of information and data for validity and relevance. Some of the data and information obtained for an audit will have to be reorganised into a more easily usable form, and judgement will have to be applied to decide what further data and information are necessary for a proper definition of the problem. Behind the summary headings, however, more detailed questions should be asked. Thus there are basically two phases which comprise the auditing process:

- Identification, measurement, collection and analysis of all the relevant facts and opinions which impinge on a company's operations.
- The application of judgement to uncertain areas which remain after this analysis.

Occasionally it may be justified to hire outside consultants to carry out a marketing audit to check that a company is getting the most out of its resources. However, it seems an unnecessary expense to have this done every year. The answer, therefore, is to have an audit carried out annually by the company's own line managers on their own areas of responsibility.

*Investment in training and institutionalising procedures facilitates the development of annual audits*

Objections to this usually centre on the problems of time and objectivity. In practice, these problems are overcome, first, by institutionalising procedures in as much detail as possible so that all managers have to conform to a disciplined approach, and second, by thorough training in the use of the procedures themselves. However, even this will not achieve the purpose of an audit unless a rigorous discipline is applied from the highest down to the lowest levels of management involved in the audit. Such a discipline is usually successful in helping managers to avoid the sort of tunnel vision that often results from a lack of critical appraisal.

Alternative names for a marketing audit are PEST analysis (Political, Economic, Sociological and Technical) and variations on this mnemonic such as STEP, but since these do not include competitor or internal analyses, they are only a part of the fuller audit referred to here.

A useful way of presenting the findings of an audit is Michael Porter's Five Forces Analysis under the headings: power of supplies; power of buyers; threat of new entrants; threat of alternative technologies; and the

*The
marketing
audit
provides the
basis for
many
decisions*

rivalry or competitive intensity of the firms in the market (for further details see Topic 20, 'Competitor Analysis')

Once completed, the information gained from a marketing audit forms the basis for many decision-making activities in the organisation. For marketing, a summary is required which highlights the key market situations and trends which will impact on the organisation's marketing strategy and programmes. The best summary is in the form of a SWOT analysis which displays the organisation's key Strengths, Weaknesses, Opportunities and Threats. Regularisation of the marketing audit will then allow for annually updated SWOTs from which developments in an organisation's strategic and tactical approaches to marketing can be made.

# Constructing a SWOT

A SWOT analysis, covering an organisation's strengths, weaknesses, opportunities and threats, is a tool often used as part of an organisation's policy and decision-making process. A well-constructed SWOT can provide powerful insights into the situation facing an organisation and can demonstrate, in a clear fashion, the direction an organisation needs to take. Poorly constructed SWOTs will, at best, provide only a bland interpretation of an organisation's position. At worst, they can be misleading and will lead to wrong conclusions and misguided policy. It is, therefore, important for marketing managers to be well-versed in the issues involved in developing a good SWOT, since it is their interpretation of the market and the organisation's position within it which will form the basis of a SWOT, whoever in the organisation performs the analysis.

A SWOT analysis must be derived from a marketing audit. In conducting an audit, it is important to remember that the results will be used to identify points which will appear in the SWOT. In this way, an audit can be given focus, and when the time comes to create the SWOT, the chances of relevant information being absent will be reduced. Poor SWOTs tend to be based on opinion or are constructed without reference to market and marketing information.

*A marketing SWOT is derived from a marketing audit*

It is also important to understand that a SWOT is constructed for a specific market, segment or customer. While it is possible to perform a SWOT for an organisation which relates to the whole range of its activities, it is unlikely that the strengths and weaknesses identified will be relevant to all the markets in which it operates. Thus, a hotel might rate its high-class restaurant facilities, which provides meals freshly cooked to order, as a strength for the 'special occasion eating-out market', but would be wrong in thinking this feature was also a strength for the 'business conference market' which required fast throughput at meal times in order to cover their meeting's agendas.

## Strengths and Weaknesses

*Strengths and weaknesses are assessed relative to performance by competitors*

Strengths and weaknesses refer to the conclusions of the internal marketing audit in relation to customer requirements. They also refer to the organisation's performance against those requirements relative to its competitors. Thus, a strength is only a strength if it is something that is of value to customers and is also something which an organisation does better than its competitors. Having the ability to deliver against the placement of an order within 48 hours is not a strength if customers require 24 hours' delivery and its major competitors are all able to fulfil this requirement. The converse situation would, of course, be a strength. Also, if a 24 hours' delivery service is the norm and all competitors fulfil this requirement, it is what is known as a 'qualifying' strength and should be omitted from the SWOT.

It is also important to distinguish between a marketing *strength* and a marketing *asset*. An asset is something which an organisation possesses which could, potentially, become a strength. A useful means of developing strengths from assets is to apply the question 'which means that . . ?' until a competitive advantage is found. Thus, high-level engineering skills are an asset from which a strength – the ability to supply against a tight specification – can be derived. Weaknesses will be associated with the absence of an asset of some form, or an asset which underperforms when compared with customer requirements and competitors' abilities.

A useful means of differentiating between strengths, weaknesses and assets is to identify **order-winning** as opposed to **order-qualifying** criteria. Qualifying criteria will be those features or benefits of goods or services which have to be present for a supplier to be a contender for a sale. Thus a holiday company might need to offer packages in Greece to qualify for consideration by a potential customer. Order-winning criteria will be related to those characteristics which it offers as unique or which outperform competitor offerings. Strengths can only refer to order-winning features and benefits,

| Competitors / Critical success factors | Weighting factor | Your organisation | Competitor A | Competitor B | Competitor C |
|---|---|---|---|---|---|
| CSF 1 | | | | | |
| CSF 2 | | | | | |
| CSF 3 | | | | | |
| CSF 4 | | | | | |
| Total weighted score | 100 | | | | |

**Figure 17.1**   Establishing competitive positions using critical success factors

whereas weaknesses can encompass both order-qualifying and order-winning factors.

A similar methodology is to use the concept of **critical success factors** (CSFs). These relate to the factors which a supplier in a market must meet if they are to compete successfully. There are usually relatively few factors that determine success. Factors such as product performance, breadth of offering, speed of service, low prices, reputation and so on, are often the most important here. A layout such as that shown in Figure 17.1 can be useful when comparing overall competitive positions using CSFs. Having identified the main CSF for a market segment, each factor should be weighted out of 100, according to its importance to customers. Total weightings should add up to 100. It is then possible to score each major competitor out of 10 on their performance against each CSF. Multiplying each score by its weight will provide a quantitative assessment of the relative strengths of each competitor within a segment. Figure 17.2 illustrates a typical calculation based on this method.

*Strengths and weaknesses focus on critical success factors*

## Opportunities and Threats

Opportunities and threats refer to external issues and are identified as a result of the external marketing audit. Thus, improving quality or creating a brand name are

| Critical success factor | Weighting % | | Strengths/Weaknesses Analysis | | | |
|---|---|---|---|---|---|---|
| The few elements of the marketing mix in which any competition has to perform well to succeed | The relative importance of each CSF scored out of 100 | | Performance against each CSF is scored out of 10 and multiplied by the weighting | | | |
| | | | | Competition | | |
| | | | You | Comp A | Comp B | Comp C |
| 1   Product | 20% | 1 | 9 = 1.8 | 6 = 1.2 | 5 = 1.0 | 4 = 0.8 |
| 2   Price | 10% | 2 | 8 = 0.8 | 5 = 0.5 | 6 = 0.6 | 10 = 1.0 |
| 3   Service | 50% | 3 | 5 = 2.5 | 9 = 4.5 | 7 = 3.5 | 6 = 3.0 |
| 4   Image | 20% | 4 | 8 = 1.6 | 8 = 1.6 | 5 = 1.0 | 3 = 0.6 |
| Totals | 100% | | 6.7 | 7.8 | 6.1 | 5.4 |

**Figure 17.2**   Strengths and weaknesses analysis

*not* opportunities and low stock turnover or poor industrial relations are *not* threats, since they all relate to internal issues for an organisation.

Apart from the problem of definition, it is also often difficult to identify *relevant* opportunities and threats. In theory, an organisation is faced with limitless opportunities and myriads of threats. These can range from the opportunities created by new markets, new products and poor performance by competitors, to the threats of war, earthquakes and competitor activities. What makes an opportunity or a threat relevant is its significance for the organisation and its likelihood of occurring. The opportunities and threats matrices depicted in Figures 17.3 and 17.4 provide a useful means of prioritising opportunities and threats for the purposes of inclusion in a SWOT analysis.

*Opportunities result from external market changes or existing needs which are poorly served*

A further means of identifying opportunities is to concentrate on those which result from one of two different situations. The first of these situations concerns changes which are occurring in the market place. These changes can take the form of legislative developments, a competitor leaving a market, infrastructural changes, market growth and so on, and can yield some very attractive opportunities. Whilst such developments may also yield threats, it is important to consider them in light of the organisation's marketing asset base. Where they go against an asset base or play to an organisation's weaknesses, they are obviously threats. If, however, they

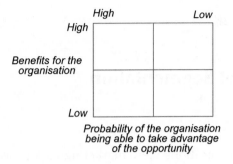

**Figure 17.3** Opportunities matrix

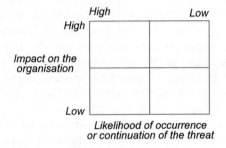

**Figure 17.4** Threats matrix

relate to strengths or capabilities, they are more likely to be opportunities.

Other opportunities derive from the second type of situation – that of an existing need being poorly served by current suppliers. If a supplier services the CSFs for its customers to a high degree of satisfaction, this is unlikely to yield an opportunity of any value. If, on the other hand, a supplier performs poorly against one CSF when compared with customer needs, then an opportunity will exist, so long as the organisation has the potential to service that need more effectively than the existing supplier.

A good SWOT, then, provides a clear presentation of an organisation's platform and position within a particular market. The issues it contains will have been refined for relevance and meaning. Each issue will have been the subject of a 'so what?' or 'which means that . . . ?' analysis, so that the true implications of each of the features included are reached. Following the presentation of a good SWOT, it should be easy to understand what the main thrust of an organisation's activities should be.

*A good SWOT should provide a clear indication of future direction*

# TOPIC 18

# Market Segmentation

Some organisations view marketing as a process which tries to persuade a faceless mass of customers to see things their way. To adopt such an orientation is to misunderstand totally what marketing is all about. Ultimately, to survive and prosper in business in the long run, organisations have to satisfy the needs of customers. Central to this need-satisfying process is what in marketing is known as 'market segmentation'.

The process of market segmentation is, itself, a continuous dialogue with specific groups of customers (market segments), whose needs are understood in depth, and for whom organisations develop specific offers that have a differential advantage over the offers of competitors. Only when this has been done should an organisation consider the array of communication and other marketing activities they have at their disposal. Market segmentation, then, is a process that links what enterprises sell to the people who buy, and as such it is without doubt the key to successful marketing.

*Market segmentation is a difficult and elusive skill*

Market segmentation, however, remains the most difficult and elusive of marketing skills, as it is both complex and multifaceted. Yet organisations must seek successful segmentation strategies, otherwise they become just another company selling what are called 'me too' products, which inevitably lead to price wars and which often turn out to be ruinous. The approach presented here, encapsulates the main points to look for when starting to think about market segmentation.

## Starting the Process

The first point to make is that no two customers are the same. Nonetheless, except in very special circumstances, it is not commercially viable to make exclusive products for single customers. Organisations thus need to find commonalties between customers so that they can group

96

them in a way that enables them to deal with such groups in a cost-effective way. Thus, the principal criteria for segmentation are as follows:

- Segments must be large enough to make it worthwhile developing products or services especially for them.
- Segments must be sufficiently different from other segments to warrant offering them something different.
- There has to be some way of describing them so that they can be communicated with in a cost-effective way.

There are basically four steps in market segmentation:

- Analysis of customer responses or behaviour.
- Analysis of customer characteristics or attributes.
- Analysis of benefits sought.
- Clustering of groups with similar needs.

## Analysis of Customer Behaviour

This is essentially the manifestation of the way customers actually behave in the market place. In respect of *what* is bought, suppliers should look for buying behaviour including: the physical characteristics of products; how they are used; where they are bought; how they are bought; the price paid; and so on. This can indicate if there are any groups of products, outlets, or price categories, which are of potential interest to a supplier (i.e., where the opportunities and problems might be). These natural groupings, whilst obvious, do at least provide clues as to what is happening in the market, as they represent different purchase combinations that actually take place. They are known as micro segments.

## Analysis of Customer Attributes

Supplying organisations also need to know **who** these customers in the micro segments are, so that they can communicate with them. In this respect **demographic** descriptors have always been found to be the most useful method. For consumer markets, important variables include: age; sex; stage in the family life-cycle; and socio-economic groupings which describe people by

*Demographic descriptors are useful for describing consumer and industrial segments*

their social status in life as defined by their jobs. It is easy to understand how demographics can be related to purchase behaviour, since people have specific needs at certain times in their lives. There is also a useful relationship between readership habits, viewing patterns, and socio-economic groupings, which is very helpful in deciding what media to use to communicate with customers. Additionally, analyses such as a classification of regional neighbourhood groups (ACORN) which classifies all households according to 38 different neighbourhood types, can be particularly useful for retail businesses, because these neighbourhood types are closely related to specific consumption patterns for different categories of goods and services.

For industrial markets, Standard Industrial Classification (SIC) categories, number of employees, turnover, production processes, and so on, are also examples of demographic descriptors.

### Analysis of Benefits Sought

The third step is to try to understand *why* customers behave in these ways, so that suppliers will then be in a better position to sell to them. In this respect, it will be important to look at what **benefits** customers derive from their purchases. These benefits will obviously be closely related to customers' attitudes, perceptions and preferences. This needs to be done for each micro segment.

### Clustering of Groups

The fourth step is to search for clusters, or groups of micro segments with similar needs. Whilst this can be done manually, it is preferable to use a computerised clustering package such as MARKET SEGMENT MASTER,* as often there can be as many as a hundred micro segments identified during the preliminary segmentation process.

---

*Details of MARKET SEGMENT MASTER can be obtained from Professor Malcolm McDonald at Cranfield School of Management, Cranfield, Bedford MK43 0AL, England.

|  |  | Worrier | Sociable | Sensory | Independent |
|---|---|---|---|---|---|
| Who buys | Socio-economic | C1 C2 | B C1 C2 | C1 C2 D | A B |
|  | Demographic | Large families 25–40 | Teens Young Smokers | Children | Males 35–50 |
|  | Psychographics | conservative: hypochondriosis | high sociability: active | high self-involvement | high autonomy: value-oriented |
| What is bought | % of total market | 50% | 30% | 15% | 5% |
|  | Product examples | Crest | McLeans Ultra Bright | Colgate (stripe) | Own label |
|  | Product physics | large canisters | large tubes | medium tubes | small tubes |
|  | Price paid | low | high | medium | low |
|  | Outlet | supermarket | supermarket | supermarket | independent |
|  | Purchase frequency | weekly | monthly | monthly | quarterly |
| Why | Benefits sought | stop decay | attract attention | flavour | price |
| Potential for growth |  | nil | high | medium | nil |

**Figure 17.1**   Example of segmentation of toothpaste market

Figure 18.1 provides a good example of actual consumer segmentation in the toothpaste market, from which it can be seen how segmentation criteria can be used to identify discrete segments.

Exactly the same principles can be followed in respect of industrial markets. Thus, the objectives of market segmentation are:

- To help to determine and to focus the direction of marketing resources through the analysis and understanding of trends and buyer behaviour.
- To help to determine realistic and obtainable marketing objectives.
- To create a basis for developing sustainable competitive advantage.

# TOPIC 19

# International Market Segmentation

The purpose of any segmentation exercise is to identify groups of purchasers who are sufficiently large, different and reachable to make them worthwhile for the investment of marketing effort. The isolation of a new segment whose needs are poorly served by existing suppliers can provide an opportunity to gain significant competitive advantage. Unfortunately, segmentation models in international marketing tend to consist of geographical groups, such as Western Europe, Eastern Europe, North America, ASEAN, Australasia and so on. Such groupings, however, are of very limited value as actionable marketing propositions, since they bear little relationship to actual consumption or usage patterns.

*Segmentation models based on geographical groups bear little resemblance to actual international markets*

Taking Europe as an example, there are typically three discrete groupings: European Union (EU); European Free Trade Association (EFTA); and Eastern Europe. Within Eastern Europe, however, there are at least three subgroups: the 'strong' group (the former Czechoslovakia and Hungary); the 'middle' group (Poland, Bulgaria, Romania and the former Yugoslavia), and the 'poor' group (the former Soviet republics). Even within Western Europe, there are significant differences arising from natural phenomena. For example, Scandinavia has short summers and long winters; Greece, Portugal, Italy and Spain have long summers and short winters; The Netherlands has low plains; and Switzerland has mountains.

Similarly, the per capita gross domestic product of Switzerland is seven times that of Portugal and, at the same time, there are significant communication and distribution differences. As examples: there is virtually no domestic television in Norway, whereas in Italy, television has very high levels of penetration; retail channel concentration is very dense in Northern Europe, whereas there is a preponderance of small, independent outlets in Southern Europe; there are also significant

cultural and linguistic differences, and so on. If, therefore, geography is to be relevant, it is more sensible to
think in terms of the Anglo Saxon North; the Latin
South; North-east France, Benelux and North-west Germany; and so on. Even this, however, is simplistic, in the
sense that there are basically three kinds of 'products'
which have to be considered when looking at such
segmentations.

## Types of International Products

### Truly Global Products

These are either products or services that are inherently
global, such as international services, world-standard
industrial products, high-technology products and so
on, or they are fashion or national products that have
become global, such as Chivas Regal, Coca-Cola, Rolls-
Royce, McDonald's, Marlborough cigarettes, and so on.
These have become global because their national appeal
is replicated in other countries.

### National Products

These typically exist where the market thrives on
supplier responsiveness, client relationships, national
preferences, and where global efficiencies are less
critical.

### Hybrid Products

Here, adaptation across countries is possible and this
requires a rethinking of simple geographical segmentation bases to ones based on customer groups with similar
needs across national boundaries. In advertising, for
example, the agency, J. Walter Thompson, discovered:

- Three broad breakfast types across Europe.
- A fashion lager market across Europe.
- Commonalities in computer software applications
  across Europe.

There are, thus, significant legal, regulatory, linguistic,
communication media and distribution channel differences across Western Europe and even throughout the

*A number of
growing
trends
amplify the
need for
international
market
segmentation*

world. There are, consequently, few truly global products and many traditional habits remain deep-rooted,
militating against international segmentation. On the
other hand (and this applies particularly to Western
Europe), there are a number of growing trends that
suggest that the need for international market segmentation will become increasingly important. These include:

- The desire for monetary union, social affairs union,
  foreign affairs union and defence policy unions.
- Increasing product and technical standardisation.
- Deregulation of transportation, telecommunications,
  pharmaceuticals and others.
- Attitude convergence towards work, individuality,
  materialism, the environment, and so on.
- Pan-European buying.
- International mergers, acquisitions and joint ventures.
- Increased international travel, education, media ex-
  posure, fashion, and so on.

The bases for international market segmentation are,
therefore, likely to be specific groupings of countries,
such as the new 'Euro Regions' outlined earlier, or
customer groups across selected countries.

Thereafter, the normal rules of market segmentation
apply (see Topic 18, 'Market Segmentation').

# TOPIC 20

# Competitor Analysis

An important aspect of a market that needs to be understood and characterised for the development of marketing policies is the substance and nature of the competition within it. In recent years, the work of Michael Porter, a Harvard Business School professor, has become synonymous with the process of such competitive analysis. His 'five forces' analytical framework provided a systematic method of exploring the competitive context of a market. Good analysis of these forces will help organisations to identify where power lies in the market, who can influence market trends, how the market is likely to develop, where to concentrate when seeking new market opportunities and the basic platforms from which it is possible to compete.

*Competitor analysis is intrinsic to the development of marketing policies*

## Components of Porter's Five Forces Framework

### The Threat of New Entrants

In analysing markets, one of the factors to be appraised is the existence, or absence, of 'barriers to entry'. In other words, how easy is it for new entrants to enter the market? Typically, barriers might be provided by high market share or economies of scale, so that without a minimum market share, unit costs will be uncompetitive. Similarly, heavy start-up costs, whether through the need for capital investment or high levels of marketing expenditure, can also provide a barrier. Conversely, markets may be easy for new competitors to enter where product differentiation is low, where technology changes can overcome cost barriers or where there is the potential for high levels of market fragmentation.

103

*Substitute Products or Services*

One factor that can considerably alter the strategic balance in a market place is the development of products that meet underlying customer needs more cost-effectively than existing products. As an example, the development of oil-based film had a major impact upon the demand for wood-based film. Similarly, the advent of fax machines virtually killed off the demand for telex, whilst fax machines themselves are under threat from computers.

*The Bargaining Power of Buyers*

The competitive climate of a market will clearly be influenced by the extent to which customers wield power through purchasing strength. Thus, a market that is dominated by a limited number of buyers, or a situation where a buyer takes a large proportion of the seller's output, will substantially limit the seller's opportunities for individual action or development. The UK and US grocery market illustrates this situation well, with a handful of major retail chains being able to exert considerable influence over manufacturing suppliers' marketing policies, and thus their profitability. Another source of competitive threat from buyers will exist when opportunities arise for backward integration, up the value chain, by buyers.

*The Bargaining Power of Suppliers*

Many of the threats that potentially exist from buyers can also come from the suppliers to an industry. If the supply of critical materials is controlled by a few suppliers, or if an individual company's purchases from a supplier constitute only a small part of that supplier's output, then freedom of manoeuvre may be limited. Again, if opportunities exist for forward integration by suppliers, this constitutes a further source of potential competitive pressure.

*The Degree of Market Competition*

Obviously, the more numerous, or equally balanced, the competitors, the more intense will be the rivalry within the market. If this is combined with a slow industry growth rate, and if fixed costs relative to variable costs are high, then the prognosis is for a high level of aggressive competition, probably accompanied by severe price-cutting. A further influencing factor will be the extent to which the competing products on offer are seen as substitutes by the market place, with few switching penalties for buyers. Of key importance in this will be the relative cost structures of the major players in the market. These will be determined not just by market share, but by capacity utilisation and production technology.

What has become increasingly obvious, however, during the severe shakeouts that occurred in the late 1990s, and are continuing to occur, is that the most meticulous analysis of an organisation's competitors is no longer an option. It is an absolute necessity in order to survive.

*Meticulous analysis of the competition is an absolute necessity*

## Performing a Competitor Analysis

A useful way to do this is to summarise the findings of a market audit in respect of major competitors. An organisation should understand the sales of each of their competitors within the particular product/market segment under consideration – their share now, and their expected share three years from now. The greater a competitor's influence over others, the greater its ability to implement its own independent strategies, hence the more successful it is. It is suggested that organisations should also identify each of their main competitors according to one of the classifications in the guide to competitive position given in Table 20.1, i.e., leadership, strong, favourable, tenable, weak.

Using the format shown in Figure 20.1 can provide a useful means of achieving this. In this, organisations need first to list their principal products or services; each major competitor's business direction and current strategies; their business directions and business strategies (see guidelines in Table 20.2); and their major strengths and weaknesses.

At a more detailed level, it is also important to develop a profile of each major competitor in terms of their contribution to the market in which an organisation

**Table 20.1**  Guide to market competitive position
classifications

- *Leadership*
  Has a major influence on the performance or behaviour of
  others.
- *Strong*
  Has a wide choice of strategies. Can adopt an independent
  strategy without endangering their short-term position. Has
  low vulnerability to competitors' actions.
- *Favourable*
  Exploits specific competitive strengths, often in a product-
  market niche. Has more than average opportunity to
  improve their position; several strategies are available.
- *Tenable*
  Performance justifies continuation in business.
- *Weak*
  Currently unsatisfactory performance; a significant compe-
  titive weakness. Inherently a short-term condition; must
  improve or withdraw.

| Products/ markets | Main competitor | Business direction, current objectives and strategies | Strengths | Weaknesses | Competitive position |
|---|---|---|---|---|---|
|  |  |  |  |  |  |
|  |  |  |  |  |  |
|  |  |  |  |  |  |

**Figure 20.1**  Competitor analysis

is interested, plus their basic capabilities. Table 20.3
illustrates some of the key areas important here. Also
extremely useful is an understanding of competitors'
performance in regard to factors which can influence
an individual customer's purchase decisions.

To collect, analyse and disseminate this information,
some kind of organised, systematic intelligence system is
necessary. It is essential to specify in advance the precise
information that is needed by the organisation about its
competitors.

**Table 20.2**   Alternative business directions

- *Enter*
  Allocate resources to a new business area. Consideration should include building from prevailing company or division strength, exploiting related opportunities and defending against perceived threats. May involve creating a new division
- *Improve*
  Apply strategies that will significantly improve the competitive position of the business. Often requires thoughtful product/market segmentation
- *Maintain*
  Maintain one's competitive position. Aggressive strategies may be required, although a defensive posture may also be assumed. Product/market position is maintained, often in a niche
- *Harvest*
  Intentionally relinquish competitive position, emphasising short-term profit and cash flow but not necessarily at the risk of losing the business in the short term. Often entails consolidating or reducing various aspects of the business to create higher performance for that which remains
- *Exit*
  Abandon a business because of its weak competitive position. The cost of staying in is prohibitive and the risk associated with improving its position is too high

**Table 20.3**   Individual competitor analysis

- Segment shares and trends
- Product line performance and quality
- Promotion strategies
- Pricing strategies
- Channel strategies
- Customer service strategies
- Management skills and philosophies
- Technological capabilities
- Financial strength

**Section D**

# UNDERSTANDING PRODUCT MANAGEMENT

# Consumer Buying Behaviour

As well as understanding a market in terms of trends, competitors, segments and so on, organisations supplying products or services also need to have an appreciation of the way customers behave when coming to a specific purchase decision. In addition, organisations need to understand how this behaviour varies between different groups of customers in order to ascertain the ways in which markets can be segmented. Without this knowledge, suppliers will find it difficult to choose between the alternative elements of the marketing mix to construct a product offering which will find favour with those customers it has decided to target.

*Knowledge of consumer buying behaviour guides the management of the marketing mix*

## Components of a Purchase Decision

The basic process can be described as an interaction between a number of external factors and a buyer's 'Black Box', which will, in turn, determine how a buyer responds to those circumstances. The outcomes of this are the different components of a purchase decision (see Figure 21.1).

*External Factors*

The external factors which may affect a potential buyer consist of the marketing mix offered by a supplier plus various environmental issues such as:

- The economic situation.
- Technological developments.
- The media.
- Political and legal influences.
- Cultural differences.
- Competitor marketing mixes.

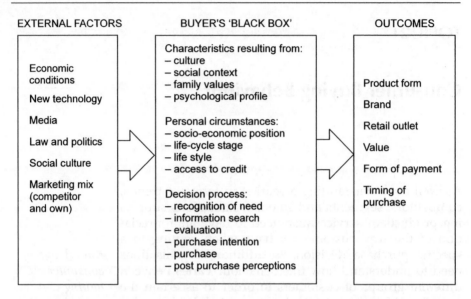

**Figure 21.1**    Components of a consumer's purchase decision

### The 'Black Box'

A buyer's 'Black Box' is really a combination of internal factors, consisting of the stages through which an individual passes on the way to a purchase decision, plus the various personal characteristics any individual will possess. These will be a combination of cultural influences; social context, such as social groups, or family values; psychological make-up; and personal circumstances. Personal circumstances will include socio-economic position, life-cycle stage, life style, access to credit facilities and so on. Psychological profiles are more complicated and will involve factors such as an individual's motivation; perception; values and attitudes.

### The Buyer's Response

The outcome of a purchase decision will consist of:

- The type of product chosen.
- The particular brand or supplier picked from the range of choices within a product type.
- The retail or dealer channel used.
- Issues such as the timing of the purchase or the volumes bought.

Together, these create a very complex situation about which to make marketing decisions. They also present supplying organisations with some fundamental options. As an example, it is reckoned that only 15 per cent of West Europeans who could benefit from a hearing aid actually use one. This is thought to result from a number of influences including, amongst others:

- Self-image.
- The social stigma associated with incapacity.
- Non-recognition of the onset of deafness.
- Ignorance of the range of aids available.
- The high cost of hearing aids.

For hearing aid manufacturers, the choices are:

- Trying to alert people to the need.
- Changing attitudes.
- Concentrating on those who are actively seeking a hearing aid.

Each alternative has its drawbacks and does not exclude action in other areas. The choices, however, do illustrate the problems inherent in making sense of, and responding to, a consumer's buying behaviour.

## Personal Involvement

In understanding consumer's buying behaviour, it is also usual to distinguish between **high involvement** and **low involvement** purchases. The degree to which purchasers will find themselves spending time, effort and thought on a purchase will depend on the frequency of the purchase, plus the level of perceived risk they experience. Feelings of risk will be driven by four main 'need' areas:

- The importance of the function the product performs for them.
- The proportion of disposable income it requires.
- The emotions aroused by the product.
- The extent to which the product reflects their self-image, or will cause others to view them in a certain light.

Thus, for a young executive with high aspirations, but with income constraints due to a large mortgage, the purchase of an electronic 'personal organiser' might be influenced by:

- Its ability to record and make available multiple information requirements without risk of losing the data.
- Feelings of importance or success.
- The cost of a good/reliable product.
- The significance of the brand.
- The way others would view possession of such a device.

Under these circumstances, the purchaser is likely to be concerned to make the 'right' decision and engage in some highly complex purchase behaviour.

If the purchaser were a young person in full-time education, behaviour is likely to be less complex and driven more by appearance, price or availability, rather than by weightier issues of brand value, functionality and social impact. Likewise, in the purchase of items such as paper clips, organisational involvement (as manifested by the purchaser's personal involvement) is likely to be extremely low and the decision process, therefore, less complex.

### The Decision-Making Process

*The decision-making process follows typical stages*

The process by which the final decision is made during a purchase tends to follow a number of stages. The extent to which each stage is included will depend on the nature of the purchase and the complexity implied. Fundamental to all purchases is **need recognition** or **arousal**, which may come in the natural course of events, or which may require effort on the part of a supplying organisation. The latter will be especially true for new products or product categories with low market penetration.

Once a need has been acknowledged, people will either start an **information search** or, in the case of low-involvement habitual purchases, move straight to a purchase. If seeking variety, this might then involve a cursory review of alternative brands. The information search may be informal and take the form of becoming open to information about the product type, or it may be active and involve talking to friends, collecting sales literature, consulting reports and experts, or actually visiting outlets to try out different offerings. This can be described as a **cognitive** stage in which beliefs and knowledge are developed about the range of alternatives available. Suppliers without high market shares, therefore, have to work hard if they wish to be included in the list from which a final choice is made.

The next stage in this process will be some form of **evaluation**, during which a customer is likely to develop a liking or preference for a particular brand or small group of brands. At some point, a customer will become **convinced** about the value of a particular offering, at which moment they can be characterised as having a **purchase intention**. This is known as an **affective** stage, during which potential buyers develop an emotional response to different offerings, which will be a reflection of their cultural, social, personal and psychological make-up. It will also be a reflection of the influences exerted by the different aspects of the market environment and the ways products have been positioned in the market by their suppliers.

Purchase intention, however, can still be altered by the **intervention** of others or by some unanticipated factor. If a buyer's intentions conflict with the attitudes of peer groups or some strong social/cultural values, they will have to work hard to maintain their intention, but could easily be persuaded not to buy if their emotional convictions are not well-grounded. Thus, an Italian male who had decided to buy a French car, might find his conviction crumbling in the face of strong nationalistic views combined with others' attitudes that such cars were designed for more 'effeminate' drivers.

*Purchase decisions are often vulnerable to deflection*

Unanticipated factors might include the arrival of new information, a change in priorities, or a change in personal circumstances. For the supplier, the implications are that clarity is of vital importance in positioning and communications, and that they should plan to reduce the impact of unanticipated factors, especially those not within their control. These could range from availability, ease of contacting a supplier, point-of-sale information, or the actions of a sales person. For high-risk purchases, customers will be more vulnerable to such deflection as a result of their heightened anxiety.

Once a purchase has been made, the final stage in the process is the customers' **post-purchase perceptions** of their acquisition. High involvement purchases, where a choice has been made between several, carefully considered alternatives, often lead to feelings of discomfort, or **cognitive dissonance**, since they will be well aware of the advantages of other offerings and the possible existence of disadvantages. Dissonance will be magnified by:

- The extent to which perceived performance is below pre-purchase expectations.
- Receiving fewer validating messages through communication such as advertising.
- Any shortfalls in after-sales service.

Customers will naturally seek to reduce their dissonance, either by confirming the wisdom of their choice, or through seeking some form of redress such as instant modification, publicising their misfortune, or taking legal action. Whatever the result, it will have a significant impact on repeat purchase decisions if the outcome is felt to be unsatisfactory.

*Consumer buying behaviour is a complex process and is difficult to predict*

Together, these factors contribute to the fact that consumers' buying behaviour is a complex process and is consequently difficult to research and predict. Apart from the models used above, there are a number of other models, more or less mathematically based, which seek to explain the formation of preferences in different ways. Thus, there is no clear picture, or universal theory, which encapsulates all aspects of consumer behaviour. What is clear, however, is the need to develop the best possible understanding of the dynamics and variations of the ways that customers approach a purchase. The more this is understood, the easier it is to see how continued sales could be jeopardised without constant attention to the careful manipulation of the marketing mix.

# TOPIC 22

# Organisational Buying Behaviour

When a business wishes to sell its products to other organisations, rather than to individuals at the end of the value chain, it faces a rather more complex marketing situation. This complexity is a result of the number of people often involved in the decision to purchase, the situation in which those people operate and the activities which, together, form the stages of the decision-making process.

*Organisational buying behaviour presents a more complex marketing challenge*

These processes are not entirely dissimilar to those followed by consumer purchasers, but tend to be characterised in different ways as a result of the contexts in which an organisation buys. For example, organisations have more formalised purchasing procedures as a consequence of the need to monitor and control purchasing activities, and they will often appraise a product in more technical terms because of the impact which a wrong purchase may have on the organisation's operations.

## Organisational Buying Stages

The major stages, or 'buy phases', of an organisational purchase are usually listed as:

- Problem recognition.
- General need determination.
- Supply specification.
- Identification of suppliers.
- Solicitation of proposals.
- Evaluation and selection of a supplier/suppliers.
- Establishment of order routines.
- Performance review.

These stages will not necessarily be followed sequentially and not every stage will be included for all purchases. In general, though, they indicate the way in

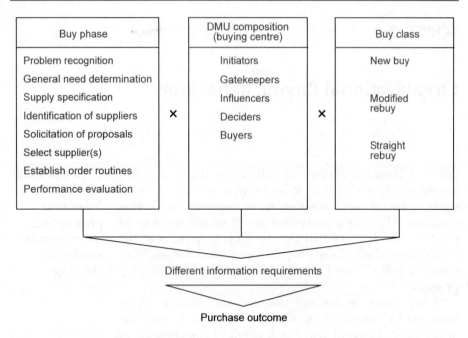

| Buy phase | | DMU composition (buying centre) | | Buy class |
|---|---|---|---|---|
| Problem recognition | | Initiators | | New buy |
| General need determination | | Gatekeepers | | |
| Supply specification | | Influencers | | Modified rebuy |
| Identification of suppliers | × | Deciders | × | |
| Solicitation of proposals | | Buyers | | |
| Select supplier(s) | | | | Straight rebuy |
| Establish order routines | | | | |
| Performance evaluation | | | | |

Different information requirements

Purchase outcome

**Figure 22.1**   Organisational buying behaviour model

which an organisation will approach a purchasing problem, but will involve different people and processes at alternative stages and in different situational contexts. The interaction of these factors will determine the information required by a purchaser and the purchase outcome (see Figure 22.1).

### Organisational Buyer Situations

To help to unravel the complexities of such purchasing, it is useful to isolate the situations in which purchases generally are made. These are frequently referred to as 'buy classes' and cover: **new buys**; **modified re-buys**; and **straight re-buys**.

#### New Buy

If making a new buy, i.e., when purchasing for the first time, or making a complete reappraisal of a particular requirement, there will be little experience in the organisation of purchasing that type of product. As a consequence, the organisation and the individuals within it will experience high levels of uncertainty and risk, which are likely to produce a number of different behaviours not so much in evidence when purchasing within the other two 'buy classes'.

Behaviours which will be of particular interest to potential suppliers will be associated with the need to reduce perceived risk. Buyers are likely to attempt risk reduction by requiring much more information about a purchase, not just in terms of the product itself, but also concerning the ability of the supplier to meet specifications, quality levels and supply continuity requirements. In addition, they will tend to seek outside opinions and recommendations about both the products and the attributes of suppliers. This can incorporate the use of paid advisers such as product experts and consultants, the collection of assessments and appraisals in technical journals, talking to existing users or customers of particular suppliers and the use of other referees such as bankers and credit reference agencies. Risk reduction is also likely to be sought through visits to suppliers' premises, inserting penalty clauses in the terms of the contract and by soliciting quotes or offers from a large number of potential suppliers to ensure that they have not missed the least risky purchase.

*Suppliers are particularly interested in behaviours associated with risk reduction*

As a consequence of this, the purchase decision often takes a long time and will probably be taken at a fairly high level in the organisation. In addition, individuals will try to reduce their own vulnerability by involving a wider range of people in the decision and passing responsibility upwards, thereby spreading the risk. A further response will be a tendency to purchase from the market leaders, or the higher priced suppliers, since these will be perceived as lower risk solutions.

### Modified Re-buys

**Modified re-buys** will occur when a purchasing organisation becomes dissatisfied with existing suppliers, or modifies its requirements in some way. Since the organisation will already have experience of sourcing the product, less risk will be perceived by higher management and the decision is likely to involve fewer people and focus on those at lower levels in the business. Those at the lower levels, however, are likely to experience greater personal risk in the absence of the involvement of their superiors. The main risk factor is the possibility of changing to an unknown supplier. The purchaser will then probably require 'out-suppliers' to demonstrate a significant advantage to break the inertia of an existing relationship.

*Straight Re-buys*

**Straight re-buys** refers to purchasing on a routine re-order basis with little risk being perceived by the purchaser. Individuals will either select a product of their choice from the offerings of 'approved suppliers' or will place orders in strict adherence to company-established specifications and relationships. Where choice can exist, it will be exercised by either the user or the purchasing department. Whilst 'in-suppliers' maintain both product and service quality, this is a difficult situation for 'out-suppliers' to penetrate. One drawback for the purchaser in this respect can be that price loses its visibility in the purchase process, which helps explain why annual purchase reviews are often institutionalised in the supplier management routines of many organisations.

### The Organisational Decision Making Unit

*The greater the perceived risk, the larger the DMU*

The risk associated with a purchase, plus the complex way in which the product will be viewed and used, means that a number of people will have the opportunity to influence the outcome of a purchase decision. As indicated, the greater the risk, the more people that are likely to be involved, with as many as 40 for an expensive, first time, purchase. Together, these constitute a decision-making unit (DMU) or 'buying centre' with individual members playing one or a number of different roles. Whilst there have been several approaches proposed for classifying these roles, there is general agreement that they will cover:

- **Initiators**, who will first propose a purchase and who could be anyone from the chief executive to an operational employee, depending on the nature of the product.

- **Policy-makers**, who will set the overall context for a purchase, or who may even initiate a purchase; policies could refer to dual sourcing, just-in-time manufacturing, preferring domestically produced products, quality requirements and so on.
- **Users**, who will actually consume the product or service as part of their job; where such people have expert knowledge, they can significantly influence the choice of supplier; for less risky purchases, they may have significant influence, both positive and negative.
- **Other influencers**, including: technical experts; the media; referral markets; financial personnel; the organisation's own customers; and so on. Exactly who influencers are will vary from one organisation to another, but the notion is important to spur suppliers to view any purchasing relationship in its wider context.
- **Deciders**, who will have the power to approve or veto a purchase decision and who will be asked to reconcile conflicting opinions within the DMU; they will tend to rely on the presentational power of the people requesting the acquisition, but will often also be driven by personal preference.
- **Gatekeepers**, through whom information is passed into the organisation. These can sit at many points in an organisation and can range from receptionists and secretaries to purchasing officials, product experts and general technocrats.

Since sales people are usually the most significant external influence on organisational purchasing, it is vitally important for them to understand, and to work with, the appropriate gatekeepers within the organisation. Once 'in', they then have to recognise the different information needs that each member of the DMU will have and the general orientations or perspectives they bring to the decision-making process. As examples: users will be concerned about ease of use, consistency and continuity of supply; influencers such as finance people will be concerned with cost, while influencers such as design engineers will more likely be interested in quality; and deciders such as the Chief Executive Officer may be concerned with reputation or status. As an example of different needs, one French supplier to hospitals segmented the market by age of purchasing

*Business must recognise the different information needs of DMU members*

officer, since those with low levels of experience required much more support to be able to satisfy the
information requirements of the various hospital admin-
istrators involved in the decision.

An outline of the complex interactions of the organisational purchasing process is shown in Figure 22.1.

It is clear from any examination of organisational
purchase behaviour, that organisations do not, in themselves, exhibit behaviour. It is the collective interactions
between individuals from the supplier and buyer organisations which are at the heart of the process, plus the
buyer's interactions with their external environment.
Such interactions will embrace the exchange of the
product, the exchange of information, social exchange,
or financial transactions, all of which can be more or less
intimate. They will be affected by the economy, regulatory changes, technology, competition and social developments, plus the culture and structure of the
organisation itself. Often, internal politics and the nature
of the personalities involved, will be as much a determinant of a purchase decision as anything else.

*Organisational
purchase
behaviour
emphasises
the notions of
relationship
marketing*

Organisational buyer behaviour, then, emphasises the
notions of relationship marketing and the need to understand both the organisation as a whole and the buying
styles of the individuals who make up the organisation.
Organisations are also tending to 'out source' more of
their requirements these days and are looking for supplier partners, rather than short-term financial gain.
Within this, many organisations now prefer total solutions or systems purchasing where suppliers provide
'turnkey solutions' either on their own or as a prime
contractor. In addition, purchasing is now seen much
more as a professional activity and is moving towards
the concept of supply chain management. Together,
these are promoting the tendency for organisational
buyers to become more demanding and even more
complex in their behaviour, which in turn leads to a
greater requirement to understand organisational buying behaviour.

# TOPIC 23

# The Product Life-Cycle

This topic is best read in conjunction with Topic 24, Diffusion of Innovation, because the two curves go together.

The product life-cycle is a conceptual tool which provides a means of describing the sales patterns of products, be they goods or service products, over their time in a market. If absolute sales are plotted on a period by period basis (usually annually), the ideal-type life-cycle approximates to an S-curve (see Figure 23.1). In reality, product life-cycles adopt a number of different shapes and are never smooth. However, a good understanding of the concept, its variations, and the determinants of its shape, can be a powerful aid to the development of marketing strategies.

*Understanding the product life-cycle can enhance marketing strategies*

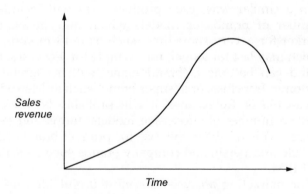

**Figure 23.1** Standard product life-cycle curve

## Life-Cycles and Product Categories

Understanding product life-cycles requires an appreciation of the different categories of product for which they could be used: product class; form; or brand. These different categories exist because a market is based on a need, which will usually be satisfied by alternative technologies over time. Each successive technology will provide a new product class and enhanced performance. The need to store information, for instance, has been satisfied by many product classes including: stone tablets; papyrus; string; ledgers; microfilm; cards; tapes; discs; and, more recently, CDs. Specific needs may, in the end, disappear, such as the need for protection against smallpox or, in some countries, executioners. At this point, a market life-cycle comes to an end. Other, more generic, needs are likely to continue for some time, for example: personal security; home entertainment; personal and mass communications; and people's social and physiological needs.

More focused examples of product classes include: televisions; bicycles; internal combustion engines; and personal computers. Each of these classes will have its own life-cycle. Within each class, there is likely to exist a number of product forms, or families, which will also experience a life-cycle. Thus, the product-class 'personal computer' has included several product forms such as: desk-tops; portables; lap-tops; notebooks; and now hand-held computers.

In a similar way, each product form will include a number of brands or models which may be on the market for a very short time, such as 6–18 months, or which may last for longer, for example for 3–9 years. If a brand can become a 'brand name' with a significant customer franchise, or a 'super brand' such as Mercedes, Coca-Cola or Rolex, then it will probably be used to cover a number of successive models, forms and even classes. This has been the case for product brands such as Tide and Persil, and company brands such as Kodak and IBM.

*The most useful life-cycle is that of the product form*

For marketing analysis, the most useful life-cycle is usually that of the product form. Product class life-cycles are often too macro to be of use, except for very long-range planning such as the 50-year strategies common amongst the larger Japanese corporations. On the other hand, product brands or models are too specific and will only map the performance of one company's activities. This will remain true even for the powerful brands which encompass a number of successive generations of a product. Sales of a particular form, such as colour televisions or neon lights, will track the activities of all suppliers to the market and will, therefore, enable judgements to be made in the context of a market as a whole. It is, nonetheless, extremely useful to plot a product or brand's performance against the life-cycle of the product form in order to ensure that nothing untoward is happening to it.

### Stages in the Product Life-Cycle

Product life-cycles will usually experience a number of successive stages (see Figure 23.2). The **introductory stage** will cover the launch of a new product form into the market to the point at which sales begin to accelerate rapidly. During this stage, sales will be relatively slow while customers get used to the new ideas it incorporates. If the form is to be a successful innovation, the product will move into its **growth phase**, during which sales volumes will increase rapidly from one time period to the next. At some point, sales growth will slow as the number of potential new purchasers reduces, at which time the life-cycle will be in its **maturity stage**. Once

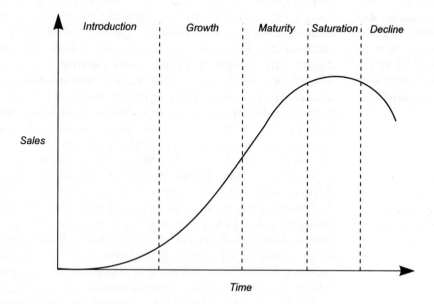

**Figure 23.2** Phases in the product life-cycle

sales growth has levelled off, the life-cycle has reached its **saturation phase** where sales are either replacements or are latecomers to the market. Since these will probably be replacing the innovators who were the first to try a new product, and who have probably moved on to replacement product forms, they will add little to the growth of the market. The final stage therefore is **decline**, either as more people migrate to the new product form or the need disappears.

Life-cycles will move into the decline phase for one of two main reasons. The first, as indicated, will be that a replacement technology, usually delivering enhanced performance, will have been developed. In this way, colour televisions replaced black-and-white versions and facsimile transmission (fax) has virtually replaced telex. The second will be a change in another aspect of the marketing environment such as fashion, legislation or standards, the development of a new industry structure or a social trend of some form.

## Deviant Product Life-Cycles

*Deviant product life-cycles are caused by the nature of a product and its patterns of consumption*

Deviations from the shape associated with a 'standard' product life-cycle (see Figure 23.3) will be caused by the nature of a product and its patterns of consumption. Some products will experience growth followed by a sharp slump before levelling out into maturity (Figure 23.3a). This is typical of the sales patterns for small kitchen appliances and will occur because saturation is achieved before replacement purchases come into play. Scalloped life-cycles (Figure 23.3b), where sales continually level off and then grow again, will be associated with products which are constantly finding new markets and new applications. Bar coding and nylon are good examples of this. Rapid growth followed by rapid decline, with sales levelling out at a low level (Figure 23.3c), describes the life-cycle of a fad such as the hardly-remembered Clackers or the infamous pet rocks. A double-humped life-cycle (Figure 23.3d) will be typical of products which come in and out of style, such as bicycles or fashions, or will be products in markets which respond well to communications so that usage will follow media or industry patterns of promotional activity.

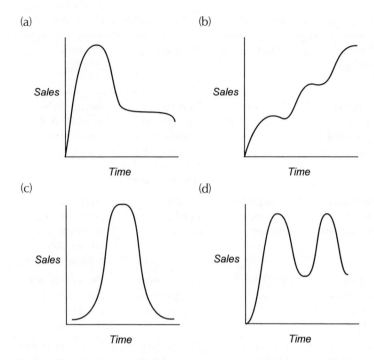

**Figure 23.3** Alternative product life-cycles

## Using the Product Life-Cycle

Whilst it is never possible to identify accurately which point a product has reached on its life-cycle, or exactly which shape the life-cycle will follow, the concept does enable organisations to consider the future – how strategies will need to alter, and what their market information needs will be. At the introductory stage, competitors will typically be limited and the focus of a marketing strategy will be educating the market. During growth, organisations are likely to face more numerous competitors and will be seeking to establish a strong position in terms of market share, niches, brands and/or reputation, while at the same time, looking for product-range extension and market development. As a market matures and becomes saturated, marketing strategy will tend to concentrate on price, brand protection and customer service. When decline begins to bite, competition will eventually reduce and the organisation will tend to concentrate on the next product form or on reducing costs, while maintaining price (see Table 23.1).

*Different strategies are needed for different life-cycle stages*

**Table 23.1**  Typical marketing-mix strategies for different life-cycle stages

| Stage in product life-cycle | Product strategy | Price strategy | Place strategy | Promotion strategy |
| --- | --- | --- | --- | --- |
| Introductory | Limited range for specialist applications | Skim or penetration | Limited to specialised outlets with service often provided by manufacturer | Educate the market and aggressive selling |
| Growth | Product range expansion | Competitive pricing for market share | Seek wide market coverage | Actively establish image or brand with competitive selling |
| Maturity | Improve quality and consolidate range | Stabilise prices | Use service for competitive differentiation | Protect brand and market position |
| Saturation | Reduce costs and range | Push price to limits | Transfer costs to distributors and automate service | Maintain brand or image at low cost |
| Decline | Further reduce costs and range | Maintain as high as possible | Reduce costs | Focused low cost communications |

The problems associated with using the product-life-cycle concept occur either from its misuse or from its misinterpretation. Misuse would result from confusing the life-cycles of product forms with organisational sales or brands, or by trying to use them as predictive tools. Misinterpretation can arise if an organisation interprets a 'glitch' in sales for the onset of decline, and pulls out of a market too early. Economic recession can have this effect, when in reality it is more likely to cause a postponement of purchasing rather than an end to it. If used sensibly, however, it can raise questions of importance such as: how fast will growth be?; what will limit growth?; what could cause the onset of decline?; and what trading conditions can be expected over the next few years? If better decisions are made as a consequence, the life-cycle can, therefore, be a valuable marketing tool.

# TOPIC 24

# Diffusion of Innovation

The shape of the standard product life-cycle implies that purchasers for a new class of product become customers at different times, and at different rates, following its introduction. This has been described by Everett Rogers as the **diffusion of innovation** or the **adoption process**. Adoption is concerned with the way that a consumer becomes a regular customer for a new product concept. Diffusion refers to the way in which the product penetrates its potential market, which, in turn, suggests that there will be different stages of adoption. Variations between the shapes of product life-cycles for different products indicate that the rate of diffusion may also vary from one product to another. Effective marketing requires a good understanding of these processes and the causes of any variations.

*Effective marketing considers variations within and between product life-cycles*

### New-Product Adoption

The adoption process for a product new to a particular consumer will tend to follow a five-stage pattern. The first stage is **awareness**, whereby a consumer learns of the existence of a product. This may happen by accident, or it may be the result of a deliberate communications campaign on the part of the supplier, or of a deliberate search on the part of the consumer. Awareness becomes **interest** if the product is perceived to offer benefits appropriate to the needs of the consumer. At this point, the consumer will actively search for information about the new product. As information is gathered, consumers will go through a process of **evaluation** as they decide whether or not to try the innovation. The next stage is therefore **trial**, where consumers will extend their evaluation by an experimental consumption. The fifth and final stage is **adoption**, whereby either the trial or the appeal of the concept is good, or strong, enough to convince consumers to buy again on a regular basis, although not necessarily from the same supplier.

Not all stages will be involved for all new products; consumers could move straight from awareness to adoption if the offer matched their particular need closely enough. More important, however, is the recognition that new purchasers will not necessarily pass from one stage to the next, and could get stuck at any one of the five stages.

### New-Product Diffusion

When plotted over time, the adoption process tends to follow a normal distribution. The mid-point of the distribution will represent the average amount of time (months or years) it took people to adopt a product. Most people will come to a new product within plus or minus one standard deviation of the average time. A minority of people, however, will either be amongst the first to become users of a product, or will be behind the rest of the market in the adoption of the innovation (see

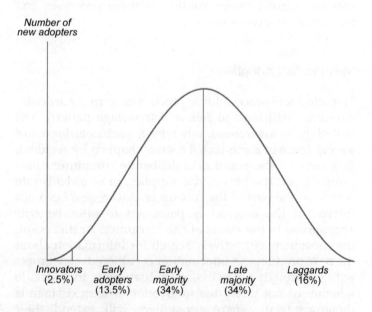

**Figure 24.1**  The diffusion of innovation curve

Figure 24.1). The various categories of adopters can be described as **innovators**, **early adopters**, **the early majority**, **the late majority**, and **laggards**.

*Consumers of new products can be placed into five 'adopter' categories*

- **Innovators** are usually characterised as being 2.5 per cent of the market and are the first to become regular users. Innovators are usually venturesome, or find value in being at the forefront of consumption. In industrial markets, innovators will either be technology-orientated, keen on seeking competitive advantage from new products, or forced into innovating as a 'distress purchase'. In consumer markets, they are usually hard to identify in terms of their demographic, psychographic or media characteristics. It is also the case that an innovator in one product area could easily be a laggard in another. Often, without knowing the individual involved, it is hard to tell who is what.
- **Early adopters**, 13.5 per cent of a market, will be keen to take up a particular innovation, but will treat it with caution. Others are likely to look up to them as they are the first of the wider market to take the risk of purchase. They will often see themselves as being significant community members and therefore at the forefront of opinion in terms of the particular product area.
- The **early majority** will comprise 34 per cent of the market and will consolidate a new product's success. They will probably see themselves as early adopters, but will tend to be more risk-averse than the early adopters. Their purchase will, therefore, be a statement of their willingness to try something new, but will be tempered by a natural conservatism.
- The **late majority**, again 34 per cent of all adoptors, will be even more conservative in their approach to the purchase of this product type, possibly even to the extent of being sceptical about the value of the innovation. Thus, as the innovation becomes more widely used, as its price falls, or as the traditional alternatives become less available, they will move to the new, increasingly acceptable, alternative.
- **Laggards**, the final category, will be the last to come to an innovation and will be the remaining 16 per cent of a market. They will occupy this position for a number of reasons, including: education level; focus of

activities; degree of isolation; attitude towards tradition; level of disposable income; lack of any alternative; and so on. For laggards, the innovation will have had to have lost its 'new product' status before they will adopt its consumption. However, there will always be some non-consumers. Even today, there are some West European and US households without a television.

### Rate of Diffusion

*The rate of diffusion depends on the product and the market*

The rate at which a new product class will penetrate a market will depend on the characteristics of both the market and the product. Market factors which will provide hurdles to penetration include:

- The absence of appropriate communications media, distribution channels or physical infrastructure (electricity, etc.).
- The slow speed of the decision-making process.
- The existence of complicated regulatory or procedural requirements.
- Adverse economic conditions.
- Sociocultural factors which mitigate against the product's adoption.

All these environmental factors need to be understood well when planning the roll-out of a new product into a market. Product factors which can hamper adoption include:

- Little relative performance or cost advantage over the present solutions to the problem which the product is designed to solve.
- Low product compatibility with existing structures in the market, be they physical, social or whatever.
- High complexity, which will make it hard for adopters to evaluate or understand the benefits on offer.
- Few possibilities to try the product before purchase, making it difficult for consumers to judge its value in advance; this is especially true of expensive goods and service products.

- Features which are hard to describe; this is often the case for products delivering abstract or intangible benefits, service products, or products which are hard to conceptualise or demonstrate, such as software consultancy or insurance services.

Within this, it should also be noted that word of mouth has often been identified as one of the key features in aiding the diffusion of an innovation throughout its potential market. Unfortunately, this is one of the most difficult aspects of promotion for an organisation to influence.

These variations help to explain the different shapes of product life-cycles, and the possible hurdles to adoption mean that not all new products will fulfil their market potential. Diffusion and adoption are not inevitable and marketing organisations have to develop strategies which will overcome the blockages they are likely to encounter.

*Diffusion and adoption are not inevitable*

# TOPIC 25

# The Ansoff Matrix

*The Ansoff Matrix is a method for structuring thinking*

The Ansoff Matrix is a $2 \times 2$ depiction of the options open to organisations if they wish to improve revenue or profitability. The matrix was first described by Igor Ansoff in 'Strategies for Diversification' (*Harvard Business Review*, September–October 1957, p. 114). It is useful because it provides a simple framework which encapsulates all the strategic directions an organisation can adopt in one analytical tool. Unlike some of the other analytical tools used in marketing, the matrix is not diagnostic; rather it is a method for structuring thinking or a means of classifying objectives.

The axes of the matrix focus on the essential relationship an organisation has to manage – the provision of products for customers. Products may be tangible or intangible and may be offered for sale in exchange for cash, or as a social benefit of some kind or another. In the latter case, the exchange will be monetary donations or some form of cooperation. Whatever the situation, the product will be either an existing offering or a product which is new to the organisation. Customers, similarly, will be either part of an existing market or members of a market not yet addressed by the organisation and, therefore, new to them. An organisation is thus faced with four choices for action:

- Concentrating on existing products for existing markets.
- Looking for new products for existing markets.
- Seeking new markets for existing products.
- Diversifying into new products for new markets. (See Figure 25.1.)

### Existing Products for Existing Markets

In developing a strategy, close attention should always be paid to existing product/market relationships.

134

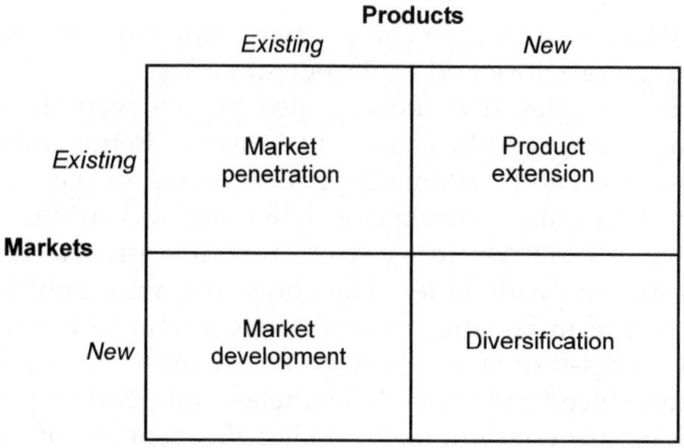

**Figure 25.1**   The Ansoff Matrix


Increased revenue in this option can be gained in a number of ways:

- The easiest method is to attract customers who share the same needs as existing purchasers, but who have not yet become regular users. This is particularly important in growth markets where new customers are appearing all the time. Strategies will concentrate on persuading such people or organisations to test a product and then, if they like it, to use your offering rather than those of direct competitors.
- In mature markets, increased sales will have to come from competitors by persuading customers to use a different supplier or brand. This will usually involve manipulating elements of the marketing mix such as lowering price, broadening a brand's appeal, or initiating sales promotion campaigns. In fact, it is more usual to focus on customer service, since price wars can be damaging to all concerned and product differentiation is often difficult to achieve.
- Improved sales can also come from persuading the market to increase usage of the products. For consumer products, this may be very appropriate, especially during periods of economic growth and increasing levels of disposable income. Thus, the notion of two-car families, two-television households and more frequent clothing purchases have an appeal during times of prosperity. In industrial markets, such a strategy may be more difficult to sell, as purchasers are likely to be seeking better value per purchase,

unless they can see competitive value from increased
usage or shortened replacement cycles.

• Higher sales revenue can also be achieved through
improved productivity, such as: a better mix of
products and customers; price increases, or reductions
in discounts; charging for deliveries; and so on.

• An alternative to seeking revenue growth is to
improve profitability. This, however, may only yield
short-term benefits, since there is a limit to the scope
for cost-reduction, and price increases cannot be
introduced too often. Nonetheless, all good organisations are continuously seeking the benefits of value
engineering, process efficiencies and the opportunity
to raise prices, and this can provide useful breathing
spaces during which an organisation can explore
other, longer-term areas, for enhancing revenue.

## New Products for Existing Markets

As the matrix shows, a second strategic option is to
introduce new products which are targeted at existing
customers with whom the organisation already has a
relationship. Within this, the better approach is to build
on some aspect of the relationship which already exists.
This can take a number of different forms:

• One option is to supply new products which are
closely associated with the products which customers
already purchase from a supplier. Thus, a computer
manufacturer could add computer peripherals, such
as printers, plotters and service contracts, or consumables such as paper, ink and discs, to its range in order
to provide a 'one-stop shopping' service.

• A similar approach particularly appropriate for
organisational customers would be to identify the
way in which they categorise their purchases and
endeavour to supply products which meet a customer's purchasing management structures. For instance, a retailer might include shampoo as a
personal care item, as a fashion accessory or as a
bathroom product. Each classification would provide
different opportunities for the shampoo producer to
expand the range of associated products they supply.

• An alternative route would be to concentrate on the
technology base used to supply existing products and

to identify other product needs customers might have which could be produced using current facilities and know-how. In this way, a packaging-tape supplier with expertise in adhesives or coating technologies might investigate other requirements which could be satisfied using similar skills.

- The other main approach is to build on the way in which existing customers use a supplier. Some relationships might be based on a partnership approach with joint problem-solving, whilst others might use a supplier for convenience or for a particular attribute of their product or service. Each type of relationship will provide different opportunities for the addition of new products to an organisation's range.

## New Markets for Existing Products

The third option in the matrix is new markets for existing products, which requires an organisation to identify users in different markets with similar needs, or new customers who would use a product in a different way. The most obvious example would be to expand from a domestic market into foreign markets (i.e., a geographical market extension). Although such a move would probably require some product adaptation, and maybe some different positioning or selling methods, the experience required to supply the product would be essentially the same. A similar example would be an expansion from say, the public sector into the private sector, or from financial services to the leisure industry. Again, whilst product modification and adaptation may be required, the core technologies of the product are unlikely to be unaltered.

*Establishing new markets for existing products is unlikely to require the alteration of core product technologies*

The same would be true for new markets where the product would be used in a different way. Raw materials, standard components and many service products would be quite easy to adapt, whereas bespoke products, or consumer goods, would be more difficult to transfer. As examples, expanded polystyrene can be used for noise insulation, heat retention in hot water tanks, as a packaging or protection material and as a floor-cushion filler; whereas the floor cushion itself would not be nearly so versatile.

### New Products for New Markets

The fourth option, new products for new markets, is the most risky diversification since it utilises little of an organisation's existing expertise or capabilities. It is also the type of expansion which has the highest failure rate. Where organisations have been successful in this domain, it is usually possible to identify some synergy in sales, distribution or product technology. The expansion by BIC, for instance, from pens into disposable razors, utilised both their understanding of the technology of mass production of cheap plastic items and their ability to sell to, and to service, multiple retail organisations. Where no synergies exist, attention to risk management becomes very important.

*Whether it is preferable to expand first into new products or new markets is a matter for debate*

The Ansoff Matrix can therefore be seen as a framework for describing the range of strategic options open to an organisation for expansion. It is also a means of conceptualising the development of a product over its market life. It provides a useful conceptual approach to expansion if there is a need to move into new markets and/or away from existing products. However, rather than moving straight to new products for new markets, organisations should see if it is possible to get there via new products or via new markets first, since these will provide experience which will reduce the risk of managing both new products and new markets simultaneously.

Whether it is preferable to expand into either new products or new markets first is a matter for debate. Some would argue for new products on the grounds that customers are more difficult to manage. Others would prefer new markets, since unfamiliar technologies are fraught with hidden problems. In the end, it is probably the option with the least degree of complexity which will determine the choice.

Overall, the Ansoff Matrix has a certain beauty in its simplicity, because it strips marketing down to its basics which are to do with getting products to market. Having said this, it does perhaps over-simplify marketing in that there are different kinds of new products and different kinds of new markets. It is important to be clear about what these are, as illustrated in Table 25.1.

**Table 25.1** Kinds of new products and markets

*Degrees of newness of the product:*

- It can stay the same
- It can be extended in some way
- It can be re-designed, modified or improved
- It can be a new product or concept entirely

*Different forms of new markets:*

- They can be the same
- They can be broader in terms of how they are defined
- They can include new coverage, but on related areas
- They can be totally new

*Newness of product*

| Product \ Market | Same product | Extended product | Modified or improved product | New product |
|---|---|---|---|---|
| Same market | | | | |
| Broader market coverage | | | | |
| New coverage but in related areas | | | | |
| New market | | | | |

*Newness of market*

**Figure 25.2** An extended product/market matrix

The Ansoff Matrix is good at reminding us that marketing life can become too complicated, but its inference that things are either old or new overlooks those middling shades of grey. One way of clarifying this is to re-draw the Ansoff Matrix as depicted in Figure 25.2.

# TOPIC 26

# The Boston Matrix

*The Boston Matrix is used to analyse markets in terms of market growth and relative market share*

The Boston Matrix (or, as it is sometimes called, the Boston Box) is a vehicle for classifying and characterising an organisation's activities in relation to the markets in which it operates. It can be used to represent strategic business units (SBUs), or product portfolios, which are then located on the matrix for analytical purposes. Such a presentation will enable the strategic management of an organisation to make judgements about how best to manage each business or product group, and to identify gaps or areas which may prove problematic as markets grow, mature or decline.

The matrix focuses on two key aspects of markets: their growth rates, and a product or SBU's relative market share by value (see Figure 26.1). Market growth

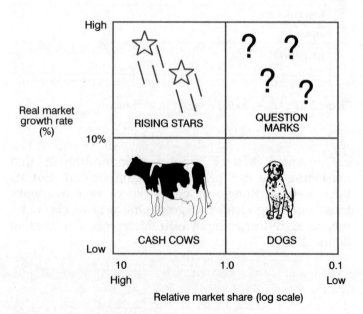

**Figure 26.1** The Boston Matrix

140

rates are ranged on the vertical axis and were originally rated between 0 per cent and 30 per cent, with a growth rate of over 10 per cent being high, and under 10 per cent low. In fact, what is considered a high or low growth rate will vary from industry to industry or market to market, and practitioners need to make their own judgements about where the breakpoints between high and low should fall. Market share is depicted on the horizontal axis on a log scale and shows a product or SBU's share **relative** to that of the largest competitor in the market. A relative market share of 1.0 means that its share is equal to that of the largest competitor; 10 will mean that it is ten times larger and 0.1 will mean that it has one tenth the share of the largest supplier. The log scale is used so that equal distances on the axis represent the same percentage increases or reductions.

The rationale behind the matrix is that growth rates will significantly affect the attractiveness of a market to an organisation for investment purposes and relative market share is a good indicator of a business's strength in that market. Growth rates are also of interest because they relate to the stages of a product life-cycle. High growth rates are associated with markets where the customer base is expanding rapidly and in which businesses have to match or exceed the growth rate to maintain their market-share position. Low growth rates indicate that the market is maturing and implies that a business does not have to compete with other suppliers for new customers entering a market, in order to maintain its share of the market.

*Relative market share is a good indicator of a business's market strength*

The importance of market share is based on the concept of the **experience curve** (see Figure 26.2). If a business can maintain the position of market-share leader, it will, by definition, have produced and sold more products than any of its competitors. This will enable it to achieve greater economies of experience and, thus, lower costs and better knowledge than competitors. Such economies and knowledge are not achieved automatically, but must be actively pursued by an organisation's management. If gained, such economies should yield cash which can be used for reinvestment in other products/SBUs; protection against price wars; other marketing efforts; or profit distribution. The knowledge gained from the experience should yield market intelligence, which should, in turn, make

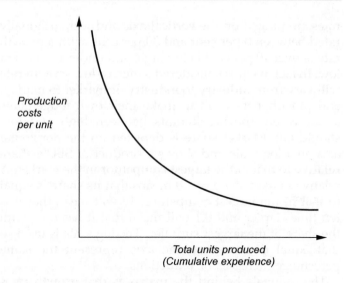

**Figure 26.2** The experience curve

competitive activities more effective. High market share also reduces the relative expenditure required for competitive marketing activities and can often provide a business with the power to influence a market in terms of price, technical standards, product development and the way competitive activities are conducted.

The products/SBUs in each quadrant of the matrix are, therefore, faced with different marketing tasks. Those in high growth markets, but with a low market share (referred to as **Question Marks** or **Problem Children**) need to seek market leadership so that when the market matures, they will be a long way down the experience curve and in a position of strength in the market. This will require investment to challenge the existing leaders and may force a business to choose between a number of products/SBUs if they are not to spread their resources too thinly.

A **Star** is a business or product which has attained market leadership in high growth markets. Here, the priority will be to invest to maintain leadership against challenges from the Question Marks of other organisations. As a market's growth slows, Stars will become **Cash Cows** if they have protected their leadership. Cash Cows still require some investment to keep their leadership position, but not to the same extent as Stars or Question Marks. Thus, they can potentially generate cash which can be used to support Question Marks seeking to challenge leaders in other markets. If a business has a low relative market share in a mature market, the matrix classifies it as a **Dog**, since it is unlikely to generate cash to the same extent as the market leader. Recently, the concept of **Cash Dogs** has been introduced to indicate products/SBUs which have a good market share and which can generate useful cash flows in spite of not being the market leaders.

An unbalanced portfolio can, therefore, have significant cash flow implications for a business either now or for the future. An absence of Stars could mean no Cash Cows in the future. The absence of Cash Cows will imply a need for external funding if it is to be in a cash-generating position in the future. Too many Question Marks may drain a business of cash if it has ambitions for leadership in each of the markets in which they are launched. Dogs consume management time and a business must consider whether they are holding them for good reasons, since they are unlikely to be contributing much to the bottom line on their own, and so on. Figure 26.3 illustrates the cash situation faced by products/SBUs in different parts of the matrix.

The implications of the matrix are that organisations need to invest heavily in Question Marks and Stars

*An unbalanced portfolio can have significant cashflow implications*

Relative market share

|  | | High | | Low | |
|---|---|---|---|---|---|
| **High** | Cash use | _ _ _ | Cash use | _ _ _ |
| | Cash generated | +++ | Cash generated | + |
| | | 0 | | _ _ |
| **Low** | Cash use | _ | Cash use | _ |
| | Cash generated | +++ | Cash generated | + |
| | | ++ | | 0 |

*Market growth* (left axis: High / Low)

**Figure 26.3**  The Boston Matrix – cash-flow implications

*Each category suggests different marketing priorities*

which they see as potential Cash Cows and only moderately in Cash Cows and Dogs. Thus, each category of product will have different cash-flow connotations and will require attention to different marketing priorities. In this way, a more rational basis for strategy development is possible and the 'health' of an organisation can be more easily assessed from a marketing viewpoint.

Like all simplifications, there are a few drawbacks to using the Boston Matrix as a diagnostic and strategic tool.

- The now-popularised names may act as demotivators for managers, especially if they feel that the organisation only views them as suitable to manage Dogs.
- Growth and market share are not the only factors which make markets attractive and which give companies strength in markets.
- The data to position products/SBUs accurately on the matrix are not always available.
- A clear and common definition of the market must be agreed so that growth and share positions are not distorted.

As an extreme illustration, it would be quite easy for a business to claim a 100 per cent share of the market if it defined the market as all those customers it supplied! In a similar way, maintaining a Cash Cow assumes that other organisations recognise the position and do not invest heavily in their Dogs and attack the Cash Cows of other organisations, thereby requiring them to spend money to defend their position. Overall, though, the tool can be extremely useful as a means of depicting an organisation's situation or market position and as a basis for internal managerial debate.

# TOPIC 27

# The Directional Policy Matrix

The Directional Policy Matrix (DPM) is a framework which can be used to classify and categorise an organisation's business activities in terms of its strengths, capabilities or market position, and the way it perceives markets to be attractive. The basic structure of a DPM is illustrated in Figure 27.1. The purpose of the matrix is to diagnose an organisation's strategic options in relation to the two composite dimensions of business strengths and market attractiveness. The DPM, therefore, enables organisations to conduct an analysis of their portfolio of products or areas of operation.

*The DPM is valuable in analysing and managing product portfolios*

The analysis is performed, first, according to the potential each product area or business has to achieve the organisation's objectives and second, according to the organisation's ability to take advantage of the range

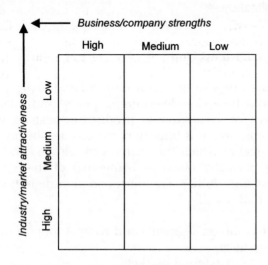

**Figure 27.1** The Directional Policy Matrix (DPM)

145

of opportunities it faces. The matrix requires its users to identify a number of factors which will act as indicators of the attractiveness of a market or opportunity to them and, similarly, a number of factors which will act as indicators of organisational strengths. These factors will obviously vary from one product or business area to another since what will be attractive to one activity may not be attractive in another area of operation, or, at least, may not be equally attractive. Similarly, a strength or capability in one area may not exist or be a strength in another.

*The DPM considers a wider range of decisional influences*

Compared with other portfolio analysis tools, such as the Boston Matrix, the DPM is a more sophisticated mechanism. Like its forerunner, the Boston Matrix, it can be used to derive quantitative comparisons between areas of activities, but, in addition, it is able to take into account a much wider range of decisional influences. In fact, the DPM was originally conceived by General Electric and developed by McKinsey (management consultants), and later Shell, as a means of overcoming some of the limitations the Boston Matrix was perceived to have. It is usually drawn as a $3 \times 3$ box matrix, rather than using the more standard $2 \times 2$ format, in order to encompass the range of strategic options it covers. In the end, the number of lines drawn is irrelevant. What is more important is defining the substance of the matrix and its axes, and adopting an orderly methodology for its application.

### Strategic Business Unit

Since the purpose of performing a DPM analysis is to provide a basis for determining policy and allocating resources for the alternative products or business within an organisation, it is important to consider the organisational level at which the analysis should be conducted. This is normally taken as being that of the 'strategic business unit' (SBU). The most common definition of a SBU is that it will:

- Have common segments and competitors for most of its products.
- Operate in external markets.

- Be identifiable as a discrete and separate unit.
- Be managed by people who will have control over most of the areas critical to success.

Thus, the process of defining an SBU can be applied all the way down to product or departmental level. It is, therefore, possible to use the DPM for any unit that has within it a number of different variables that can be usefully plotted using a two-dimensional matrix. There must obviously be two or more markets or segments between which managers wish to choose, and these can be either existing or potential markets. It is usually felt that there should be at least three and a maximum of ten areas for analysis if using the DPM is to be of value.

## Market Attractiveness

The vertical axis of a DPM represents the degree to which a market is attractive to an organisation. The key determinant of market attractiveness is its potential to yield growth in sales and profits. Although what constitutes a market for the purposes of DPM analysis will vary, a useful definition is: 'An identifiable group of customers with requirements in common that are, or may become, significant in determining a separate strategy.'

*The key determinant of market attractiveness is its potential to yield growth in sales and profits*

Thus, there is a large element of management judgement required at an early stage in the construction of a DPM which will be critical to the quality of the analysis. To avoid unnecessary bias, it is vital that market definition and the identification of market attractiveness criteria be done in as objective a way as possible. It is also the case that both these judgements need to be made in isolation from the organisation's position in its markets. This is difficult to achieve since most of the managers involved in such an exercise will have views about the organisation's position, which will potentially influence their judgements. To make the exercise worthwhile, however, as much objectivity as possible should be striven for.

For some examples of what might constitute market attractiveness criteria, see Table 27.1. The most important are usually the first four.

**Table 27.1**   Criteria which might make a market attractive*

- Growth rate
- Accessible market size
- Competitive intensity
- Profit margins
- Differences between competitive offerings
- Existence of technical standards
- Compatible infrastructure
- Ease of obtaining payment
- Sensitivity to interest rates
- General volatility
- Degree of regulation
- Barriers to entry
- Rate of technological change
- Likelihood of political stability
- Potential for supply 'partnerships'
- Availability of market intelligence

* List non-exclusive

## Business Strength or Position

*Ideally, judgements about business strength or position should be validated by independent market research*

The horizontal axis of a DPM is a measure of an organisation's strengths, or potential strengths, in the market place. The criteria used to judge a product's strengths must be related to customer requirements if they are to have any meaning. The criteria will vary between markets and will need to be assessed against the performance of competitors. The purpose of identifying the criteria is to evaluate the degree to which the organisation can take advantage of a market opportunity. As for market attractiveness, business strengths or position need to be judged in as objective a way as possible to avoid all the products or business areas falling within the same sector of the matrix. Ideally, such judgements should be validated by independent market research.

A list of factors which might be considered when assessing business strengths is shown in Table 27.2.

It is usual, however, to translate these into capability to deliver what the market or segment requires. For guidelines on how to do this, see Topic 17 on SWOT analyses.

**Table 27.2**  Factors which might be considered, or which may
yield, business strengths*

- Relative quality
- Production capacity
- Production flexibility
- Product adaptability
- Unit cost of production
- Price position
- R&D capabilities
- Brands owned
- Company image
- Market share
- Range of commercial contacts
- Influence on regulatory bodies
- Delivery performance
- Service facilities
- Channel access or distribution network
- Size/quality of sales force

* List non-exclusive

## Constructing a DPM Portfolio

Having identified the criteria which will make a market
attractive and which will yield business strengths, these
can then be judged quantitatively by weighting each
factor and then scoring each factor in terms of relative
performance or attractiveness. By multiplying each
factor's weight by its rating, a numerical value can be
obtained. When the values for each factor are totalled,
the product or activity can be positioned on the Matrix.

To avoid all products ending up on the left-hand side
of a $2 \times 2$ form of the matrix, scores for performance can
be expressed as a ratio where the value is set against a
similar value for the best-performing organisation in the
market. If a log scale is used for this axis, ranging from,
say, 3 to 1 to 0.3, this tendency can be overcome.

The use of a $2 \times 2$ form of the matrix yields four
strategic categories as shown in Figure 27.2. Each category will have a strategy choice associated with it which
managers will have to translate into specific objectives
and marketing programmes for that area. Illustrations of
what these might be for each quadrant are shown in
Figure 27.3. In addition, the steps required for the
creation of a DPM are summarised in Table 27.3.

Notes:

*Invest for growth* – businesses that are relatively high in business strengths and market attractiveness.

*Manage for sustained earnings* – businesses with medium strengths in markets of medium to low attractiveness. Maintain strong position in moderately attractive markets, but do not invest to increase market share.

*Manage for cash* – businesses with a relatively weak position in a relatively unattractive market. Harvest for current profitability or divest.

*Opportunistic* – businesses with low business strength, but high market attractiveness.

**Figure 27.2**    Four strategic categories

**Table 27.3**    The ten steps involved in producing a DPM

| | |
|---|---|
| Step 1 | Define the products/services for markets that are to be used during the analysis. |
| Step 2 | Define the criteria for market attractiveness. |
| Step 3 | Score the relevant product/services for market. |
| Step 4 | Define the organisation's relative strengths for each product/service for market. |
| Step 5 | Analyse and draw conclusions from the relative position of each product/service for market. |
| Step 6 | Draw conclusions from the analysis with a view to generating objectives and strategies. |
| Step 7 | (Optional) Position the circles on the box assuming no change to current policies. That is to say, a *forecast* should be made of the future position of the circles. |
| Step 8 | Redraw the portfolio to position the circles where the organisation wants them to be. That is to say, the *objectives* they wish to achieve for each product/service for market. |
| Step 9 | Detail the strategies to be implemented to achieve the objectives. |
| Step 10 | Calculate the appropriate financial consequences of changes by product. |

| Main thrust | Invest for growth | Manage for sustained earnings | Manage for cash | Opportunistic development |
|---|---|---|---|---|
| Market share | Maintain or increase dominance | Maintain or slightly milk for earnings | Forgo share for profit | Invest selectively in share |
| Products | Differentiation – line expansion | Prune less successful Differentiate for key segments | Aggressively prune | Differentiation – line expansion |
| Price | Lead – aggressive pricing for share | Stabilise prices/raise | Raise | Aggressive – price for share |
| Promotion | Aggressive marketing | Limit | Minimise | Aggressive marketing |
| Distribution | Broaden distribution | Hold wide distribution pattern | Gradually withdraw distribution | Limited coverage |
| Cost control | Tight control – go for scale economies | Emphasise cost-reduction viz. variable costs | Aggressively reduce both fixed and variable | Tight – but not at expense of entrepreneurship |
| Production | Expand, invest (organic acquisition, joint venture) | Maximise capacity and utilisation | Free up capacity | Invest |
| R&D | Expand – invest | Focus on specific projects | None | Invest |
| Personnel | Upgrade management in key functional areas | Maintain, reward efficiency, tighten organisation | Cut back organisation | Invest |
| Investment | Fund growth | Limit fixed investment | Minimise and divest opportunistically | Fund growth |
| Working capital | Reduce in process – extend credit | Tighten credit – reduce accounts receivable Increase inventory turn | Aggressively reduce | Invest |

**Figure 27.3** Programme guidelines suggested for different positioning on the DPM

# Developing New Products

A significant proportion of most organisations' revenue is derived from products introduced in the recent past. Such new products can take many different forms and can be derived from a number of different external and internal sources. Their development or acquisition, however, is costly and there is a great danger of failure. This danger can be reduced if marketing principles and personnel can be involved at every stage of the acquisition, development and launch of new products.

## Types of New Products

*New products have different degrees of 'newness'*

New products which are not just the acquisition of another organisation's established products will have different degrees of 'newness' associated with them. A common way of classifying new products is:

- *Revolutionary new products*: products the like of which have never been seen before and which create entirely new markets.
- *Improved products*: existing products which have been enhanced to provide better performance or greater perceived value; often referred to as the 'next generation'.
- *Modified products*: where current models are replaced by new ones which combine features of a number of different models.
- *Adapted products*: products which have been changed to address needs in other markets or market segments, but whose key functionality remains the same.
- *New brands*: successful new products often stimulate the launch of similar competitive products by other organisations under different brand names or alternative positions.

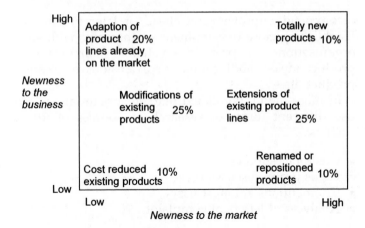

**Figure 28.1** New product classification

An alternative classification based on 'newness' to markets and the businesses launching them is shown in Figure 28.1. The percentages shown for each category demonstrate that only a small proportion (10 per cent) of all new product launches concern products which are totally new concepts or in any way revolutionary. This suggests that new product management must cover a wide range of different situations.

## Sources of New Product Ideas

Organisations which are open to new ideas and which actively pursue new product opportunities are usually systematic in their search. They recognise that there are a number of different sources which can generate good ideas and that sometimes a proactive approach needs to be adopted. Appropriate sources, however, will vary from industry to industry and may require different types of approach, although all ideas must be closely linked with customer needs and wants if they are to be successful commercially.

For many organisations, **customers** are, in fact, the most profitable source of new ideas. This is certainly true in industrial markets, where customers often produce the highest percentage of new ideas, particularly if they are **lead users** (i.e., organisations which make the most use of a new product). Lead users are also, therefore, likely to see the limitations of a product first and can recommend improvements ahead of later purchasers. Establishing close development partnerships with such organisations can provide a valuable source of new product ideas, modifications or extensions of existing product lines.

In more highly populated markets, organisations can use different forms of **research** as sources of ideas, such as:

- Customer surveys.
- Focus group discussions.
- Competitions amongst users.
- Analyses of letters of complaint.

As an example, when Toyota decided it wished to enter the US automobile market it decided to use the VW Beetle as its **benchmark** product. Thus, it closely questioned existing users about the problems they experienced with the Beetle. The result was a car positioned as a 'fun' product for drivers who were prepared to buy foreign cars, with none of the drawbacks of a Beetle, but all the advantages.

Other **external** sources of new product ideas include:

- Competitors.
- Patent offices.
- Intermediaries.
- Universities.
- Commercial laboratories.
- Consultants.
- Market research firms.

*Organisations must be willing to explore new ideas*

The Japanese have often analysed competitor products (a process known as reverse engineering) as a source of new ideas and are net importers of licenses for various technologies, which they often improve for their own commercial purposes. In some countries, as a means of facilitating this process, publications exist which are devoted to advertisers seeking ideas or inventors searching for a business willing to exploit their discoveries. **Internal** sources can be equally valuable and can include: research laboratories; sales representatives; and other employees.

Sometimes, the chief executive, as the founder or key technical force within the business, is the main source of innovation. Whatever the source, the organisation must

**Figure 28.2**  Cultural blockages to new product initiatives

be willing to explore new ideas. In many enterprises, their organisational culture can act as a damper and stifle initiatives which could be the future life-blood of the business (see Figure 28.2).

## Stages in Product Development

Once an idea for a new product has been conceived, the process of development and placing it on the market needs to be carefully managed to reduce the risk and costs of failure. The initial stage is a preliminary market and technical assessment of the concept to judge whether its creation and sale seem feasible. This should be performed fairly quickly and be at minimal cost. The next step is a detailed technical product analysis and the creation of prototypes, in parallel with some more detailed market research, to test the assumptions made during the initial feasibility or concept test.

Once an organisation is satisfied that a new idea has sufficient potential, the technical side of the business should move towards a pilot production stage while marketing begins to establish the springboard from which the product will be launched. This may involve preparing the media, identifying appropriate channels of distribution, understanding the target-market buyer-behaviour, and establishing a market position. Pilot production and a test marketing exercise are often employed as the next stage to confirm or deny the potential before full investment is made in production facilities and the market as a whole.

*The task of marketing is to reduce new product risk by pursuing market knowledge*

As can be inferred, the cost of developing a new product for commercialisation will increase dramatically as an organisation moves towards full commercialisation. The task of marketing is to reduce the risk by pursuing market knowledge which will enable a project to be dropped before expenditure becomes too high. For mass market consumer products, the cumulative expenditure at the point of full launch can be as high as £5 million. Of this, 50 per cent can be accounted for by the national **roll-out** of the product. The importance of rigorous procedures to prevent the inappropriate launch of a new product can, therefore, be seen to be vital (see Figure 28.3).

It has also been estimated that for every successful new product, between 50 and 70 new ideas have to be considered and that only one in four products which are test-marketed prove successful once launched nationally. When products are successful, they tend to be ones which:

- Deliver a significant differentiated benefit.
- Have a good technological fit with the supplying organisation.
- Stem from businesses which have 'done their marketing well'.

Modern management practices indicate that these factors are more likely to be achieved where new product teams are set up which consist of representa-

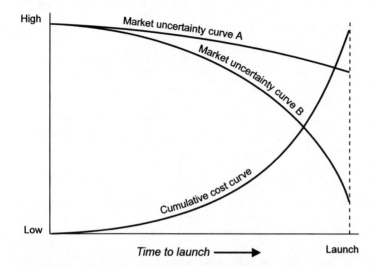

**Figure 28.3** Risk and new product development

tives from the major management disciplines in the organisation: operations; engineering; finance; human resources; and marketing. In addition, where development is managed as a parallel process between engineering, production and marketing, as opposed to a serial development process, success is even more likely. Whatever the process, however, without good marketing input, new products become a game of Russian roulette rather than a disciplined management contribution to the organisation.

*Without good marketing input, new products become a game of Russian roulette*

**Section E**

# UNDERSTANDING POSITIONING

# TOPIC 29

# Branding

When making a purchase, a customer is influenced by a whole range of factors associated with the complete product offer. One of these may be the product's brand name. In spite of its intangibility, a well-developed brand can be a powerful influence on both customers and competitors alike, and will be a key contributor to the way a product, company, or whatever, is positioned in the market place. It is, therefore, important to understand the scope of branding, including the difference between a major brand and lesser brands, or commodities, which do not command the same power, the specific components of a brand name and the differences between successful and unsuccessful brands.

## The Scope of Branding

When considering brands, it should first be stressed that the term 'brand' is used to encompass not only consumer products such as Persil or Nescafé, but a host of offerings, which include places (such as Bangkok), ships (such as the *Queen Elizabeth*), companies (such as BMW and Kodak), industrial products, service products, and even individual people. Second, a distinction should be drawn between a 'brand' and a 'commodity'.

*The scope of branding is wide*

Typically, commodity markets are characterised by a lack of perceived differentiation by customers between competing offerings. Whilst there may be quality differences, the suggestion is that within a given specification this carton of milk, for example, is just the same as any other carton of milk. In situations such as these, one finds that purchase decisions tend to be taken on the basis of price or availability, and not on the basis of the brand or the manufacturer's name. Thus, one could

161

argue that the purchase of petrol falls into the commodity category, and whilst the petrol companies do try to promote 'image', they inevitably end up relying upon promotions such as wine glasses and games to try to generate repeat purchase.

There are examples, however, of taking a commodity and making it a brand. A good example is provided by Perrier Water: the contents are naturally occurring spring water which, whilst possessing certain distinctive characteristics, at the end of the day is still spring water. Yet through packaging and, more particularly, promotion, an international brand has been created with high brand loyalty. Consequently, it sells for a price well in excess of the costs of the ingredients.

*The difference between a brand and a commodity is the idea of added values*

The difference between a brand and a commodity can be summed up in the phrase 'added values'. A brand is more than just the sum of its component parts. It embodies for the purchaser or user, additional attributes which, whilst they might be considered by some to be 'intangible', are still very real. To illustrate the power of these added values, it is only necessary to consider the preference given by consumers to successful brands by dint of the brand name, rather than because of any functional superiority that can be discerned in objective comparisons.

## Successful and Unsuccessful Brands

Successful brand building aids profitability by helping to create stable, long-term, demand and by adding values that entice customers to buy. They also provide a firm base for expansion into product improvements, variants, added services, new countries, and so on, and can help to protect organisations against the growing power of intermediaries. A strong brand name may also help organisations to transform themselves from being faceless bureaucracies into firms that are attractive both as employers and as businesses with which to associate.

It is important, then, not to make the mistake of confusing successful and unsuccessful brands. The world is full of products and services that have brand names, but which are not successful brands. Successful brands tend to:

- Have a unique identity which is widely recognised by members of the target market.
- Provide sustainable competitive advantage by being more attractive than most other identities or positions in the market.
- Add significantly to the asset value of an organisation as demonstrated when the organisation is sold or acquired.
- Require continuous investment to avoid the diminution experienced by some previously powerful brands, such as Hoover, Singer, Biro, and so on.

## The Components of a Brand

The first component of a brand is its **brand positioning**. This is concerned with what the brand actually *does* and with what it competes. In other words, brand positioning starts with the physical, or functional, aspects of the product. For instance, Canada Dry is positioned in the UK as a mixer for brandies and whiskies, rather than as a soft drink competing with Coca-Cola, Pepsi-Cola and 7Up. Similarly, Tide is presented as a tough, general purpose detergent, rather than as a powder for woollens. Marks & Spencer also goes to great lengths to support its image as a high-quality multiple rather than a low price chainstore and SAS is carefully positioned as the business person's airline. Positioning is usually performed against identifiable motivators in any market, only one or two of which are of real importance when developing a brand. These dimensions are best seen as bipolar scales along which brands can be positioned. Examples of these are provided in Table 29.1.

**Table 29.1**   Bipolar scales for brand positioning

| | |
|---|---|
| Expensive | Inexpensive |
| Strong | Mild |
| Big | Small |
| Hot | Cold |
| Fast | Slow |
| Male | Female |

The second component of a brand is its **personality**. This is a useful descriptor for the total impression that consumers have of brands and indicates that in many ways brands are like people in that they have their own physical, emotional and attitudinal characteristics. Thus, they are a complex blend of different characteristics which together create a brand identity. In this way, two brands can be very similar in terms of their functions, yet have very different personalities. As an example, the Ford Fiesta, the Peugeot 205 and the Rover Metro all perform about the same along the functional dimensions of size, speed and price. Yet each one has a totally different personality, which is the result of a blend of three sorts of appeal: sensual, rational, and emotional.

- *Sensual appeal*: refers to the way the product or service looks, sounds or feels. It is easy to imagine how this appeal can differ in the case of, say, cigarettes or cars.
- *Rational appeal*: concerns the way the product or service performs (what they contain, their relative costs and so on).
- *Emotional appeal*: is perhaps the most important aspect of a brand, and has a lot to do with the psychological rewards it offers, the moods it conjures up, the associations it evokes and so on; it is easy to see the overt appeal of certain products as being, for instance, particularly masculine, feminine, chic, workmanlike, or 'flashy'.

*A brand converts a commodity into something which can command a higher price*

Brand personality is also the result of a whole gamut of influences, such as: the places where it is sold; the price that is charged; other brands from the same manufacturer; how it is used; the kind of people who buy and use it; after-sales service; the name of the brand; advertising; point of sale material; PR; sponsorship; and many others.

However, for any brand to be successful, all these elements have to be consistent, since they will all affect the brand's personality and it is this personality, above all else, that represents the brand's totality and which makes one brand more desirable than another. At its simplest, it is a brand's personality that converts a commodity into something unique and enables a higher price to be charged for it.

Overall, then, a good brand is an identifiable product, service, company, person, or place, augmented in such a way that buyers or users perceive a personality which incorporates relevant and unique added values which closely match their needs. A brand's success results from being able to sustain these added values against competitors over time.

*Brand success lies in its sustainability*

# TOPIC 30

# Pricing Strategies

A customer's response to an offering from a supplier is affected by all aspects of the marketing mix which constitutes that offer. Amongst these variables, price is always an important feature since it is one of the determinants of a product's value. Price is thus one of the evaluative criteria utilised by potential customers, as are the costs which will be incurred in both making the purchase and owning or utilising the product. Price and associated costs are, therefore, an important adjunct to positioning.

*Creating a strategy first requires an understanding of the strategic alternatives available*

At the same time, price is a very difficult aspect of the marketing mix to manage. This is because it is subject to many pressures which are independent of marketing objectives. These can be both internal (from financial, operations, sales and other senior managers) and external (from customers, competitors and government agencies, etc.). To maintain the integrity of prices, a sound pricing strategy is required to act as a yardstick against which to make pricing decisions. A strategy for pricing is also required to support an organisation's overall marketing strategy and to protect profitability. The strategy adopted will be determined by the circumstances an individual organisation faces, and requires marketing managers to possess a good understanding of the alternative strategies available.

## Market Skimming

A market-skimming strategy is one where a supplying organisation positions itself at the top of the market against its competitors. If there are no competitors, then skimming suggests a price at which only a small number of the potential customers for a product will be prepared to buy. The implication of a skimming strategy is that an organisation will be targeting a niche in the market for

166

whom the benefits of a product have a high value. A further implication is that product volumes and market share will never be high, but that margins should be good.

Following a skimming strategy is appropriate for products or offerings which are unique or which attract high quality ratings. Uniqueness may be derived from: proprietary access to materials, facilities or the technology a product incorporates; the way in which the product is produced; or its particular formulation. Uniqueness can be protected by patents or by keeping processes and recipes a secret. Quality will be associated with the care with which a product or service is produced, the materials it incorporates or the customer service which accompanies the product. Quality can also be associated with: precision; reliability; longevity; finish; presentation; robustness; and many other features, depending on the product's application. *Skimming strategies are appropriate for unique products or offerings*

Maintaining a pricing strategy of skimming over the life of a product obviously requires support from other positioning variables such as image, brand value, relationship management and the way in which a price is presented. It also requires efforts to distance a product away from competitors and a strategy for maintaining differentiation over the product life-cycle. Where significant economies of scale and/or experience are potentially available, skimming and sustaining high price levels becomes difficult unless a really powerful brand has been created, there is a wide patent platform or propriety access to the supply of non-substitutable materials or facilities exists.

## Sliding or Reducing Skim

As the name implies, this strategy involves an initial high price which is dropped either as new entrants make a market more competitive or as a market matures. Whilst it does not imply continuing as the most expensive in a market, it does mean that the organisation will seek to be towards the upper reaches of the continuum of prices which prevail in a market. In this way, an enterprise can seek to address larger sections of a market with the object of becoming one of the market leaders suppliers, if not *the* market leader.

A sliding or reducing skim strategy is also appropriate when it is difficult to sustain a technological advantage or where costs are sensitive to economies of scale and/or experience. Both these factors will make a product attractive to competitors and require price adjustments as the market evolves. In this case, the organisation will be following the market and trying to recover product development and investment costs in as short a period as possible. At the same time, it will be seeking to position itself as a dominant player through branding or service quality while using price as a support for its ambitions.

## Market Penetration

*Market penetration strategy uses low price to obtain volume sales and market share*

A strategy of market penetration is the opposite of a skimming approach. Here a low price is used to obtain volume sales and to attain market share. The price, however, must not be so low that it becomes indicative of poor quality or unacceptable performance. Sometimes, this can be used as an entry strategy into an already established market, or it might be used to create a market or speed up its development by making a product accessible to a wide audience early in its lifecycle. In some cases, organisations have been known to price ahead of expected cost gains from economies of experience in order to achieve this.

Such a strategy requires an organisation to maintain its price advantage in the face of changes in the general market price structure. It also requires that the benefit to price ratio between supplying organisations is sufficiently different to be significant in the eyes of the consumer: i.e., that whatever products act as benchmarks for customers appear to them to be significantly more expensive. The developing Malaysian and Korean automobile manufacturers provide good examples of organisations adopting this type of approach.

### Floor Pricing

This strategy implies keeping prices right at the lower end of the price spectrum and will be used to appeal to those who are very price-conscious. High sensitivity to price will be a result of the customer seeing little differential value between the various offerings in the market or having restricted disposable incomes. The perceived benefits of the offer must still match the price adopted. Such benefits are more likely to be presented in isolation from other benefits which may exist since they will have less value for this particular type of customer. Such a strategy requires close attention to costs at all times and is typical of the bargain basement, no frills, type of operation. Enterprises which can survive on low margins, whether because of high turnover, lower profit requirements, or insignificant overheads, are best able to pursue this type of strategy.

## Competitor Pricing

An alternative to adopting a proactive pricing strategy is to position an organisation a specific distance from a market leader's price. This distance may be large or small, and may be above or below the market leader chosen, depending on the way in which the business wishes to be perceived. Any price changes initiated by the leader will then be followed by the competitor organisation, either immediately or at the next available opportunity. In the case of forecourt or retail prices, this may be the following day. Where prices are not openly stated or are part of a competitive tendering process, this can take much longer.

Such an approach is rarely operated in isolation and may be used as part of a penetration or skimming strategy. If the distance adopted is large, then it is likely that a product is being used as a loss leader to attract customers who would then purchase other products at prices closer to the norm. If the distance is significant, but remains constant over time, the position may be held to attract a particular segment of the market by offering a specific value proposition. Whatever the case, the overall benefits offered are likely to be similar to those offered by the leader, who will be providing a 'price umbrella' under which others in the market can 'shelter'.

*Competitor pricing may form part of a penetration or skimming strategy*

## Cost-based Pricing

Under all the strategies discussed above, there is an implication that costs should be managed in the light of the strategy adopted rather than the other way round. In some cases, however, cost will be a significant determinant of price. As an example, where products use expensive capital equipment to be produced, skimming or floor pricing may not be possible options. In other areas, such as some types of government procurement, or where suppliers have been developed as partnerships, prices may be determined and discussed on the basis of costs.

It is also the case that, in the end, income must exceed total costs. These, and other reasons, as illustrated in Table 30.1, make costs a very appealing base from which to set prices. Setting prices according to costs however, is, fraught with dangers (see Table 30.2), and can lead to suboptimism or the absence of any clear market position.

**Table 30.1**   Appeal of a cost approach to pricing

- Managers usually feel more certain about costs than about what customers will pay.
- Prices are easier to justify in terms of cost rather than benefits.
- A cost-based approach to pricing is administratively easier than judging market-based issues.
- Prices based on cost appear socially more acceptable and are less open to accusations of exploitation.
- A cost-plus approach should ensure that an organisation remains profitable.

**Table 30.2**   Problems of a cost approach to pricing

- Costs are not always easy to identify.
- It ignores the way customers use price.
- It ignores the relative value of an offering compared with competitors.
- Costs will often vary with volume.
- Market objectives are not usually related to costs.
- Costings between products is highly dependent on the way costs are allocated.

The strategy adopted should also, clearly, be appropriate to an organisation's marketing objectives, be they in terms of market share, defending markets, establishing a position, managing relationships, stabilising a market, expanding a market or whatever. Within strategies, there is also the opportunity to decide whether an organisation will operate fixed prices with no discounts, or whether they will adopt a more flexible approach. As a general rule, however, no matter what strategy is adopted, in a buoyant market with rising or excess demand, a business should always seek to raise prices, since it will find it hard, or even impossible, when times are not so good.

*It is difficult, or even impossible, to raise prices when times are hard*

## TOPIC 31

# Setting a Price

*Pricing decisions should always be made in the context of pricing strategy*

Any specific pricing decision should always be made in the context of the pricing strategy an organisation has opted to follow. These can vary from a skimming or penetration approach to being the cheapest in the market, or simply following the lead of a major player. Costs are also used as a basis for pricing, but are not usually considered to be a sound basis although prices must, in the end, yield income in excess of total operating expenses.

As well as strategy, there are a number of situational factors which will also influence the exact price chosen. Thus, when the occasion arises which requires a pricing decision, an organisation's pricing strategy will provide the main approach to be adopted, but situational variables will determine the actual price paid.

### Occasions Requiring Price Decision

The most obvious occasion demanding a pricing decision is when a business sets a price for the **first time**. This can occur when a business launches a product which is either new to them *and* the market, which is just new to them, or when they move an existing product into a new market. In some of these situations, a price structure will already exist, and the organisation's strategy will determine approximately where it will be positioned relative to competitor products on the price continuum (see Figure 31.1).

In situations where a product is completely new to a market, then pricing becomes more difficult, although still driven by the organisation's strategy. Here it is sometimes possible to benchmark against similar but non-competing products. Alternatively, it may be possible to establish how target customers evaluate a potential purchase (payback, return on investment, up front

172

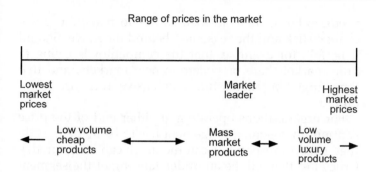

**Figure 31.1**  The price continuum

price, life-cycle cost, etc.) or how they perceive value (reliability, availability, brand, security, gaining competitive advantage, associated attitudes, social prestige, etc.). In the absence of these, it may be justifiable to use costs as an indicator for price, in which case it should be acknowledged that improvements to the quality of the organisation's marketing are probably required!

Costs however, *are* a significant issue, when they change. When **costs increase**, it is wise to attempt to maintain margins if the increase is likely to be permanent. This may simply require marginal changes to price lists. In more sensitive markets, it may be necessary to find ways of adding value to justify a price rise. Where costs are likely to be volatile, as is often the case for commodity raw materials or where prices are sensitive to exchange rates, it can be wise to use hedging arrangements, although these can be expensive. Whatever the cause, there is still a decision as to how margins can be maintained without alienating customers. If, on the other hand, **costs drop**, there is an awkward choice to be made between appearing to be exploitative, using the extra profits for investment and using the price flexibility which has become available for competitive advantage.

A price decision will also have to be made when **competitors initiate a price change**. If the initiator is a 'benchmark' competitor, then the response will be fairly straightforward. This will be particularly true for price followers who have adopted a set position in relation to certain key market players. If the initiator has traditionally occupied the role of a follower, then an assessment

*Costs are a significant issue when they change*

needs to be made as to their power to make the price-change stick and the reasoning behind the move. Should it be felt, for example, that the competitor is trying to grab market-share or penetrate new markets, and that they might be successful, a defensive response is required.

For organisations operating at either end of the price continuum, a similar judgement has to be made (i.e., do they need to respond or can the move can be ignored?). Crucial to this will be an understanding of the segment in which the competitor is operating, the likely response of customers and the relationship between the competitor and the responding organisation in the minds of the customer.

The most difficult situation is when a **customer asks for a price reduction**. This may occur during regular negotiations or as a request for a discount from normal prices. Here, it is useful to establish reference points against which to negotiate, such as well-known competitors' prices and the benefits of the product under discussion. It is also useful to establish what has motivated the request, since this could help to formulate a response which was not a cut in price. This may be more difficult if the relationship with the customer is distant or 'transaction-based'.

If such a situation leads to price negotiations, it is important for the supplier to look for trade-offs which could be made in exchange for price cuts, but which would save the supplier money or gain them advantage. These could include prompt payment, higher volumes, less frequent deliveries, joint promotions, taking a broader mix of products, and so on. This, however, does require a good understanding of operational costs on the part of the supplier to avoid reduced profitability.

### Price Presentation

*Price can be presented to customers in different ways to enhance acceptability*

When quoting a price to a customer, it must also be remembered that a price is not just an isolated figure, but can be presented in a number of different ways which will make it more or less acceptable. Some prices can be made to look more acceptable if they are 'unbundled' and broken down into component parts. This can include separated delivery charges, packaging requirements, service costs, warranties, upgrades and so on. The more complex the product, the more scope there is for this type of approach. Some customers, however, may be more interested in the total cost for budgeting or comparison purposes.

Prices can also be made acceptable by providing initial comparisons with other products which are outside a particular customer's price band. If a customer felt, for instance, that the absolute top acceptable price for a suit of clothing was $350 and a supplier was trying to sell one at $375, the supplier may help his case by referring to $750 high brand suits which the customer would never purchase, but which would make $375 seem a fair price.

In some businesses, it is also often worth deliberately presenting a range of models which fall into basic, standard and de luxe categories, in order to enhance the value of the standard model. This also has the advantage of being able to move de luxe features into the standard model to enhance value over time. Where a product has a tendency to move towards commodity status as customers become more familiar with it, or as a market matures, this can be a useful tactic.

Psychological elements can also be used to enhance the acceptability of a price. This can involve the use of 'attractive numbers' (although what is attractive will vary between different cultural environments) or pricing in relation to certain 'break points' in the market. The existence of such points help explain the use of $X.99 prices and the significance of keeping below certain price thresholds in a market. Again, such thresholds will vary from market to market.

## Transaction Price Management

Studies of prices which have compared invoice pricing with the prices customers actually pay have noted that there are often a number of 'off-invoice' concessions which have the effect of reducing the profitability of a customer. These can include:

- Prompt payment discounts.
- Promotional allowances.
- Retrospective volume discounts.

- Free delivery for orders over certain values.
- Sales promotion campaigns.
- Unofficial extended credit.

Since most customer profit calculations are based on invoices, organisations can easily overestimate the profitability of individual customers. The difference between invoice price and the price effectively paid has been shown to be as much as 29 per cent in some cases.

Advantage can be gained by monitoring such income 'leakages' and targeting those customers who incur fewer 'off-invoice' price discounts. It is sometimes also possible to move particular elements of 'off-invoice' reductions on to the invoice to demonstrate to customers the real value of their purchase for comparison purposes. In addition, different customers will be sensitive to different elements of 'off-invoice' costs. As an example, one distributor or retailer may be more attracted to promotional discounts than credit allowances. In this case, it may be possible to engineer prices to achieve better results for the supplier by focusing on appropriate elements for specific tactical ends.

*What is important is the price customers end up paying*

For all organisations, what is important is the price the customer ends up paying. However, setting a price, obtaining sales in the right volumes and collecting the income is not a simple matter. What is important is consistency, which should be driven by adherence to a pricing strategy and which sets the context for a pricing decision. Situations, however, will vary from one customer to another, from one market to another and from one time period to another. Such situational variables will determine which tactics are appropriate and how an organisation should respond to the specific circumstances it faces.

# TOPIC 32

# Advertising

Advertising is one of the four major communications and promotions activities in which organisations can engage. Of the four, advertising is probably the most glamorous, although the others (sales promotions, public relations, and personal selling) are nonetheless potent promotional tools! A useful definition which differentiates advertising from other methods of communication are that it is: any paid form of non-personal presentation in a measured media by an identifiable sponsor. It is also, probably, the most powerful aid to positioning, certainly from within the promotional mix.

Even though there are many relatively cheap forms of advertising, such as small advertisements in local newspapers, any 'serious' advertising campaign is usually an expensive undertaking. This is particularly true for major consumer goods and service companies for whom branding is a major contributor to competitive advantage, although advertising is also important for industrial suppliers, government agencies and other non-profit organisations.

*Any 'serious' advertising campaign is usually expensive*

For commercial organisations that see advertising as an important aspect of their promotional activities, expenditures of 5 per cent up to 30 per cent of sales are not unusual. The potential cost and contribution of advertising requires marketing managers to make careful media choices, to understand what advertising can realistically achieve, and to know how to make advertising effective.

## Advertising Media

The medium most commonly associated with advertising is television. It is the communications channel to which more people are exposed than any other, although, in absolute terms, more money is generally spent on newspaper advertising. Television, however, tends to arouse more excitement in marketing executives because of its life style, creative and entertainment associations. Other media include:

- Magazines.
- Radio.
- Outdoor displays.
- Direct mail.
- Novelties.
- Catalogues.
- Directories.
- Circulars.

Marketing communications managers consequently face a wide range of media choices when putting together an advertising campaign. Their decision should depend upon whom they wish to reach, the product they are promoting, the type of message being sent and the cost-effectiveness of the alternatives. An organisation's target audience might, for example, be difficult to identify, may not spend much time reading newspapers or magazines, and may respond better to light-hearted messages. In this case, television or radio might be required to reach them. A special interest group such as joggers or accountants, who take their interest seriously, might be better reached via targeted magazines.

The media chosen should also be able to demonstrate the selling properties of a product, and this again will vary between media. Thus, a complicated message will require magazines or mailings if it is to be communicated effectively, whilst announcements of limited events such as sales or the opening of a new store can be successfully advertised over television and radio or in daily newspapers and hoardings.

*A combination of advertising media is often required to overcome the limitations of each*

Whichever media is chosen, the important financial consideration is the cost per thousand exposures, preferably to the organisation's target market, and the impact the advertisement will have. Often, a combination of media is required to overcome the limitations each might have such as: clutter; fleetingness of exposure; wasted exposures; plus the image impact which might be implied by the choice of media. Some organisations, for instance, might not want to be associated with high-cost television advertisements or 'junk mail'.

## Types of Advertising Objectives

There are three main types of advertising campaigns which an organisation can adopt depending on the marketing situation it faces. The first of these is **informative advertising** which is particularly important when trying to introduce new product forms or classes. The purpose of informative advertising is, normally, to build primary demand by educating a market or by encouraging the formation of attitudes. Such objectives, however, are not only appropriate for new products, but may also be helpful for mature products to reduce false impressions held by consumers; suggest new applications for a product; make consumers aware of upgrades, improvements, new outlets, or special events; and so on. Whatever the case, the information selected for communication, plus the way in which it is communicated, will also support a product or organisation's positioning.

Positioning is more usually supported by **persuasive advertising**. This is commonly observed in competitive markets where a technology or product form is already established and accepted. The objective will be to create selective demand by building preferences or promoting particular attributes or benefits to differentiate an organisation. As part of this, advertisers can compare their offering with those of their competitors, although competitor denigrations and criticism can reflect badly on an advertiser. In addition to positioning and brand preference, persuasive advertising may be used to encourage immediate or early purchase, promote product enquiries or sales appointments, and stimulate a trial purchase or attendance at a demonstration. Of these, the majority of advertising used by, say, holiday time-share firms is of this final kind. Consumer goods suppliers tend to focus on encouraging a purchase whilst industrial organisations usually concentrate on enquiry generation.

*Advertising is an important aid to positioning*

The third form of advertising is based on **reminding** consumers of a brand's values or **reinforcing** positioning and other messages already implanted in people's minds. This is often evident in mature markets or where reassurance is an important aspect of post-purchase evaluation for the customer. Established brand names tend to be protected by their owners with this type of advertising. The brochures which come with expensive items are equally concerned with convincing purchasers that they have made the right choice as with persuading people to buy. Where products are subject to seasonal influences, reminder advertising is also important to prevent any loss of position between seasons.

## Making Advertising Effective

Like any other form of communication, to be effective, advertising must get people's attention, keep their interest, have a clear message and avoid distortion. In addition, advertisers must start with a good understanding of the effect they wish to achieve.

Although the obvious objective is to generate sales, it is hard to link advertising directly with purchases, especially where other objectives are involved, such as education or positioning. The main exception to this is direct response advertising, where it is easier to identify sales resulting from campaigns. Objectives are, therefore, better couched in terms of awareness, brand recall, comparisons, knowledge and attitudes.

*Effective advertising conveys a clear message via a creative proposition*

Once the context of a campaign is established, effective advertising requires the development of a clear message which the advertisers wish to convey. This should be converted into a creative proposition which does not compromise the essentials of effective communications. Much time and effort is usually spent on this aspect to ensure the communicability of the message. Here style, time, language and presentation are important to match consumers' situations. In this, choice of media is also significant, since it will affect the possibility for distortion and the chances that the message will reach the right target group. Good advertising agencies are important contributors to decision-making in these areas. Organisational managers, however, need to be careful not to get too carried away by the artistic and creative sides of advertising at the expense of the original objectives.

Advertising, of course, should never be performed in isolation and requires market research to help define and evaluate its activities. Such research should be conducted both before and after any campaign to identify the directions it should take and the effect it has had. Too often, organisations concentrate on the creation and delivery of a campaign, and whether it obtained sufficient exposure, at the expense of trying to understand what needs to be achieved. Overall, though, there is no substitute for a well-developed advertising plan which follows a logical process of decision-making. The contents and structure of such a plan are illustrated in Table 32.1.

**Table 32.1**  Suggested pro-forma for an advertising plan

- **General objectives**
  What are the overall objectives we wish to achieve?
  Should they focus on conveying information, developing attitudes, giving reasons for buying or what?
  What other promotional activities might be needed to support these objectives?
  Are these objectives consistent with activities in other areas of the marketing mix?
  Is it possible to achieve the objectives set through advertising alone? (If not they are not an appropriate objective for advertising.)

- **Target audience**
  Who are they? How do we describe/identify them?
  What do they already know/feel about us/our competition?
  Where are they? What are their reading/viewing (etc.) habits?

- **Response required**
  What response do we require from the target audience?
  What do we want them to feel/believe/know about our product?
  Is there anything we wish to avoid conveying?
  Are these responses incorporated in the *specific* objectives set for our advertising activities?

- **Creative platform**
  How are the key messages translated into a communicable presentation?
  Is the creative platform clearly linked with our specific objectives?
  Does the presentation link clearly with the responses required?
  What evidence is there that the presentation is acceptable and appropriate to our audiences?

*continued overleaf*

**Table 32.1** *continued*

- **Media platform**
  What medium or combination of media are to be utilised for the campaign?
  Why is this choice appropriate?
  What criteria have been used to determine cost-effectiveness?
  Do the media chosen match the 'quality' of our product?

- **Timings**
  When are our communications to be displayed/conveyed to our audience?
  What is the pattern of activities to be?
  Have we considered all the alternative patterns?
  What is the reasoning behind the scheduling adopted?
  How do the timings adopted coordinate with:
  - promotions of the other products we sell?
  - competitor promotional and other marketing activities?
  - seasonal trends?
  - special events in the market?

- **Budget**
  How much will the planned campaigns cost?
  When is the money going to be required?
  How is expenditure going to be monitored and controlled?
  What is the cost justification for spending this amount?

- **Measuring expected results**
  How do we intend to measure the results?
  Have we established any benchmarks required to establish change?
  Are all objectives sufficiently quantified to be measurable?
  What are our criteria for success/failure?

# TOPIC 33

# Public Relations

As the name suggests, 'public relations' as an area of marketing is concerned with an organisation's relationships with the various groups, or 'publics', that affect its ability to achieve its goals and objectives. The aspects of these relationships which act as a focus for public relations, are the image and information a market holds about an organisation. In other words, its **position** in the market. At a simple level, this is achieved through publicity in various print and broadcast media. However, the broader views being encouraged by moves towards **relationship marketing** require public relations activities to be more specific in their targeting and objectives. Public relations, therefore, is an important support for both relationship marketing and positioning.

Interest in public relations is also being stimulated by the reducing power and cost effectiveness of mass media advertising. As the volume of communications aimed at the public increases and media channels proliferate, public relations offers an alternative means of reaching the audiences which an organisation would like to influence. A message received, for instance, via an editorial can be up to five times more influential than one received via an advertisement. Public relations, however, is unlikely to replace advertising or other means of communication and promotion. A more likely development is that it will increase its significance as an integral part of a communications or promotions mix.

*Public relations messages can be far more influential than advertising*

## Public Relations Communications Tools

Public relations activities cover a number of different areas.

### News Generation

One of the most widely used is the **generation of news**. News is best structured around a story which can

183

incorporate information about an organisation or its products. Stories can be created around discoveries, achievements, personalities or changes. Often surveys or projects are commissioned to provide objective reports about topics of relevance to both the sponsoring organisation's products and its image. Thus, toothpaste manufacturers might support dental health research or a financial services organisation might investigate people's attitudes towards saving. News can also be used to make consumers aware of the existence of a product or service in order to stimulate enquiries from interested parties. It must also be remembered, however, that placing news where it will be accepted for publication is as important a skill as spotting and reporting newsworthy activities.

*Events*

Organisations can also gain people's attention through staging or sponsoring **events**. These can range from simple news conferences and seminars to exhibitions, competitive activities, anniversary dinners and stunts. All are likely to gain media coverage and draw attention to the sponsoring organisation's name. They can also aid the achievement of credibility or establish images with which an organisation would like to be associated. Events are also good opportunities to develop relationships with suppliers, opinion leaders and associates, as well as customers.

*Publications*

An organisation's **publications** are another method of communication in which public relations will have an active interest. Sales support material is an obvious example, which can include brochures, manuals and presentations, usable by all personnel who have contact with the outside world. Annual reports, other public interest communiqués and special publications such as cookery books and children's stories also provide vehicles for influencing both customers and those who can affect customers' perceptions. Internal audiences and significant stakeholders are often addressed by organisational newsletters and magazines.

## Support for Good Causes

Organisational **support for good causes** is another means of promoting an image and associating an organisation with a certain set of values. This can include charity donations in return for product coupons, the sponsorship of public service activities such as festivals and individual executives' support for local community interests such as educational establishments, hospitals or crime prevention.

## Expert Opinion

Individuals within an organisation can also act as sources of **expert opinion** for journalists, public enquiries or other forms of research and investigation. Public relations managers may seek to promote the expertise in their organisation through the dissemination of contact lists and by grooming individuals' interviewing and presentational skills.

## Visual Identity

Organisations also often seek to establish a **visual identity** through either conformity of design or logos. While design can make it easier for customers to recognise an organisation's products when they come across one, logos and other identification marks can be more important for internal markets as a means of signifying change or commonalty of purpose.

### Scope of Public Relations

Public relations can provide a powerful support for an organisation's positioning objectives. As examples, **events** can be used to reinforce brand values, or **publications** can help to draw the public's attention to features such as the stability or innovative nature of an organisation. Less directly, but still importantly, public relations can be used to establish credibility for either an organisation or its technologies, on the back of which a position can be established. Similarly, public relations may be used to build awareness of new products, new processes or other changes which will enhance an

*Public relations are a powerful support to positioning*

organisation's ability to serve its customers. Public relations can thus prepare the way for more direct positioning activities such as sales force campaigns; advertising; pricing mechanisms and packaging.

Developing **relationships** with both customer and other markets can also benefit from public relations activities. At one level, good relationships involve sharing information, and public relations tools such as sales support materials, specialist publications and research results are useful vehicles here. At another level, relationships should involve demonstrations of commitment and, again, public relations can provide support. This can be through inviting individuals from targeted markets, be they customer markets, influencer markets, referral markets or third party intermediaries, to events. Alternatively this could be achieved by acknowledging their activities with awards, mentions in press releases or by referrals of media enquiries to them. These can be further supported by sales force and sales promotions activities.

A further role for public relations is in dealing with special problems or disasters and **limiting the damage** such events can have on an organisation. In this respect, the tobacco industry maintains a vigilant public relations campaign to limit the effects of adverse health publicity and government restrictions on advertising. An alternative example was provided by Perrier, when it became known that some of their mineral water had become contaminated with poisonous chemicals. To limit the potential damage to its brand name, it immediately embarked on a widespread public relations campaign to show that this was an isolated event and that the public were in no danger.

*Public relations can be a powerful means of shaping attitudes and opinions*

Public relations, then, can be a significant aspect of an organisation's promotional mix and can be very influential in shaping attitudes and opinions. Relatively speaking, it is also a cheap means of gaining publicity and access to media channels. As an example, the value to Fuji of advertising on a modern airship was not the direct effect on the people it flew over, but the television coverage it gained from the novelty of the presentation. On a lesser scale, public relations are also very useful for smaller organisations with limited promotional budgets, although the exact results of public relations spending are always hard to quantify.

**Section F**

# UNDERSTANDING MARKETING RELATIONSHIPS

# TOPIC 34

# Personal Selling

Personal selling is normally seen as part of the communications mix. This is because the key role of the sales person is to present the organisation's offer and to engage in two-way communications which negotiate the terms of a sale. However, in order to effect these presentations and negotiations satisfactorily, sales people have to develop and maintain good relationships with their customers, particularly if repeat purchases are part of the desired outcome. Personal selling is, therefore, also an important aspect of the relationship market approach to business management.

The majority of sales people operate in the field of industrial or trade marketing. However, personal selling is also a part of some areas of consumer marketing such as personal financial services or home improvements. Whatever the arena, the sales process is very similar and the tasks which the sales person has to undertake are effectively the same. For organisational customers, the main difference is that there is an added degree of complexity. This results from the greater number of people involved in the decision-making process, the more formalised procedures involved and the distinct steps which an organisation tends to follow in the purchase decision.

For business-to-business selling, it is also important to distinguish between a new buy, a straight re-buy and a modified re-buy. The higher the degree of 'newness', the more people tend to be involved and the more involved the selling task becomes. If, in addition, the product is complex, the greater the range of roles the sales person has to play. The way such roles are performed is often critical in determining the strength of the relationship between buyer and seller. Under these circumstances, where there may need to be dealings with engineers, technologists and senior management, as well as finan-

*Sales people are often critical in determining the strength of the relationship between buyer and seller*

cial personnel and purchasing officers, a team approach is often a suitable sales response. Thus sales people might have to become technical consultants; systems designers or integrators; cost accountants; administrative experts; or business strategists in order to deal satisfactorily with the whole range of customers' concerns that are likely to influence the purchase decisions.

*The earlier a sales person becomes involved in a decision, the better he or she will be able to influence the outcome*

The earlier a sales person can become involved in the decision-making process, the better he or she will be able to influence the outcome. This is particularly important given that commitment to a supplier usually grows through the successive stages of the buying process. The commitment of existing customers can also be strengthened if straight re-buy situations can be converted into modified re-buys as this is likely to enhance the involvement of the supplier with the customer and, therefore, the strength of the relationship.

### The Sales Process

Prior to any selling encounter, the sales people need to understand as much as possible about their **prospects**. Often, a great deal of effort is involved in such research, but can save much time in the long run if it means that sales people see the right people at the right time and can provide relevant information. The sales process, however, starts with **territory planning** and obtaining **interviews**. This is particularly important to ensure that the maximum time is spent selling as opposed to travelling, administration, wasted calls, and so on. In addition, a systematic approach to territory planning is needed to ensure that all customers receive enough regular visits to maintain good relationships.

Although some calls will be made 'on spec', the majority will be by appointment. Appointments between customers and sales people are usually arranged on the telephone. Thorough preparation is needed before the call to enable the sales person to decide who is to be spoken to, what is the objective for the call and what is the lever which is to be used to arouse the prospect's interest. It is not always easy to get through to prospects or, once connected, to persuade them to agree to an appointment. This is equally true for consumer sales calls.

Sales people will only succeed if they handle their **sales interviews** effectively. They must establish clear objectives for each call and have a plan of how they intend to achieve these objectives. A useful sequence to follow in any call is the '*ABC*' sequence in order to achieve the required objectives. The sales person should gain the prospect's Attention (*A*), sell Benefits (*B*), and move to a Close (*C*). The sales offer also has to be preplanned and the necessary facts, information and supporting sales-kit of literature, samples, data and other aids needed to achieve the interview objectives must be assembled.

Since customers buy products and services for what they will do for them, that is, the **benefits** of having those products or services, the sales person must focus on selling these benefits rather than the features. For the sales person, a simple formula to ensure this customer-orientated approach is adopted is always to use the phrase 'which means that' to link a feature to the benefit it brings. In this, sales people should seek to identify *standard benefits* (those benefits which arise directly from the features of what they offer), *company benefits* (benefits which are offered by the sales person's company) and *differential benefits* (those benefits which differentiate between the sales person's product or service and those of their competitors). A 'benefit analysis form' can be used to ensure a methodical analysis is conducted and proof should be given to substantiate every claim.

*The sales person must focus on selling customer benefits, rather than product features*

A buyer will almost invariably raise **objections** during a sales interview. An objection is a statement or question which puts an obstacle in the path leading towards closure of the sale. Buyers may raise fundamental objections when they cannot see a need for the product or service on offer. They may raise standard objections when they recognise their need, but either wish to delay a decision, or need further convincing before concluding a deal.

When faced with a fundamental objection, the sales person has to sell the need for the product in question rather than the benefits entailed. There is a range of techniques for dealing with standard objections but if the buyer continues to raise objections without actually concluding the interview, there may be a hidden objection. It is often possible to discover what this is by asking an incomplete question, such as, '*and your other reason for not deciding is . . .?'* Other objections, such as a price objection, can usually be overcome by talking in terms of value rather than cost.

The sale is **closed** when the buyer makes a firm commitment to place an order. The sales person should constantly look for opportunities to close the sale. The buyer will often show interest, make committing statements and ask questions; these are **buying signals** which the sales person should follow up by asking a question in order to confirm that they have correctly interpreted the buying signals.

**Trial closes** can be used throughout the sales offer to test the buyer's reactions, uncover objections, determine buyer interest and speed the sale. Trial closes also help the sales person to retain the initiative and accumulate small commitments from the buyer. The sales person may also use direct and indirect questions to obtain buyer commitment. It is sometimes possible to offer alternatives which lead the buyer into stating a preference which, once expressed, can pave the way to an immediate close. Other opportunities to close can be created by the summary technique, giving a quotation or by offering a concession.

The close, however, is not the end of the matter, it is just a step in a continuous process. Sales people must always remember that their objective is not only to close the sale, but also to open up a **lasting relationship** with the customer. In the final analysis, this is what makes a successful sales person.

*Personal selling is a relatively expensive form of relationship building*

Running a sales force, however, is an expensive form of communications and relationship building. The decision to use personal selling must, therefore, be carefully considered and will be based on the appropriateness of the advantages a sales force can provide (see Table 34.1). Clearly, in different markets, different weightings will be given to the various forms of communication available. In industries with few customers such as capital goods or specialised process materials, an in-depth understanding of customers is required and personal contact is of paramount importance. In contrast, many fast-moving industrial or consumer goods are sold into fragmented markets for diverse uses. In these areas, other forms of communications are likely to be more cost-effective.

**Table 34.1** The advantages of personal selling

- It is a two-way form of communication, giving the prospective purchaser the opportunity to ask questions of the sales person about the product or service.
- The sales message itself can be made more flexible and therefore can be more closely tailored to the needs of individual customers.
- The sales person can use in-depth product knowledge to relate their messages to the perceived needs of the buyers and to deal with objections as they arise.
- As a purchase is concluded, the sales person can move rapidly from persuasion to reinforcement and maintain appropriate relationships.
- Most important of all, the sales representatives can ask for an order and perhaps negotiate on price, delivery or special requirements.

## TOPIC 35

# Managing the Sales Team

As the importance of managing relationships with customers has increased, organisations have had to pay particular attention to the productivity of one of their scarcest and most expensive resources: the group of individuals who have the greatest amount of direct contact with customers, otherwise known as the sales force. The standard measures of sales force productivity have traditionally included call rates; revenue targets; volume targets; and an increased client base. In more enlightened organisations, results-oriented sales managers have come to recognise that other objectives and productivity yardsticks are also required. In addition, this has led to the understanding that organisations also have to address issues of motivation and training to complement this expanded set of requirements.

### Sales Force Objectives

*Sales force objectives should be as precise as possible*

One of the major problems in achieving sales force productivity is that the way sales people have to spend their day leaves comparatively little time available for selling. Much time is occupied in planning, travelling, sales administration and so on. In these circumstances, it is crucial that an organisation should know as precisely as possible what objectives it wants its sales force to achieve. The sophistication of these objectives has led to the development of both quantitative and qualitative targets for sales activities.

The principal quantitative objectives employed are usually concerned with:

- How much to sell (the value of unit sales volume).
- What to sell (the mix of unit sales volume).

194

- Where to sell (the markets and the individual customers that will take the company towards its marketing objectives).
- The desired profit contribution (where relevant and where the company is organised to compute this).
- Selling costs (in compensation, expenses and supervision).

The first three types of objectives are derived directly from an organisation's marketing objectives, and constitute the principal components of the sales plan. However, there are many other kinds of quantitative objectives which can be set for the sales force; these are summarised in Table 35.1.

Qualitative objectives are more intangible in nature and can be a potential source of problems if sales managers try to assess the performance of the sales force along dimensions which include abstract terms such as 'loyalty', 'enthusiasm' and 'cooperation', since such terms are difficult to measure objectively. Thus, in seeking qualitative measurements of performance, managers often resort to highly subjective interpretations which cause resentment and frustration amongst those being assessed.

However, it is perfectly possible for managers to set and measure qualitative objectives which actually relate to the performance of the sales force on the job. It is

**Table 35.1**  Further quantitative objectives for a sales force

---

- Number of point-of-sale displays organised
- Number of letters written to prospects
- Number of telephone calls to prospects
- Number of reports turned or not turned in
- Number of trade meetings held
- Use of sales aids in presentations
- Number of service calls made
- Number of customer complaints
- Safety record
- Collections made
- Training meetings conducted
- Competitive activity reports submitted
- General market condition reports delivered

---

possible, for example, to assess the skill with which a person applies his or her product knowledge for a customer, the skill with which the work is planned, or the skill with which objections are overcome by the representative during a sales interview. While still qualitative in nature, these measures relate to standards of performance which are likely to be understood and accepted by the sales force.

Given such standards, it is not too difficult for a competent field sales manager to identify deficiencies; get agreement on them; coach in skills and techniques; build attitudes of professionalism; show how to self-train; determine which training requirements cannot be tackled in the field; and evaluate improvements in performance and the effect of any past training. Table 35.2 shows an example of setting objectives for an individual sales representative.

## Motivating the Sales Force

Sales force motivation has received a great deal of attention in recent times, largely as a result of the work undertaken by psychologists in other fields of management. It is, therefore, now widely accepted that it is not enough to give someone a title and an office and expect them to achieve good sales results. Effective leadership is as much 'follower determined' as it is determined by management, and it is important to remember some of the main factors that contribute to effective management of the sales force.

*Believing a job to be worthwhile contributes to enhanced performance*

If a sales manager's job is to improve the performance of his or her sales force, and if performance is a function of incentives minus 'disincentives', then the more he or she can increase incentives and reduce disincentives, the better will be performance. Research has also shown that an important element of sales force motivation is a sense of doing a worthwhile job. In other words, the desire for praise and recognition, the avoidance of boredom and monotony, the enhancement of self-image, the freedom from fear and worry and the desire to belong to something believed to be worthwhile, all contribute to enhanced performance.

**Table 35.2**  Setting objectives for an individual sales representative

| Task | Standard | How to set standard | How to measure performance | Performance shortfalls |
|---|---|---|---|---|
| • To achieve personal sales target | Sales target per period of time for individual groups and/or products | Analysis of: – territory potential – individual customer's potential Discussions and agreement between salesman and manager | Comparison of individual salesman's product sales against targets | Significant shortfall between target and achievement over a meaningful period |
| • To sell the required range and quantity to individual customers | The achievement of specified range and quantity of sales to a particular customer or group of customers within an agreed time period | Analysis of individual customer records of: – potential – present sales Discussion and agreement between manager and salesman | Scrutiny of: – individual customer records – observation of selling in the field | Failure to achieve agreed objectives. Complacency with range of sales made to individual customers |
| • To plan journeys and call frequencies to achieve minimum practicable selling cost | To achieve appropriate call frequency on individual customers. Number of live customer calls during a given time period. | Analysis of individual customer's potential. Analysis of order/call ratios. Discussion and agreement between manager and salesman | Scrutiny of: – individual customer records Analysis of order/call ratio Examination of call reports | High ratio of calls to individual customer relative to that customer's yield. Shortfall on agreed total number of calls made over an agreed time period |
| • To acquire new customers | Number of prospect calls during time period. Selling new products to existing customers | Identify total number of potential and actual customers who could produce results. Identify opportunity areas for prospecting | Examination of – call reports – records of new accounts opened – ratio of existing to potential customers | Shortfall in number of prospect calls from agreed standard. Low ratio of existing to potential customers |
| • To make a sales approach of the required quality | To exercise the necessary skills and techniques required to achieve the identified objective of each element of the sales approach | Standards to be agreed in discussion between manager and salesman related to company standards laid down | Regular observations of field selling using a systematic analysis of performance in each stage of the sales approach | Failure to identify: – objective of each stage of sales approach – specific areas of skill, weakness – use of support material |

Based on original work of Stephen P. Morse when at Urwick Orr and Partners

Other methods and ideas that have been used to improve the productivity of sales forces during the last decade have included:

- The development of imaginative and thorough training modules covering areas such as communication techniques, body language, human behaviour and motivation, observation skills, transactional analysis and effective planning.
- The introduction of performance measurement, supported by evaluation procedures.
- The design of creative and productive sales aids.
- The establishment of systems for tapping and cross-fertilising creative ideas generated by the firm's sales force.
- The development of effective incentive systems.

## Remuneration

However, remuneration will always be a most important determinant of motivation. This does not necessarily mean paying the most money, although clearly, unless there are significant financial motivations within a company, it is unlikely that people will stay. In drawing up a remuneration plan, which would normally include a basic salary plus some element for special effort such as bonus or commission, the objectives summarised in the following list should be considered:

*Money is not the only motivator*

- To attract and keep effective people.
- To remain competitive.
- To reward sales people in accordance with their individual performance.
- To provide a guaranteed income plus an orderly individual growth rate.
- To generate individual sales initiative.
- To encourage team work.
- To encourage the performance of essential non-selling tasks.
- To ensure that management can fairly administer and adjust compensation levels as a means of achieving sales objectives.

A central concept of sales force motivation is that the individual sales person will exert more effort if he or she is led to concentrate on:

- *Expectations* of accomplishing the sales objectives.
- *Personal benefits* derived from accomplishing those objectives.

The theory of sales force motivation is known as the *path–goal* approach because it is based on the particular path which the sales representative follows to a particular sales objective – and the particular goals associated with successfully travelling down that path. Representatives estimate the probability of success of travelling down various paths or sales approaches, and estimate the probability that their superiors will recognise their goal accomplishments and will reward them accordingly. Stated less formally, the motivational functions of the sales manager consist of increasing personal pay-offs to sales representatives for work-goal attainment, making the path to these pay-offs easier to travel by clarifying it, reducing road-blocks and pitfalls and increasing the opportunities for personal satisfaction *en route*.

*Sales managers must constantly seek ways of increasing the personal satisfaction experienced by their sales people*

# TOPIC 36

# Key Account Management: Understanding the Concept

The concept of Key Account Management (KAM) has evolved as a natural development of greater customer focus and relationship marketing in business-to-business markets. The emphasis is on moving away from one-off, 'exploitative' transactions to longer-term synergistic relationships. The significance of this for business is that the development of a KAM relationship allows buyer/seller companies to come together and create value in the market place over and above that which either could create individually. The evolutionary nature of KAM makes it possible to identify five distinct stages in the relationship between selling and buying companies. Identifying which stage the company is at is helpful in preparing for the challenges ahead and their implications for company organisation and staffing.

## Developmental Stages of KAM

As the nature of the relationship with the customer develops from being an 'anonymous buyer' to something approaching a 'business partner', the level of involvement with them becomes correspondingly more complex. This gives rise to some characteristic positions on the evolutionary path which are labelled Exploratory KAM, Basic KAM, Cooperative KAM, Interdependent KAM and Integrated KAM, as shown in Figure 36.1.

Each stage is distinguished by the nature of the problems faced by the selling company and how it organises itself in response. As with personal relationships, those between businesses can founder for a number of reasons. The market position and priorities of the buying or selling company may also change over time in a way which negates the strategic necessity for a

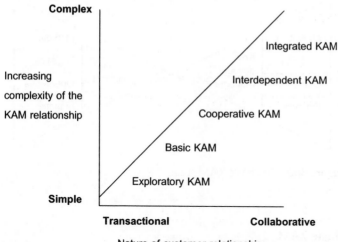

**Figure 36.1** Evolutionary nature of KAM relationships

*Source:* Adapted from a model developed by A. F. Millman and K. J. Wilson (1994) 'From Key Account Selling to Key Account Management', 10th annual conference on industrial marketing and purchasing, University of Groningen, Netherlands.

close working relationship. The evolutionary stages provide an overview of what can happen if all mishaps are avoided, rather than any form of practical model.

## Exploratory KAM

This is a 'scanning and attraction' stage, where both seller and buyer are sending out signals and exchanging messages prior to the decision to get together. Both parties are interested in reducing costs. Commercial issues such as product quality and organisational capability are more important than establishing social bonds. Negotiation skills are paramount in the inevitable discussions that take place about price. It is unlikely that either party will disclose truly confidential information at this stage.

Here one of the greatest organisational problems is the ability of a key account manager to persuade the selling company to improve its production processes or to change its internal procedures in a way which makes them genuinely more customer focused.

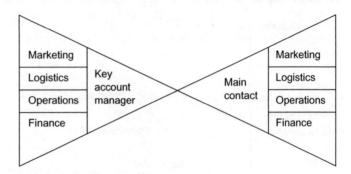

**Figure 36.2** The Basic KAM stage

## Basic KAM

Transactions have begun and the supplier's emphasis shifts to identifying opportunities for account penetration. In turn, the buying company will still be market testing other suppliers for price as it seeks value for money. It is essential, therefore, that the selling company concentrates on the core product/service, including all the intangibles, in an attempt to tailor-make a customer-specific package.

Although there may still be a lack of trust, there has been a subtle change organisationally. The key account manager and the main contact in the supplier organisation are closer to each other and their organisations are aligned behind them, as shown in Figure 36.2.

## Cooperative KAM

By this stage trust will be developing and the selling company may have become a 'preferred' supplier. However, the buying company may still periodically test the market to check alternative sources of supply. With this increasing trust comes a willingness to share information about markets, short-term plans and schedules, internal operating systems and so on. Staff in the selling company are likely to be involved in discussion with their counterparts in the buying company, forging links at all levels from the shop floor to the boardroom. There is often a social context also, sometimes in the form of organised events such as golf days.

It is this network of interactions which brings a new strength to the relationship. With it comes the realisation that customer service operates at many levels and should be driven by a desire not to let down personal contacts. The relationship is still fragile, however, because of the difficulties in making the transition to higher levels of trust and mutual regard. It is not a highly organised relationship and there are many things that can go badly wrong, particularly as a result of staff turnover.

## Interdependent KAM

When this stage is reached, the selling company is seen by the buying company as a strategic external resource. The two should be sharing sensitive information and engaging in joint problem solving. Each will allow the other to profit from their relationship and there is also a tacit understanding that expertise will be shared.

At this stage, the selling and buying companies are closely aligned and communicating at all levels, as shown in Figure 36.3.

The various functions in each partner communicate directly. The role of the key account manager and the main buyer contact is to 'oversee' the various interfaces and ensure that nothing occurs to discredit the partnership, rather than being the mainstays of the relationship.

The partnership agreement will have long-term profit margins, although there will usually be several

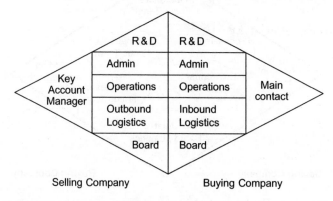

**Figure 36.3** The Interdependent KAM stage

*Source:* As Figure 36.1.

categories of performance expectations reviewed and renewed on a regular basis. It will be in the 'spirit of partnership' for the selling company to meet all of these consistently and to the highest possible standards.

### Integrated KAM

If the seller/buyer relationship can extend beyond partnership so that in effect the two companies operate as an integrated whole, but maintain their separate identities, a more synergistic situation can be created.

The interfaces between the two organisations at all levels will function as focus teams in a way which is largely independent of the key account manager. These teams, made up of personnel from both companies, will generate creative ideas and overcome problems. These may be functional, issue based, project based or perhaps serve a motivational purpose. Electronic data systems become integrated, information flows are streamlined, business plans are linked and even the unthinkable is explored.

*The brand should be sacrosanct*

About the only issue which remains sacrosanct for the selling company is likely to be its brand. Any requests from the buying company which could undermine this will probably be greeted with great suspicion.

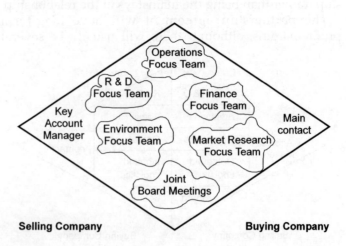

**Figure 36.4** The Integrated KAM stage

*Source:* As Figure 36.1.

## Challenges for the Future

Although transforming the tactics of repeat business into a strategic thrust sounds deceptively simple, the implementation of KAM has proved to be more problematic. Many organisations have tried the partnership approach whilst failing to recognise the demands that true partnership brings. There are obvious benefits to be had, but it is important to acknowledge that managing the transition from traditional selling to general accounts to KAM will not be easy.

Indeed, as shown in Table 36.1, there are a number of key questions which need to be addressed if the KAM approach is to provide a relevant model for organisations faced with the changing demands of continuously evolving markets.

**Table 36.1** Key questions for the future of KAM

- How are organisations going to find or develop KAM executives with sufficient skills to build buyer/seller relationships?
- Is Integrated KAM the ultimate stage in the evolutionary development of KAM or will another form emerge?
- What is the best way to build key account teams?
- What are the particular problems for key account managers operating in complex supply chains or on a global basis?
- What are the organisational implications of global KAM?
- What kind of decision support systems are required for effective KAM?
- How should the differences between key accounts and non-key accounts be managed?
- At what level may the KAM relationship be seen as a barrier to competition and fair trade?

# Key Account Management: Implementing the Concept

In order to implement KAM effectively, organisations need a clear understanding of the areas in which KAM differs from traditional account policies.

## Difference Between KAM and Traditional Selling to General Accounts

Account management has long been recognised as an important sales function in business-to-business markets. However, general account management systems are notorious for being difficult to extend beyond a sales-based relationship. The tendency is for the performance of the account manager to be measured in terms of numbers of transactions and contract renewals. Negotiations are invariably focused on cost, product availability and quality issues. The aim of sellers is to keep their liabilities to a minimum whilst buyers are focused on value for money and are keen to keep options open. Under a general account management system, account turnover is accepted as a fact of life, new customers are constantly being sought and little differentiation is made between customers except, maybe, in terms of size or location.

*KAM focuses on customer retention, rather than customer acquisition*

Recasting these efforts as a KAM system recognises that it may be more cost-effective for a supplier to focus resources on retaining existing profitable accounts rather than constantly signing up new customers. Further, it recognises that not all customers have the potential to be long-term partners and that developing such relationships requires the allocation of disproportionate resources. The emphasis becomes one of tailored service rather than sales, and supply coordination rather than delivery. Accounts are considered whole entities instead of buying points and key account managers become

206

responsible for the quality of the relationship as well as the negotiation of sales.

As an example of the flexibility required, DHL operate a Global Account policy that enables them to offer a strategic partnership to customers, with a Global Account Team located either in the country that the customer prefers to deal with or based at DHL's headquarters.

## Strategic Marketing Benefits of KAM

The first benefit of successfully developing a KAM system is that less profitable accounts are identified and managed accordingly, thereby consuming fewer resources. Similarly, if key accounts are identified and kept for longer, less effort is required to attract new customers, except for those with the potential to become longer-term customers.

Broadening the relationship so that it goes beyond sales negotiations will increase the amount of two-way communications between the seller and buyer organisations. As communications increase, then so do the chances of doing more business.

If customer satisfaction levels can be raised in this way, a virtuous circle can be created in which it becomes easier to sell to satisfied customers, as shown in Figure 37.1.

Organisations which use KAM systems to evolve accounts successfully into business partners also become more strategically secure. Their customers become less fickle and more willing to accommodate mistakes. Mutual problem solving will reduce the costs of 'doing business' and resources can be devoted to creating value for customers further along the supply chain. *KAM systems offer strategic security*

In addition, buying companies will benefit by having their supplies safeguarded, in terms of both quality

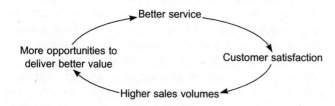

**Figure 37.1** Customer satisfaction virtuous circle

and quantity, and are able to concentrate their resources on operations rather than procurement or supply management.

### Skills required of a Key Account Manager

*Key account managers require a repertoire of skills and knowledge*

Key account managers must be able to recognise how a relationship with a customer changes and how to respond positively to events in a way that enhances the relationship. This requires an ever-increasing repertoire of skills and knowledge as the scope of KAM widens and becomes more complex, particularly in global markets. Different skills are needed at each stage of the KAM relationship.

- In the early stages, as the main point of contact for a buying company, key account managers must represent the selling organisation in a way that makes it appear competent. In this, they must appear likeable, approachable and trustworthy while at the same time demonstrating sound selling skills and good product knowledge.
- As the relationship moves to interfaces at all levels, high-level business skills are required of key account managers, since they have to act as a key facilitator between the different areas of the business. They will also need to develop an understanding of department or functional issues and how these might impact on the key account.
- Key account managers also require general management skills so that they are equipped to deal with any tensions that arise over differing organisational priorities. These can occur as a result of demands on staff who report to other functional managers as well as the key account manager, and the cross-functional nature of advanced KAM.
- Where key account managers have team responsibilities, they must keep all the members fully briefed about operational and strategic issues that have a bearing on the KAM relationship. This requires high level organisational and team skills.
- Key account managers also require strategic business skills to deal with a key account's specific problems or needs, particularly as they become more involved in all aspects of managing an account.

## Organisational Positioning

Organisationally, KAM must be positioned at the highest level as a result of its potential strategic impact and the authority that the key account manager requires in order to call in resources from across the organisation. This positioning should reflect the significance of the role in bringing about and maintaining large tranches of long-term business. In order to be effective, KAM cannot be perceived within the organisation as a simple re-titling of the existing sales group.

The authority and status of the key account manager can easily be undermined if the buying organisation is allowed to gain the ear of somebody higher in the business. Thus, when dealing with key accounts, more senior managers and directors should be seen to defer to the account manager.

*Key account managers must be given authority and status commensurate with their strategic role*

Such authority will help to overcome adversity within the selling organisation during the early stages of the KAM relationship as other managers seek to fight proposed changes to the internal procedures needed to support the development of the relationship.

## Implementation Issues

For the effective implementation of KAM, organisations need to address all of the above areas and develop policies to accommodate them. In particular, it is important that specific measurements are put in place to measure its success. These might include: key account sales relative to general accounts; industry and own customer satisfaction systems; and executive feedback and development procedures.

Ignoring the differences between KAM and traditional selling to general accounts, the skills required, or the strategic organisational positioning of KAM, are likely to create difficulties in implementation. At the same time it is important that the entire organisation appreciates the benefits that adopting KAM can bring to the long-term profitability of the business.

# TOPIC 38

# Channel Strategy

A major concern for any producing organisation is how they can best make their products available to the market place. The options available are many and the wrong choice can have significant consequences for an organisation's success. In addition, once made, such choices tend to be long term, in that a distribution system takes time to build and make effective and, once established, is not easily changed. The development of a strategy for the channels through which products will be placed on the market is, therefore, an important aspect of marketing.

### Evaluating the Use of Intermediaries

*The basic channel strategy decision is whether or not to use intermediaries*

The basic channel strategy decision is whether to sell direct to users or whether to use some form of intermediary. The choice may be straightforward in that the costs incurred by selling direct may be just too high. Thus Volkswagen would have difficulty finding enough capital to fund a retail network for the sale of its cars in Germany, its home market, let alone the rest of Europe or the rest of the world. Similarly, the German consumer electronics company, Braun, would have to sell a large number of competitor manufacturers' products in addition to its own before it could consider owning retail outlets which would be of interest to shoppers and have sufficient turnover to cover the overheads of retail premises.

When the decision is not so clear-cut, the choice will depend on an evaluation of the advantages and disadvantages of using intermediaries. The main advantages include:

- Reduced **distribution costs** since an intermediary will be able to use the same transport and storage facilities

210

for the output of a number of suppliers and spread the costs across a greater number of products.

- Better **access** to remote or fragmented markets, which would be too costly to service directly, or markets about which an intermediary has special knowledge and in which they can operate more efficiently.
- Reduced financial and physical problems associated with **stock holding**. If intermediaries pay for goods on receipt, rather than when sold, and operate warehouse facilities which match the particular requirements of local markets, original suppliers gain working capital benefits without having to invest in supply chain facilities.
- Improved **service response** can be achieved by intermediaries who are closer to customers geographically, or who possess better local knowledge of the needs of customers in their area.
- Enhanced **value** can be provided by intermediaries for customers via a number of different means. These may include one-stop shopping; systems integration; special packaging; or just simply breaking bulk and supplying in smaller quantities.

The disadvantages to a supplier of using intermediaries are smaller in number, but can have significant consequences. Since intermediaries tend to be independent organisations, there is an inevitable **loss of control** on the part of the supplier. Thus, there will be no guarantee that the products will be presented or positioned in the most appropriate way, or that intermediaries will actively sell one supplier's products rather than another. The other problem which can result from the use of intermediaries is a **loss of customer contact** and the information such contacts provide. Apart from the inconvenience involved in passing information to a supplier, intermediaries will often be keen to hold on to information for the power it can add to their side of the relationship.

The functions performed by intermediaries are not usually optional; they are all required in order that the final customer finds the overall offer worthwhile. Strategic decisions about channels are, therefore, concerned with who should perform these functions and where they should be located. The decisions will be based on efficiency in terms of who can best execute a function,

*The functions performed by intermediaries must be done by somebody*

plus the other marketing requirements of a supplier.
Thus, apart from being more cost-effective, an intermediary should also complement the supplier's product
range, pricing aspirations and service policies.

### Channel and Intermediary Alternatives

There is a very wide range of channel intermediaries
who will perform sales, distribution and service functions on behalf of a supplier. The exact number and
appropriate forms will vary enormously between industries. However, the major types in existence are
illustrated in Table 38.1.

Any particular intermediary may be a combination of
two or more of the types listed in Table 38.1. In reality,
*Many*
*companies*
*utilise a*
*combination*
*of*
*intermediaries*
for strategic purposes, form is irrelevant. More important are the costs they incur and the advantages they
provide. In general, many organisations utilise a
combination of intermediaries, and may even operate a
direct sales activity as well, to match the different
markets in which they desire a presence.

In addition to varying the types of intermediary, an
organisation will also include the number of intermediaries as part of their strategy. The first strategic option is
to seek **intensive distribution** by stocking their products
in as many outlets as possible. Thus, milk can be made
available through doorstep delivery; supermarkets; convenience retailers; vending machines; garages; caterers;
and in some cases, directly from the farmer, to match
consumer need and utilisation. The second option is
**selective distribution** which involves some, but not all,
of the intermediaries who would be willing to supply a

**Table 38.1** Major forms of intermediaries

| | |
|---|---|
| • Retailers in or out of town | • Catalogue distributors |
| • Wholesalers | • Direct mail retailers |
| • Distributors | • Franchised outlets |
| • Dealers | • Freight forwarders |
| • Agents | • Merchandise clubs |
| • Value added re-sellers | • Party sales organisers |
| • Original equipment manufacturers | • Licensed manufacturers/ service operators |

product. This can be a cheaper option and allows a producer to concentrate his or her efforts more effectively and thereby maintain greater control. Many financial services and products with a high brand value are marketed in this way. The third option is to offer **exclusive distribution** by limiting the number of intermediaries who handle a product. While this will reduce market coverage, it offers the supplier the possibility of greater control, better access to information, and can encourage intermediaries not to stock competing products or brands. New automobiles, plant and equipment, spare parts, major appliances and high brand apparel are often distributed in this way.

Developing a channel strategy thus requires an organisation to make some long-term decisions about how to make its products available to their end-user markets. The decisions are long term because each party will require commitment from the other and the creation of any arrangement will involve considerable investment of both time and money. This can include:

*Channel strategy involves long-term decisions*

- Familiarisation.
- Training.
- Establishment of routines.
- Even an investment in special tools, equipment or facilities.

The basis of the decision will be the trade-offs involved between control, cost and market objectives.

A supplier must also decide where to focus marketing efforts: on a **push strategy**, whereby attention is concentrated on the intermediary to 'sell-in' more products, or on a **pull strategy**, whereby the supplier emphasises the creation of demand so that intermediaries are encouraged to deal in that product. The strategy might also involve the development of different channels over time. For example, a direct sales force can help an organisation to prove that a market exists through obtaining early market penetration, but is then replaced by dealers to obtain intensive distribution as a market grows. This may be followed by a move to exclusive distribution to create brand value in a mature market. Whatever the case, the decisions involved are not easy, but can significantly influence success in the market.

**TOPIC 39**

# Channel Management

Having devised a channel strategy, a supplier organisation has to develop appropriate relationships with its intermediaries to enable it to take good advantage of the opportunities it wishes to address. The major drawbacks to using intermediaries, rather than supplying direct, are the loss of control which intermediaries imply and the lack of access to direct feedback from user markets. Channel management must, therefore, seek to work with intermediaries so that they complement the suppliers' marketing objectives and minimise the problems of control and access to market information. Organisations can achieve this through attention to channel motivation, treating intermediaries as business partners and managing channel conflict.

*Treating intermediaries as business partners enhances channel management*

## Motivating Intermediaries

Intermediaries' prime focus of attention is *their* customers, since it is they who provide them with their income. Apart from the usual marketing issues involved in attracting and retaining such customers, the nature of the job performed by intermediaries also highlights issues of stock turnover and margins. Stock turnover will be an important issue as a result of the working-capital implications of holding inventories. Margins are important since production costs are outside an intermediary's control, which means that profitability is very dependent on the bought-in price and margin management. In addition, intermediaries will tend to concentrate their efforts on the products which sell most easily.

Suppliers must work hard if they are to motivate intermediaries under these circumstances. The simple solution is to reduce prices or make the margin available to the intermediary more inviting. Efforts will also be required from suppliers to reduce the risk of stock-outs on the part of the intermediaries, which may result from their reluctance to hold large inventories. At the same time, suppliers must encourage intermediaries to promote *their* products rather than just wait for customers to turn up.

Possibly the most important aspect of motivating intermediaries is to remember that they are, themselves, a market and not just middlemen being paid to provide a service for the supplier. If the latter approach is adopted, the tendency will be for suppliers to seek the **compliance** of their channel members rather than any more substantial form of **cooperation**. This can lead to interactions based on transactions rather than a relationship built on mutual long-term needs. In transaction mode, motivation will tend to be 'deal-orientated' and focus on discounts, advertising allowances, merchandising arrangements, and sales incentives. While these tools are not, in themselves, inappropriate, they need to be used as part of a wider marketing approach if they are to provide longer-term cooperation and stability.

*Intermediaries form a market in themselves*

As a market, intermediaries' problems need to be solved in a way which encourages them to become 'advocates' for their suppliers. This requires an understanding of how value can be supplied, rather than looking at the problem as one of efficiency or a simple transfer of cost. Important areas of value to middlemen which go beyond the approaches implied by a deal-orientation include:

- Sales support materials.
- Market research about intermediaries' markets.
- Advanced information about product development.
- Fast responses to technical queries.
- The creation of market pull.
- Rapid fault tracing.
- Product training.

### Developing Partnerships

An organisation's relationships with its intermediaries are often better managed if they can be formed into **partnerships**. Under a partnership arrangement, intermediaries are more likely to see themselves as a meaningful part of their supplier's enterprise. The essence of this will be **agreement** between supplier and intermediary about the supplier's general market policies plus positive demonstrations of **commitment**. Agreement and commitment between supplier and middleman will reduce the need to exert control, since channel markets should now, voluntarily, implement supplier policies and increase the flow of information from end-users to suppliers. Having the incentive to collect it they should be more willing to pass it back.

*Commitment to channel partnerships needs to be positively demonstrated by suppliers*

One way of promoting agreement within channel partnerships is through the creation of distributor panels, in the same way that equipment suppliers might set up user groups. Two-way communications between people at different levels of each organisation will also be a means of cementing relationships. At a deeper level, this might include cross-board membership, personnel exchanges and participation in the marketing planning process.

Commitment to creating a feeling of partnership can be demonstrated in a number of ways. One significant action is the referral of customer enquiries to the relevant intermediary. Others can be:

- Inclusion in public statements.
- Mentions in company newsletters.
- Invitations to trade entertainment events.
- Acknowledgement of achievements.
- Consultancy advice.
- Not opening competing outlets in their territory.

A significant demonstration is to devote a specific part of the supplier's marketing management structures to channel marketing to show that the relationships are important.

This is not to say that channel partnerships cannot be changed. As a product matures through its life-cycle in the market, different arrangements may be required to match different market developments. As a simple example, mass markets need to be addressed in a different way from niche markets, and products which are tending towards commodity status do not require the same level of dealer sophistication to be competitive. Similarly, as the competitive status of a product improves through, for instance, brand value development, different types of intermediary may be required to maintain product positioning. In the early 1990s in the UK, both Nissan and Mazda (Japanese car manufacturers) made significant changes to their franchised dealer network; the former to gain better control, the latter to upgrade the quality of their dealers in order to complement better the perceived quality and status of their newer models.

## Channel Conflict

Since channel members are normally independent organisations there is always the potential for conflict, either between channel members themselves or between an intermediary and their supplier. Resolution of such conflict is important so that intermediaries will remain responsive to efforts to motivate them and a partnership relationship can be maintained.

The majority of the conflict between intermediaries and suppliers usually occurs because suppliers have not paid proper attention to, or are inconsistent about, their channel management policies. As an example, equipment manufacturers will naturally want distributors to offer high levels of service, local advertising and competitive prices. They will also want their products promoted, presented and displayed, to the disadvantage of their competitors. If intermediaries were to adopt such policies unconditionally, they would incur significant costs, but not necessarily fulfil their own profit objectives or provide the right type of service for their customers. As indicated above, suppliers need to take channel members' ambitions and problems into account before demanding gold-star service for knock-down prices from them.

*Conflicts between intermediaries and suppliers usually arise from supplier neglect or inconsistent channel management*

Inconsistent channel management can also arise when suppliers make their products available through a number of competing intermediaries. In the more extreme cases, suppliers find themselves competing directly with their intermediaries, which tends to leave channel members feeling a little betrayed. During the 'shake-outs' in the world personal computer markets in the late 1980s and early 1990s, many manufacturers and volume wholesalers started by-passing their intermediaries in an effort to survive. This put many intermediaries out of business and left much bitterness. It must be added that this was only necessary as a result of poor channel relationships and short-sighted channel management in the first place.

Conflict between channel members, rather than between intermediary and supplier, can occur for a number of reasons. One cause can be the appointment of too many intermediaries in one geographical area so that they end up competing with each other and find it difficult to sustain sufficient volume to make it worthwhile doing business. Another can result from the supplier seeming to favour one channel member against another.

*Conflict is best resolved by anticipating its occurrence*

Alternatively, individual channel members may start 'letting the side down' by engaging in over-vigorous competitive activities or reductions in quality. Here, suppliers must fulfil a role of **channel captain** and seek to maintain a state of distribution equilibrium.

Conflict is best resolved by anticipating its occurrence and trying to pre-empt the causes. Well-motivated intermediaries who see themselves as partners can significantly reduce the potential for such conflict. A well-developed strategy should seek to balance the needs of suppliers and intermediaries so that it adds value to products beyond the costs they generate and advance the strategies of both.

# TOPIC 40

# Sales Promotion

The term *advertising* (often referred to as 'above-the-line expenditure') can be defined as all non-personal communication in measured media by an identifiable sponsor. This includes television, cinema, radio, print, and outdoor media. *Sales promotion*, for which the term 'below-the-line expenditure' is often used as a synonym, is not so easily defined. For example, Americans use the term to describe all forms of communication, including advertising and personal selling. In Europe, some use the term to describe any non-face-to-face activity concerned with the promotion of sales; some use it to describe any non-media expenditure; whilst others use it specifically to mean in-store merchandising. Managers concerned with sales promotions must, therefore, be clear about the nature and scope of such activities and how they can best contribute to the organisation's marketing goals.

## Nature and Scope of Sales Promotion Activities

In practice, sales promotion is a specific activity, which can be described as the making of a featured offer to defined customers within a specific time limit. In other words, to qualify as a sales promotion, someone must be offered something which is featured, rather than just being an everyday aspect of trade. Furthermore, the offer must include benefits not inherent in the product or service, as opposed to the intangible benefits offered in advertising, such as adding value through appeals to imagery. As such, it is an important tool in developing relationships with the various markets an organisation wishes to address.

*Sales promotion is the making of a featured offer to defined customers within a specific time period*

Seen this way, every other element of the marketing mix, including advertising, personal selling, point-of-sale material, pricing, after-sales service, and so on, can

219

*Sales
promotions
are designed
to alter
customer
behaviour*

be used as part of a structured sales promotion in order
to achieve specified objectives. Thus sales promotion is
essentially a problem-solving activity designed to get
customers to behave more in line with the economic
interests of the company. Typical tasks for sales
promotion include:

- Clearing slow moving stock
- Counteracting competitive activity
- Encouraging repeat purchase
- Securing marginal buyers
- Getting bills paid on time
- Inducing trial purchase.

From this, it will be seen that sales promotion is not
just concerned with volume increases. It is, for example,
often used to assist production and distribution scheduling by persuading customers to bring forward their
peak-buying from one period to another. In this way,
sales promotion can seek to influence many different
audiences in a number of different ways:

| | | |
|---|---|---|
| *Salespeople* | to sell | ⎫ |
| *Customers* | to buy | ⎪ |
| *Customers* | to sell | ⎬  more, earlier, faster, etc. |
| *Users* | to buy | ⎪ |
| *Users* | to use | ⎭ |

The many and varied types of sales promotions are
listed in Table 40.1. Each of these different types is
appropriate for different circumstances and each has
advantages and disadvantages. A typical example can be
provided by a promotion that consists of a free case
bonus: it is possible to measure precisely both the cost of
the extra cases and the additional volume resulting from
the offer; it is fast and flexible; it is effective where the
customer is profit-conscious; it can be made to last as
long as required; and it is simple to set up, administer
and sell. On the other hand, it has no cumulative value
to the customer, is unimaginative, and can often be seen
as a prelude to a permanent price reduction.

Amongst the alternatives available, points schemes in
their various forms became increasingly popular in the
1990s. Their advantages to the sponsoring organisation
cover their wide appeal; the absence of any need to hold

**Table 40.1** Types of sales promotions

| Target market | Price promotions | | Product promotions | | Services promotions | |
|---|---|---|---|---|---|---|
| | *Direct* | *Indirect* | *Direct* | *Indirect* | *Direct* | *Indirect* |
| *Consumer* | Price reduction | Coupons<br>Vouchers<br>Money equivalent<br>Competitions | Free goods<br>Premium offers (e.g., 13 for 12)<br>Free gifts<br>Trade-in offers | Stamps<br>Coupons<br>Vouchers<br>Money equivalent<br>Competitions | Guarantees<br>Group participation events<br>Special exhibitions and displays | Cooperative advertising<br>Stamps<br>Coupons<br>Vouchers for services<br>Events admission<br>Competitions |
| *Trade* | Dealer loaders<br>Loyalty schemes<br>Incentives<br>Full-range buying | Extended credit<br>Delayed invoicing<br>Sale or return<br>Coupons<br>Vouchers<br>Money equivalent | Free gifts<br>Trial offers<br>Trade-in offers | Coupons<br>Vouchers<br>Money equivalent<br>Competitions | Guarantees<br>Group participation events<br>Free services<br>Risk reduction schemes<br>Training<br>Special exhibitions and displays<br>Reciprocal trading schemes | Stamps<br>Coupons<br>Vouchers for services<br>Competitions |
| *Sales force* | Bonus<br>Commission | Coupons<br>Vouchers<br>Points system<br>Money equivalent<br>Competitions | Free gifts | Coupons<br>Vouchers<br>Points system<br>Money equivalent<br>Competitions | Free services<br>Group participation events | Coupons<br>Vouchers<br>Points systems for services<br>Events admission<br>Competitions |

stocks of gifts; the difficulty faced by customers who try to cross-value gifts; and their ease of administration. On the other hand, they offer no advantages in bulk-buying, are difficult to budget, and lack the immediacy of dealer-loaders. Great care is necessary, therefore, in selecting a scheme appropriate to the objective sought.

Although in recent years sales promotion activity has increased to such an extent that it now often accounts for as much expenditure as above-the-line advertising, it is important to realise that, on its own, sales promotion will not replace selling, change long-term trends, or build long-term customer loyalty.

### Sales Promotion Strategy and Tactics

Unfortunately, the tactical nature of most sales-promotion activities means that they often amount to little more than a series of spasmodic gimmicks lacking in any coherence. This is a stark contrast to the commonly held belief that advertising should conform to some overall strategy. Perhaps this is because advertising has always been based on a philosophy of building long-term brand franchises in a consistent manner, whereas the basic rationale of sales promotion is usually to help the company to retain a tactical initiative. In fact, there is no reason why there should not be a strategy for sales promotion, so that each promotion increases the effectiveness of the next, so that a bond between seller and buyer is built up, so that tactical objectives can be linked in with some overall plan, and so that there is, generally, a better application of resources.

*Sales promotion activity is easily undermined by lack of strategy*

In spite of this, there is widespread acknowledgement that sales promotion is one of the most mismanaged of all marketing functions. This is mainly due to the absence of any strategy, which contributes to the confusion about what sales promotion is and which, in turn, often results in sales-promotion expenditure being inadequately recorded. One of these problems may be in locating the expenditure, let alone evaluating it. Some companies include the expenditure with advertising, others as part of sales-force cost; some as a general marketing expense, others as a manufacturing expense (as in the case of extra product, special labels, or promotional packaging), whilst the loss of revenue from special price reductions is often not recorded at all.

Such failures can be extremely damaging, especially since sales promotion can be such an important part of marketing strategy. Indeed, with increasing global competition, troubled economic conditions, and growing pressures from distribution channels, the focused nature of sales promotion is turning into a more attractive, widespread and acceptable marketing tool. This highlights the need for organisations to set good objectives, to evaluate results after the event, and to have some organisational guidelines for their sales promotion campaigns. For example, a $1 case allowance on a product with a contribution rate of $3 per case has to increase sales by 50 per cent just to maintain the same level of contribution. Failure at least to realise this, or to set alternative objectives for the promotion, can easily result in loss of control and a consequent reduction in profits.

*The objectives of each promotion should be clearly stated from the outset*

Managing an organisation's sales-promotion expenditure effectively thus requires an objective for each individual sales promotion to be established in the same way that an objective is developed for advertising, pricing, or distribution activities. The objectives for each promotion should be clearly stated, in terms such as product trial, repeat purchase, increased distribution, more prominent display, a shift in buying peaks, combating competition, and so on. Thereafter, the following process should apply:

- Select the appropriate technique.
- Pretest.
- Mount the promotion.
- Evaluate in depth.

The in-depth evaluation requires spending to be analysed and categorised by type of activity (e.g., special packaging, special point-of-sale material, loss of revenue through price reductions, and so on). For the sales promotional plan itself, objectives, strategy and brief details of timing and costs should also be included. It is important, however, that the activities planned are compatible with, and complement, other activities within an organisation's promotions or communications mix.

# TOPIC 41

# Customer Retention
# Strategies

Much marketing attention is directed at developing strategies to expand sales through market share dominance; market penetration; finding new markets; and product range expansion. The main reason for concentrating on these is that size, revenue growth and dominance have been shown to be positively correlated with long-term survival and profitability. Recent work, however, has questioned the universality of the these approaches, arguing that the cost of winning new customers is high and that, for many organisations, it will be more cost-effective to concentrate on retaining existing customers than attracting new ones.

*The profitability gained from improved customer retention can be quite startling*

For some industries, the increased profitability which can be gained from improved rates of customer retention are quite startling. Improvements of a few percentage points in customer retention yield large percentage increases in profits. The basis of this is the mathematical relationship between retention rates and the average life of a customer. Thus, a 90 per cent retention rate implies that 10 per cent of a business's customers are lost each year. In 10 years, the equivalent of all of its customers will have to have been recruited just to maintain the size of its customer base. The average life of a customer can thus be seen to be 10 years. If retention rates are increased to 95 per cent, the average life of a customer doubles to 20 years, since only 5 per cent will be lost each year. Where recruiting new customers costs significantly more than selling to existing customers (five times more in many cases), customer retention may prove a more profitable strategic objective.

Apart from the costs of recruitment, retained customers can also benefit supplier organisations in a number of other ways, although this assumes that such customers become loyal out of choice rather than through some device which 'locks them in'. Such benefits will be obtained because:

- Regular customers will tend to spend less time comparing prices with those of competitors and can become less price-sensitive, providing the opportunity for premium pricing.
- Voluntarily retained customers are more likely to be a source of positive referrals, which can provide a cost-effective source of new customers.
- Administrative procedures and other activities which affect the cost of a sale will be more routinised and, for the supplier as well as the customer, less expensive.
- There is a tendency for loyal customers to make a larger proportion of their purchases with a single supplier and thus boost turnover.

Before focusing on customer retention as a strategic objective, however, it is important for any particular business to understand the relevance of customer retention activities for their customer base. In some markets, customers value the ability to move between suppliers for similar purchases and would resent efforts on the part of suppliers to develop longer-term relationships. In others, many customers are unprofitable, or merely contribute to overheads, rather than adding to the 'bottom line', as is the case for many bank current accounts which are effectively dormant from one year to the next. In addition, the nature of some products means that the majority of sales are only ever going to be 'one-offs', or, at least, very infrequent purchases, as is the case for double glazing, some large projects and time-share holiday accommodation. Under these circumstances, strategies designed to improve customer retention are likely to reduce customer satisfaction levels and have little impact on profitability.

Where it appears that customer retention is an appropriate strategy, the next step is to identify the type of customers the business wishes to retain. This will provide the focus for both customer recruitment and retention endeavours. In general, the 'right type' of customers will have a particular need in common, so that the costs of servicing these customers can benefit from economies of scale and the organisation's positioning will not become too diffused. This essentially requires a benefit segmentation exercise, with the identification of asso-

*Retention strategies must focus on the 'right type' of customer*

ciated needs and benefits enabling subsegments to be developed. Many such subsegments can be adequately managed via the advances being made in database marketing.

Other types of customer who will be a suitable focus for retention strategies include ones who like stable relationships, are reasonable in their demands of suppliers and who have the potential for long-term purchase or usage.

Customers not attracted to stable relationships, often referred to as 'promiscuous customers', will tend to be those who are very price-sensitive, who value change and variety, or who respond well to sales-promotion initiatives. Predictions of 'promiscuity', however, do not tend to be very robust and characteristics such as income, sex and socio-economic class, cannot be easily used for this purpose and, indeed, will vary from one industry sector to another. What is true, however, is that loyalty is sometimes a 'default situation' caused by the inability of a customer to purchase elsewhere through legal restrictions, company policy, poverty, or awareness limitations and who may well turn out to be 'promiscuous' under other circumstances.

The term 'reasonable customers' refers to those who do not cause a supplier to incur costs significantly beyond those associated with the provision of the product. Unreasonable customers would include those for whom the cost of sale was high, who made excessive use of warranty or after-sales services, or who were late payers. Those with the potential to be 'long-term customers' would include customers who recognise that they have a long-term need, who can be easy to locate or keep in touch with and who are likely to experience or maintain an appropriate level of disposable income.

*Personal recommendations generate more better-quality customers*

These characteristics highlight the importance of personal recommendations, which have been found to generate more of the better-quality customers than other sources of new customers. They also emphasise the need to target consumers with stable life-styles or organisations which do not suffer wild fluctuations in their activities, who seem to be well-positioned for growth, or who are diversified enough to survive changing market circumstances. In this context, the value of identifying and developing campaigns for referral markets becomes apparent.

In addition to identifying potentially loyal and profitable customers, it is also important to understand the causes of customer defection, since these will underpin the development of any strategies for retention. Essentially, there are only two causes of customers ceasing to purchase: their need ends, or the product-offering fails in some way or another.

Needs can end for a number of reasons such as children growing up; retirement; death; bankruptcy; legislative changes; in-house provisions; and so on. Together, these will be either a move from one stage in a life-cycle to another, or changed circumstances.

A failure in a product-offering will be due to the product (including service products) failing to deliver the performances required, a failure in customer service or a competitor offering superior benefits in terms of product performance, service or value. Table 41.1 provides examples of industries with traditionally high defection rates. It is, therefore, very important for an organisation to monitor defection patterns as clues to the causes both of customer satisfaction and dissatisfaction levels. These can be supplemented by the use of 'root cause analysis' to get to the heart of defections, rather than just accepting stated reasons, which are not always the real ones.

Once the rationale and focus for customer retention has been identified, attention must then turn to the choice of strategic options. The main aim of such options will be to convert a potential or actual purchaser into a loyal, long-term customer. This is the process of

*The causes of customer defection underpin retention strategies*

**Table 41.1** Industries with traditionally high defection rates, where customer retention improvements can have a significant impact

- Personal, home and motor insurance
- Credit and charge cards
- Hotels
- Airlines
- Grocery retailing
- Travel and real estate agencies
- Courier services
- Management training and consultancy

*Strategic options fall into three categories*

converting the relationship from that of a simple transaction to something approaching a partnership, which is then maintained over time. The options available fall into three different categories: **validating** the customer's **choice** of supplier; **enhancing** the **value** of the exchange; or creating **interdependency**.

*Validating choice* means finding ways of reassuring a customer that they have chosen wisely and providing them with clear views as to why their decision was, and is, correct. This will reduce the likelihood of their considering alternative offerings and will enhance their ability to explain their choice to others. Verbalising the reasons for using a supplier is, in itself, a powerful means of reinforcing personal opinions and beliefs, but does require a high degree of clarity. Validation can be achieved via:

- Influencer markets such as the media, trade associations and intermediaries.
- Customer communications such as advertising, PR and direct mail.
- Post-purchase service activities, including instruction manuals, product maintenance or emergency assistance.

Perceptions of *enhanced value* will result from building something extra into the overall product offer which will increase the utility the customer derives from its consumption. Value is provided in either tangible or intangible form. Tangible value can be:

- Monetary, such as loyalty discounts, or terminal bonuses.
- Gifts donated on a periodic or cumulative basis, such as Air Miles schemes.
- Christmas shopping deals.
- Some form of points collection activity.

Intangible value is more likely to be provided through customer service or database marketing, which makes purchase, use, or ownership of the product satisfying and/or ego boosting.

*Interdependency* requires both the supplier and the purchaser to recognise that they rely on each other for either product or revenue. This can be achieved on the part of the supplier by:

- Acknowledging, both publicly and privately, the contribution a customer makes to their business.
- Seeking help from customers so that they become more involved in the organisation's activities.
- Finding ways of demonstrating commitment to customers by 'bending rules', public pronouncements or extraordinary efforts to meet individual requests.

Focusing on interdependency is probably the issue closest to ideas of partnership, since any partnership should involve the sharing of risk, information and commitment.

As a final point, and as previously noted, it must be remembered that customer retention should not be taken to involve schemes which 'lock customers' into a supplier. While the idea has appeal in terms of reducing competition and enhancing supplier power, the long-term impact on customer perceptions can be dysfunctional. Locking mechanisms include: financial exit penalties; propriety technology which is incompatible with other products; or just the sheer administrative problems involved in abandoning a supplier. One only has to think of the problems involved in transferring a house-purchase mortgage from one lender to another to understand the frustrations such barriers can cause.

*Customer retention activity should avoid 'locking' customers into a supplier*

Recent research has also indicated that an alternative way of approaching customer retention is to ensure product offerings match purchasers' values: values on deep-seated responses which categorise things as 'good' or 'bad', 'right' or 'wrong', and so on. When an offer or brand mirrors the values of a target market above and beyond a competitor product, loyalty is much easier to sustain.

# TOPIC 42

# Customer Service Strategies

*Customer service is a key differentiation factor*

Customer service is an increasingly important factor both for competitive advantage and customer retention. Indeed, the service element of many product offerings is sometimes the only aspect which distinguishes one organisation's marketing efforts from those of another. In addition, once a supplier/customer relationship has been established, customer service provides a significant contribution to the augmented product offering which enhances the value of a purchase and cements relationships. To manage this adequately, in some organisations, customer service is treated as a separate aspect of the marketing mix for which individual plans and strategies are created.

Customer service can most easily be thought of as all those activities which support a customer's purchase from the time they decide to buy from a particular organisation to the point at which they take full ownership and responsibility for the product. Whilst this is obviously a simplification, the approach covers most of the major elements which need to be considered when devising an organisation's customer service strategy.

## Elements of Customer Service

The key elements of customer service include:

- The organisation's response to **placing the order**, which provides the initial encounter. The ease by which an order is taken and facilitated can provide a lasting impression, and can win and sustain customers if managed more effectively than by other organisations. Apart from just being accessible, this can also involve advice, assistance in creating a specification and personal attention.

- The **information** provided by a supplier while an order is being processed and delivered will also influence a customer's experience of an organisation. Such information could include: order confirmation; delivery notification and delivery variations; plus information which will facilitate installation or utilisation. Regular contacts with a supplier will reduce the possibility of customers feeling isolated or forgotten and can increase a customer's feelings of being important to a supplier.

- **Delivering** the goods or service, which will also affect a purchaser's experience of a supplier. This does not just involve availability and delivery lead times, but also the way in which the product is delivered. Thus, the ability to deliver at specific times, the degree of delivery time variability, the completeness of an order and fill rates (the percentage of orders shipped complete), will all contribute to customer service levels.

- The support provided **after** sales have been completed, which can substantially enhance or reduce the value of a purchase. In fact, customer service is often taken to mean after-sales service, despite the other elements which customer service covers. Post-sales support ranges from straightforward maintenance and repairs to training activities; helplines; assistance with, and notification of, upgrades; instruction manuals; returns policy; and fault tracing.

- **Problem-solving**, which can be the true test of an organisation's commitment to customer service. This is particularly the case for many service organisations such as insurance, transport and hotels where the core product is, to a large extent, customer service, but where customers often only learn of an organisation's true qualities when something goes wrong. This is also true where tangible products are concerned and can cover action on complaints, crisis repairs and an organisation's ability to respond to emergency orders. Also included here will be the way in which an organisation deals with problems such as design faults, contamination or other supply problems which may arise from time to time.

## Developing a Strategy

Forming a customer service strategy first involves the identification of the critical elements of service associated with an organisation's activities. Some of these will be 'order-qualifying-type' activities, in that they have to be provided for an organisation to be on the shortlist of potential suppliers. For most computer vendors, for instance, the ability to offer service contracts falls into this category. Others can be characterised as 'order winning', in that they will act to differentiate one supplier from another.

Once identified, an enterprise can then compare its performance in these customer service elements with the expectations of customers and the performance of competitors. This will provide appropriate targets for customer service levels, for which policies and processes can be established. As an example, many organisations now operate a 'three-rings' policy which tries to ensure that any telephone call is answered on, or by, the third ring to avoid the frustration a caller can experience from not knowing whether they have the right number, or from just feeling ignored. Other targets may involve on-time delivery levels, minimum notification times for late deliveries, emergency response times, and so on.

*Customer service priorities should reflect customer preferences*

A good method for establishing customer service priorities is to perform **trade-off analysis** with customers. This asks respondents to prioritise different aspects of customer service against each other, such as delivery time variability against order lead times (see Figure 42.1). In this example, it is assumed that all customers would find a short order lead time with no delivery time variability the most preferable combination (scored 1), and the converse the least acceptable (scored 9). Customers are then asked to complete the remaining boxes with the numbers 2 to 8 to represent their order of preference. These rankings will show exactly where customer preferences lie. If this is performed for the half-dozen or so elements which are critical for attracting new customers or retaining existing ones, it is possible to develop quite sophisticated customer service programmes. It is also possible to use such an analysis for segmentation purposes, so that differing requirements can be serviced at the appropriate levels, should distinct patterns of need appear.

Delivery time variability

| Order lead times | | On time | ± One day | ± Two days |
|---|---|---|---|---|
| | One week | 1 | | |
| | Two weeks | | | |
| | Three weeks | | | 9 |

**Figure 42.1**  Example of customer service trade-off matrix

The final decision in creating a customer service strategy revolves around the implementation of the service programme. The basic options are contracting out, or doing it yourself.

Here, the decisions will depend on the resources available to an organisation, plus the trade-offs between costs, quality and control. As an example, whilst it may be cheaper to subcontract repairs, it may be hard to monitor quality. Similarly, whilst good asset management might dictate using third parties for infrequently used and expensive service operations, a situation of rapid change might make it more desirable to keep the activity in-house to retain control over market or new product developments.

One answer to the problems of managing customer service has been to reduce the need for service by allowing customers to perform certain activities themselves. Thus, the developments in Electronic Data Interchange (EDI) have enabled customers to place orders direct via terminals on their own premises, thereby reducing the need to order during opening hours, etc. Similarly, central diagnosis facilities via EDI can locate equipment faults and perform tests which can save much time and expense for both parties. In addition, 'plug-in maintenance', whereby a whole module or aspect of a product is replaced, sometimes by the customers themselves, rather than sending out a specialist to locate a faulty part, has reduced the need for service calls.

*Self-service is one answer to the problems of managing customer service*

*Customer
service
facilitates a
customer's
experience of
dealing with
a supplier*

Overall, then, customer service can be a powerful contributor to the competitive position of an organisation and its ability to maintain good customer relationships. As product reliability improves, the need for after-sales service decreases. However, a customer service package covers more than just after-sales service and should facilitate much of a customer's experience of dealing with a supplier.

# TOPIC 43

# Database Marketing

Databases have traditionally been too large and expensive, and their performance too slow, for them to be cost-justifiable. Consequently, many of the marketing information systems in use today are limited to summary sales reporting systems. However, with the increased importance attached to direct marketing, telemarketing and sales performance management (using laptop computers), many companies are actively engaged in building customer databases. These databases are then used to enhance the quality of an organisation's relationship with its customers. Good databases will enable the personalisation of communications; marketing managers to be alerted to needs automatically; and comprehensive customer records to be available at the 'touch of a button'. In addition, good databases can allow for micro segmentation based on such criteria as buying patterns, customer-initiated communications, fine-tuned demographics and other, normally difficult-to-discern, characteristics.

## Problems with Databases

One drawback to using databases is that they often represent a compromise between the strategic requirements of an organisation's planners and the tactical requirements of other managers. Another problem for newcomers to the world of databases is that they sometimes fall prey to the many pitfalls, and believe many of the myths which are associated with them, as illustrated in Table 43.1. The consequence of these problems is that databases often hold data that does not fit the purpose of the tacticians, far less the needs of strategic planners. The attempt to develop databases that serve both strategic and tactical purposes is often referred to as **database marketing**.

*Database marketing seeks to develop databases that serve both strategic and tactical purposes*

**Table 43.1** Myths and realities about databases

| Myth | Reality |
|------|---------|
| The database collects what we need. | We collect what is easily available. |
| The database measures what matters. | We measure what is least embarrassing. |
| The database users understand what data they need. | We know what we used last, what the textbooks say and what might be interesting on a rainy day. |
| The database needs to hold more and more data. | We feel safer with 'loadsadata', even when we haven't a clue how to use it. |
| The database must integrate the data physically. | We like neat solutions, whatever the cost. |
| The database will save staff time. | We need more and more staff to analyse data. |
| The database will harmonise marketing, finance and sales. | We all compete for scarce resources, and this involves fighting. |
| The database is the one source of our market intelligence. | We haven't thought through the business problems. |

One of the most acute problems is that of reconciling the internal and external views of markets. The usual problem is that data retrieved from the sales ledger rarely possesses the details needed to link customer records to market segments. Some of the problems are described in Table 43.2 against the key issues involved in identifying a market segment: what is bought; by whom; and for what reason?

*The costs of developing data-fusion routines emphasises the need to collect data at source*

Fusing together data from external sources and internal data is becoming increasingly common as a solution to this external–internal problem. This is often referred to as data fusion. Where large volumes of data are involved, computer programmes, known as **deduplication routines**, are used to automate the matching of the data. However, automation rarely achieves more than 80 per cent accuracy in matching, and manual matching has to be applied to the remaining data.

The cost of matching external and internal market-coding schemes is driving some companies to collect

**Table 43.2**   Problems of reconciling internal and external
market audits

| External audit variable | Problem with internal audit |
|---|---|
| What is bought | Internal systems have rich detail on accounts and stock-keeping units. However, information about products such as colour, style, etc., can often be missing. Information on the outlets or channels through which they were sold is also very often lacking. |
| Who buys | Internal systems record who paid the invoice and who received delivery of the goods. They rarely record who made the buying decision or who influenced it. Even when buyer details are on the system, it is rarely easy to determine their characteristics such as age, sex and so on. |
| Why | Internal sources of information on why people purchase is scarce. Enquiries can be qualified, using survey techniques, to provide some clues about why people respond to an advertising campaign. Customer satisfaction surveys may also yield clues. Call reports from field sales and telesales can also provide valuable clues, especially if survey disciplines can be observed by the sales staff. |
| Reconciling variables | Reconciling external with internal variables involves:<br>• matching accounts to customers<br>• matching stock-keeping units to products<br>• matching external variables to internal records<br>• collecting data from sources other than the sales ledger (e.g., from surveys of sales representatives) |

customer profiles at source. This occurs either when they
first enquire, or when their sales ledger records are first
created. However, the cost of making changes to the
sales ledger, and the fact that it is 'owned' by the Finance
Department, are often barriers to success. In the future,
Marketing will need to work much more closely with
Finance and IT Departments if it is to develop databases
successfully.

### Avoiding Badly Constructed Databases

Information, in the minds of most marketing managers, lies in a strange 'no man's land', part way between the 'nitty-gritty' stuff of marketing management and the abstractions of technologists, cyberneticists and 'boffins'. Widely misunderstood, or equated to 'keyboard literacy' or 'technology awareness', the management of marketing information often ends up neglected or delegated to the most junior member of the marketing team. In reality, this should be a responsibility addressed by senior marketing managers (i.e., those who have a good view of the decision areas a database will be required to support).

In addition, it must be remembered that information is not all hard, objective data, and organisations will not necessarily become better-informed by collecting more and more raw data and storing it until they end up knowing 'everything'. The belief tends to be that accounting systems are a source of hard facts, since most accounting transactions have to be audited and therefore must be reasonably accurate. Constructing good marketing databases must take into consideration the fact that most accounting data has little direct relevance for marketing strategy.

### What Information is Needed to Support a Marketing Strategy?

*Different marketing objectives require different supporting information*

The answer to this question is something of a conundrum, since the information needed depends upon the marketing objectives for which a strategy is developed and the tactical decisions which have to be made on an ongoing basis. If the strategic marketing objectives are changed, then different kinds of information are needed to support the new strategy that will have to be developed. Table 43.3, illustrates how different objectives require different supporting information. At this point, the sales or marketing director might feel that because the situation changes so radically every year there can be no hope of developing an effective system or procedure for obtaining marketing information.

**Table 43.3**  Examples of business objectives and
segmentation methods

| Business objective | Segmentation method | Information source |
|---|---|---|
| Market extension | | |
| • new locations | Geodemographics | Electoral roll (consumer) |
| • new channels | Prospect profiles | Companies house (business) |
| • new segments | Survey analysis | Prospect lists and surveys |
| Market development | Customer profiling | Sales ledger and added profile data |
| | Behavioural scoring | Models from internal data source |
| Product development | Factor analysis Surveys Qualitative methods Panels/discussion groups | |

However, without seriously addressing the problem, marketing managers will end up ill-informed when they come to develop their marketing strategies or make tactical decisions.

For all the problems, there are, in practice, a limited number of basic underlying marketing issues with which all companies have to contend. Furthermore, the solutions usually adopted can be seen as variations on relatively few themes. The basic model of information flows to support a marketing system can, therefore, be visualised as shown in Figure 43.1. The main components of this system are explained in Table 43.4.

The critical issue, then, when building such a system is that it is not self-contained within marketing. It requires interface programmes that will alter the systems used by Finance, Sales and other internal departments, so that information can be produced which will be of direct relevance to marketing management. In addition, it will need to capture appropriate data-feeds from external sources to provide other supporting information. The

*A marketing information system should not be self-contained within marketing*

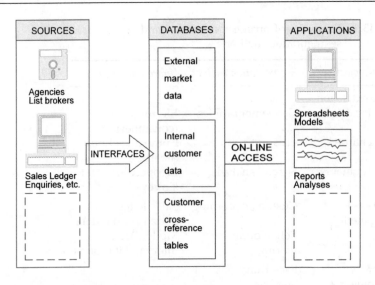

**Figure 43.1** Information flows in a marketing system

secrets of success in developing such systems for marketing are:

- Understanding the information needs of marketing and particularly how internal and external views of a market will be reconciled.
- Developing a strong cost–benefit case for the development of information systems, given that other systems, including financial ones, will have to be altered to accommodate the needs of marketing.
- Working continuously with internal IT staff until the system is built whilst recognising that they are/will be under pressure from other sources, especially Finance, and that unless marketing maintains momentum and direction, then other priorities will inevitably win.

*Cross-functional cooperation is an essential prerequisite for the creation of marketing databases*

Marketing planners need to become far less insular and parochial if they are to obtain the information they require to plan effectively. Cross-functional understanding and cooperation must be secured by the Marketing Department if it is to develop the systems it needs. In many companies, Marketing staff are, at best, tolerated by their colleagues in Finance, Operations, IT, and on the Board. Building the interdepartmental bridges to secure data, information and knowledge is possibly one of the greatest challenges facing marketing today.

**Table 43.4**  The main components of a market database system

---

**External market data**: which is purchased from external agencies. These include governmental agencies, market research firms, list brokers and so on.

**Internal customer data**: which is collected from the sales ledger and other internal sources such as customer service, field sales, telesales, etc. It is coded and segmented in such a way that market-share figures can be created by comparison with external data.

**Customer reference table**: which is needed to make the system work effectively. It identifies customers (as defined by Marketing) and provides a cross-reference to sales ledger accounts. Whenever a new sales ledger account is created, the cross-reference table is used to determine the customer associated with that account. This avoids the need for costly manual matching or deduplication after the account is created. It is also used by marketing applications as a standard reference table for customers.

**Databases**: refer to all three of the above data types. They need to be structured using a technique known as *data modelling* which organises the data into the component types that Marketing wants, and not the structure that Finance or anyone else provides. Usually, the data is held using *relational database* software, since this provides for maximum flexibility and choice of analysis tools.

**Interfaces**: refers to the computer programs that grab the data from the source systems and restructure it into the components to go onto the marketing database. These programs have to be written by the in-house IT staff, since they obtain and restructure data from the in-house sales ledger, and other in-house systems.

**Applications**: are the software programs that the planners use to analyse the data and develop their plans. They include data-grabbing tools that grab the items of data from their storage locations; reporting tools that summarise the data according to categories that Marketing defines; spreadsheets that carry out calculations; and 'what-if' analyses on the reported summary data.

---

Tables 43.1 to 43.3 and Figure 43.1 are reproduced with the kind permission of Dr Robert Shaw of Shaw Consulting, London.

# TOPIC 44

# Category Management

Category management (CM) is a concept that has developed as a radical alternative to brand management in retail marketing since the mid-1990s. The process of CM can be summarised as: 'The strategic management of a group of products clustered around a specific customer need. This group, or category, is managed as a strategic business unit with clearly defined profitability goals.' The impact of CM is that it shifts the focus of managers from individual brands to the management of overall categories as defined by local customer needs.

CM emerged from the development of ideas within the concept of Efficient Customer Response (ECR) that was initiated industry-wide in the US market from the mid-1980s onwards. The emphasis of ECR is on sales profitability rather than sales volume and spans the entire business process from the purchase of raw materials to manufacturing, distribution and sale. Its bases are the recent improvements to be found in technology which have allowed suppliers and buyers to reduce waste and stockholding and to reduce discounts as a means of generating sales. The focus of the concept is the business processes to be found in retail organisations.

## Growth of CM

Brand management focuses on individual brands from the manufacturer's perspective, grouping all functions that affect a brand's profitability under one manager. Retailers however, will often group brands together by product (e.g., soap powder) because that is more convenient for their customers and reflects the way in which customers shop.

The resultant categories are therefore defined by customers, but this can lead to problems of definition. For instance, when a customer wants a cleaner for the bathroom, does he or she categorise it as a bathroom

242

product, a cleaner, or a home safety product? In addition, categories tend to vary regionally and according to customer types, rather than on a broader cross-cultural basis. In response some manufacturers have had to recast their brands for categories, but this raises the question of whether some products should appear in more than one category (for instance, should herbs be categorised with fresh produce, baking goods or both?).

In the final analysis, what is important to retailers is that their shelf space sells more than it would if managed another way. Retailers' expertise lies in providing the space to sell products and services to facilitate that. By appointing an external supplier as category manager, and making them responsible for optimising sales from that space, retailers are exploiting manufacturer skills in such areas as display, sales promotion and merchandising.

The retailer will normally set minimum standards for the category such as demanding that there must be at least one major brand name and one 'own label' product displayed. After that, the category managers make their own stocking and communications decisions on behalf of their assigned category. For example, if SmithKline Beecham were to identify opportunities for increased toothbrush sales within the oral hygiene category for which they acted as category manager, they could spend their own budget on promoting them.

Contrary to traditional practices, CM obliges manufacturers to consider the profitability of an entire product segment rather than that of just their own brands. The fact that retailers have forced this change is another example of the evolution of retailers from passive distributors to proactive marketers and the shift of power from manufacturer to retailer.

*CM reflects the shift of power from manufacturer to retailer*

### From Brand Management to CM

The trend towards CM has also required a shift from the traditionally narrow focus of brand management. Looked at from a category perspective, it is possible to see that the consumer choice is not just about selecting from competing brands such as Coca-Cola or Pepsi, but involves an entire drinks portfolio of soft drinks, juices, beverages and alcohol. Heinz began realigning its business along category management principles in 1997 and now has eight global categories: ketchups and sauces, infant feeding, seafood, food service, petfood, weight control, frozen food and convenience meals.

Rather than relying on the power of their brand names, organisations need to ensure that all of their support systems demonstrate to retailers that they are capable of managing categories to advantage. This might mean a review of all of the organisation's systems for retail supply such as, for instance, the logistics of keeping the shelves fully supplied, or maintaining efficient electronic data interchange systems for stocks.

### Limitations of CM

Viewed purely as a strategy to reduce waste and therefore costs, CM loses its focus on the end customer as the absolute priority. Concentrating on the maximisation of shelf space profitability may not improve customer satisfaction levels and that, in the long run, may reduce profits.

One recent report concluded that the availability of a wide selection of goods is a major determinant in customers' decisions about where to shop. CM limits the product choice to those which are most profitable for the retailer and this can have a negative impact on the customers' shopping experience. If customers feel hindered in their purchase decisions by the inability to compare prices of different brands, the CM process will ultimately rebound.

Further difficulties arise from the issue of positioning different product categories. Should paper tissues, for instance, be categorised with bathroom products or health and beauty? And, should the two categories be set next to each other or apart? In addition, different retailers and manufacturers could well work to different category definitions.

*CM's emphasis on the manufacturer/ retailer relationship can demote a customer focus*

These limitations reflect the fact that much of the emphasis of CM has been on the manufacturer/retailer relationship. A 1994 *Financial Times* survey found that consumers have effectively been demoted as the focus of marketing strategy as retailers have grown in importance, with consumers attracting 30 per cent of marketing expenditure against retailers at 54 per cent.

## Challenges for the Future

One of the most difficult challenges facing CM is reducing the number of superfluous items on the shelves. This is in opposition to traditional brand marketing which aims to prolong the life of the brand by extending the product range. Possible ways of evolution are demonstrated by Figure 44.1.

Mass customisation has been made possible by the increased sophistication in consumer information which has allowed marketers to provide variations on the central product to suit each customer. The growth of retailers' own label products (e.g., Tesco's 'finest' and 'value') reflects this, but further limits the available shelf space for branded supplies. The difficulty for retailers is to ensure that limiting consumers' brand choice is not perceived as limiting their category choice just because they cannot find their favourite products.

The future of CM must necessarily take account of the distribution systems for an increasingly 'global village' market. Many mass retailers are unable to market so

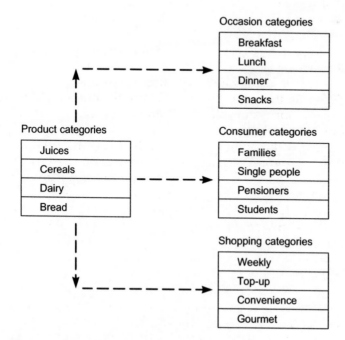

**Figure 44.1** Category management evolution

many products properly, even when redefined as categories. Providing marketing expertise is therefore one way in which manufacturers can hope to retain some kind of balance in the relationship with such international retailers.

In order to sustain a customer focus, manufacturers need free access to customer information. This can be obtained through large panel companies such as Nielsen, or through the development of a manufacturer's own database, such as Heinz. Manufacturers can also try to establish a reputation for themselves as leaders in ECR, carefully positioning themselves in retail perception.

*CM can help deliver customer satisfaction by focusing retailers on customer preferences*

Future emphasis will probably be on targeting customer satisfaction more effectively, in order to maximise long-term profit. CM can help by focusing on the retail audience and the way in which category sales are driven. This in turn helps retailers build an effective vehicle for appealing to the variety of customers' product decisions and needs. The challenge is to make this happen on a store-by-store basis, at an affordable cost.

**Group G**

# UNDERSTANDING MARKETING PLANNING AND CONTROL

# TOPIC 45

# Forecasting Sales

The size and complexity of the marketing task in all kinds of enterprise has substantially increased in recent years. The growing diversity of customer needs in a rapidly changing environment has resulted in shorter product life-cycles. Distribution patterns have changed dramatically in most markets, and have been complicated by the geographical dispersion of operations and the growing internationalisation and scale of businesses. In addition, the sociocultural, legal and political environments in which managers have to operate have become more volatile and the volume of data and information available has mushroomed. Added to this is the ever-present difficulty of measuring the behavioural aspects, such as organisational and psychological influences, which impact on marketing decisions.

The result of all this is that it is becoming increasingly difficult to forecast with anything like the accuracy that was possible when markets were more stable. Nevertheless, this is a necessary task and one which has to be done well, since the consequences of being wrong can be very severe indeed. Crucial to this is a good understanding of the differences between **macro** and **micro** forecasting and the ability to utilise both qualitative and quantitative methods.

The selection of an appropriate forecasting approach or set of techniques is dependent on four main factors:

- The **degree of accuracy** required, which, in turn, will depend on the risk associated with the decisions which will be based on the forecast.
- The **availability of data** and information, which will determine the techniques which can be utilised for making forecasts.
- The **time-horizon required**, which will, again, affect the approach to be adopted.

249

- The **position of a product in its life-cycle**, which will influence both the time-horizons sought and the types of data and information which will be available.

### Macro and Micro Forecasting

**Macro forecasting** is essentially concerned with forecasting markets in total. In adopting a macro approach, the emphasis is on observing the broad picture and, from that, deducing the implications for the products and markets in which an organisation is interested. Some form of macro forecasting has to precede the setting of marketing objectives and strategies. Other forecasts should come after the company has decided which specific market opportunities it wants to take advantage of and how best this can be done.

**Micro forecasting** is more concerned with detailed unit forecasts and should normally come after the organisation has set its major objectives and strategies. These obviously deal with shorter time-horizons such as an organisation's sales predictions for the next period. For this type of forecast, qualitative extrapolative techniques may be appropriate, although, in general, simple extrapolations are fraught with dangers. It must be recognised here that such projections are based on the assumption that what has happened in the past will be a guide to what will happen in the future. A more appropriate micro approach is to build up, from an individual customer level, an estimate of what the total sales of a product could be in a given period.

*Macro forecasting precedes the setting of marketing objectives and strategies, whereas micro forecasting follows such activity*

### Forecasting Techniques

Whilst there are many techniques which can be applied to the making of forecasts, they usually fall into one of two categories: **quantitative techniques**; and **qualitative methods**. Quantitative approaches, as the name implies, refer to a forecast made on a numerical basis of some kind and usually involve some form of statistical analysis. Qualitative estimates are more intuitive in nature and rely on the skills of individuals in interpreting the world around them as they see it, based on their experience, the quality of their imagination and their knowledge of the area under discussion. In the end, the outcome of a qualitative forecast should, of course, also be quantitative in nature. It is the methods of arriving at the projection which differ.

It is also the case that, particularly at a macro level, it would be unusual if either of these methods were used entirely on their own, mainly because of the inherent dangers in each. Thus a combination of approaches is usually far more appropriate. As an example, it is comparatively easy to develop an equation which will extrapolate statistically the world population up to, say, the year 2010. The problem here is that the method would not have taken account of likely changes in past trends. Better would be an approach which listed a whole series of possible events which could affect world population, and then assigned probabilities to the likelihood of those events happening. From this, a more sophisticated and more realistic forecast could be produced.

*A combination of forecasting techniques is usually required for any one forecast*

A similar approach is adopted by many business forecasters, who use leading indicators: that is, indices of related or even non-related activities as aids to estimating changes in market conditions at a macro level. Examples include:

- The *Financial Times* Ordinary Share Index, which is reckoned to provide a lead of about six months.
- New housing starts, which can give a lead of about 10 months.
- The net acquisition of financial assets by companies, which can be used as a lead for about 12 months.

Such indicators will only provide approximate pictures of general business conditions and cannot be guaranteed to offer consistent correlations. On the other hand, forecasters may discern, from their experience and their understanding of business, that there is a close fit between seemingly unrelated activity and the sales performance of a particular product.

In recent years, there has also been a considerable growth in the use of marketing models to provide a macro-type basis for sales estimation. Generally, these models incorporate a number of statistically derived relationships drawn from empirical observations, the purpose of which is to explain the observed market behaviour in terms of marketing trends. However, not everybody is enthusiastic about such models, particularly if they are used for large scale situations, because of the problems of quantifying what are often qualitative and intangible relationships. In addition, such relationships will often change considerably over time, thus making the model obsolete. Another factor mitigating against the use of models is the considerable expense involved in collecting the necessary data.

An example of a qualitative macro estimation technique is the Delphi forecast (named after the Greek oracle who foretold the future). Here, a group of experts discuss a problem, such as, 'what will be the major marketing features of the year 2010?', and who give their consensus of the answer to this problem.

As noted, good micro approaches are based on building up, from an individual customer level, an estimate of what total sales of the product could be in a given period. Quantitative micro methods sometimes involve surveys of actual and/or potential customers or seek to extract information from internal sources. Although the procedures involved may be very sophisticated, these studies basically rely on indications from respondents as to their likely purchasing behaviour. An example of a qualitative micro estimate would be an estimate based on the judgement of members of the sales force concerning future sales.

### Forecasting and Uncertainty

*The output of a forecast should be a range of scenarios*

Forecasts deal with uncertainties, which require market forecasters to establish the nature of the 'either/or' associated with the area under study. Thus, the output of a forecast should be expressed in terms of a range of possible outcomes. Beyond this, it should also be recognised that the process by which any market prediction is achieved is essentially probabilistic. Forecasts thus can and should be made to incorporate the probabilities that are implicit in the marketing environment in which the organisation operates.

As an example, sales forecasters are concerned to establish what proportion of a total market potential will be represented as their sales estimates. This will be based on an assessment of the effect of a specific marketing mix and marketing programme in competition with alternative means of satisfying the same need. The danger here is that it can be possible for such estimates to become self-fulfilling prophecies, in that both the estimate and the marketing mix programmes are dependent on each other. In this sense, a given level of market achievement is predicted by what an organisation believes to be potentially achievable. More useful, here, would be alternative scenarios based on different probabilities so that optimum levels of investment can be assessed, and risk factors built into the various activities of the organisation.

The task of marketing managers, then, when adopting a forecasting role, is to take whatever relevant data are available to help to predict the future. They must apply to them whatever quantitative techniques are appropriate, but then use qualitative methods, such as: expert opinions; market research; analogy; and so on, to predict what will be the likely discontinuities in the same time series. It is only through sensible use of the available tools that management will begin to understand what has to be done to match its own capabilities with carefully selected market needs. Without such an understanding, any form of forecasting is likely to be a sterile exercise.

*Marketing managers should ensure that predictive tools are used sensibly and appropriately*

# TOPIC 46

# Marketing Planning

All organisations operate in a complex environment, in which hundreds of external and internal factors interact to affect their ability to achieve their objectives. Managers need some understanding, or view, about how all these variables interact and they must try to be rational about their decisions, no matter how important intuition, feel and experience are as contributory factors in this process of rationality. Most managers accept that some kind of formalised procedure for planning the organisation's marketing helps to sharpen this rationality so as to reduce the complexity of business operations and add a dimension of realism to the organisation's hopes for the future.

### The Essence of Marketing Planning

The contribution of marketing planning to organisational success, whatever its area of activity, lies in its commitment to detailed analysis of future opportunities to meet customer needs and a wholly professional approach to selling to well-defined market segments, those products or services that deliver the sought-after benefits. Such commitment and activities, however, must not be mistaken for budgets and forecasts. These have always been a commercial necessity. The process of marketing planning is a more sophisticated approach which is concerned with identifying what, and to whom, sales are going to be made in the longer term to give revenue budgets and sales forecasts any chance of being achieved.

*Marketing planning is a managerial process leading to a marketing plan*

In essence, marketing planning is a managerial process, the output of which is a marketing plan. As such, it is a logical sequence and a series of activities leading to the setting of marketing objectives and the formulation of plans for achieving them. Conceptually, the process is very simple and is achieved by means of a planning system. The system is little more than a structured way

254

of identifying a range of options for the organisation, of making them explicit in writing, of formulating marketing objectives which are consistent with the company's over-all objectives and of scheduling and costing the specific activities most likely to bring about the achievement of the objectives. It is the systemisation of this process which lies at the heart of the theory of marketing planning.

## Types of Marketing Plan

There are two principal kinds of marketing plan:

- The strategic marketing plan.
- The tactical marketing plan.

The **strategic marketing plan** is a plan for three or more years. It is the written document which outlines how managers perceive their own position in their markets relative to their competitors (with competitive advantage accurately defined), what objectives they want to achieve, how they intend to achieve them (strategies), what resources are required, and with what results (budget). Three years is the most frequent planning period for the strategic marketing plan. Five years is the longest period and this is becoming less common as a result of the speed of technological and environmental change. The exceptions here are the very-long-range plans formulated by a number of Japanese companies which may often have planning horizons of between 50 and 200 years!

The **tactical marketing plan** is the detailed scheduling and costing of the specific actions necessary for the achievement of the first year of the strategic marketing plan. The tactical plan is thus usually for one year.

*Preparing a detailed plan before a strategic plan is completed can indicate a confusion between strategic marketing planning and budgeting*

Research into the marketing planning practices of organisations shows that successful ones complete the strategic plan before the tactical plan. Unsuccessful organisations frequently do not bother with a strategic marketing plan at all, relying largely on sales forecasts and the associated budgets. The problem with this approach is that many managers sell the products and services they find easiest to sell, to those customers who offer the least line of resistance. By developing short-term, tactical marketing plans first and then extrapolating them, managers merely succeed in extrapolating their own shortcomings. Preoccupation with preparing a detailed marketing plan first is typical of those companies that confuse sales forecasting and budgeting with strategic marketing planning.

## The Contents of a Strategic Marketing Plan

The contents of a strategic marketing plan are as follows:

- *Mission Statement*   This sets out the *raison d'être* of the organisation and covers its role, business definition, distinctive competence, and future indications.
- *Financial Summary*   This summarises the financial implications over the full planning period.
- *Market Overview*   This provides a brief picture of the market and includes: market structure; market trends; key market segments; and (sometimes) gap analysis.
- *SWOT Analyses*   These are the strengths and weaknesses of the organisation compared with competitors against key customer success factors plus the organisation's opportunities and threats; they are normally completed for each key product, or segment.
- *Issues to be addressed*   These are derived from the SWOT analyses and are usually specific to each product or segment.
- *Portfolio Summary*   This is a pictorial summary of the SWOT analyses that makes it easy to see, at a glance, the relative importance of each; it is often a two-dimensional matrix in which the horizontal axis measures the organisation's comparative strengths and the vertical axis measures its relative attractiveness.
- *Assumptions*   These are the assumptions which are critical to the planned marketing objectives and strategies.
- *Marketing Objectives*   These are usually quantitative statements in terms of profit, volume, value and market share, of what the organisation wishes to achieve. They are usually stated by product; by segment; and overall.
- *Marketing Strategies*   These state how the objectives are to be achieved and often involve the four Ps of marketing: product; price; place; and promotion.
- *Resource Requirements and Budget*   This is the full planning period budget, showing in detail, for each year, the revenues and associated costs.

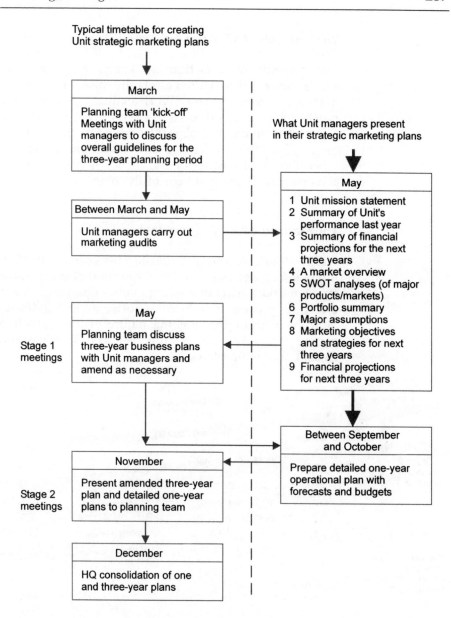

Typical timetable for creating
Unit strategic marketing plans

**March**

Planning team 'kick-off'
Meetings with Unit
managers to discuss
overall guidelines for the
three-year planning period

What Unit managers present
in their strategic marketing plans

**Between March and May**

Unit managers carry out
marketing audits

**May**

1 Unit mission statement
2 Summary of Unit's
   performance last year
3 Summary of financial
   projections for the next
   three years
4 A market overview
5 SWOT analyses (of major
   products/markets)
6 Portfolio summary
7 Major assumptions
8 Marketing objectives
   and strategies for next
   three years
9 Financial projections
   for next three years

Stage 1
meetings

**May**

Planning team discuss
three-year business plans
with Unit managers and
amend as necessary

**Between September
and October**

Prepare detailed one-year
operational plan with
forecasts and budgets

Stage 2
meetings

**November**

Present amended three-year
plan and detailed one-year
plans to planning team

**December**

HQ consolidation of one
and three-year plans

*Note:* The marketing planning process must not be confused with what appears in the plan
itself, which is described on the right.

**Figure 46.1** Strategic and tactical marketing plans

## The Contents of a Tactical Marketing Plan

The contents of a tactical marketing plan are very similar, except that it often omits the mission statement, the market overview and SWOT analyses, and goes into much more detailed quantification by product and segment of marketing objectives and associated strategies. An additional feature is a much more detailed scheduling and costing of the tactics necessary to the achievement of the first year of the plan.

## The Marketing Planning Timetable

Figure 46.1 depicts the relationship between the marketing planning process and the output of that process: the strategic and tactical marketing plans. Figure 46.2 shows the same process in a circular form, as this indicates more realistically the ongoing nature of the marketing planning process and the link between strategic and tactical marketing plans.

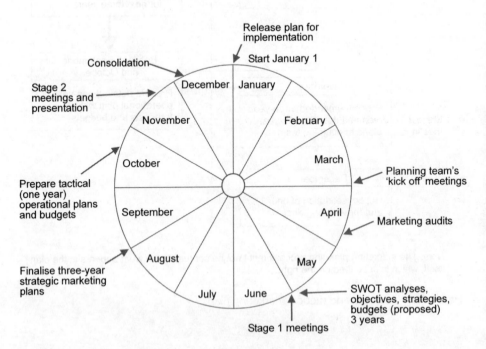

**Figure 46.2** Strategic and operational planning cycle

# TOPIC 47

# International Product Planning

Although there are many factors which inhibit success-ful international marketing, inadequate product plan-ning is one of the more significant contributions to poor international marketing performance. This is because the product is at the heart of the marketing mix which constitutes a supplier's offer, and to which customers and consumers respond. Since trade is about selling products into markets, the product, as the leading edge of the marketing mix, must be as 'right' as possible to avoid becoming another example of products which fail once they move outside their home territory. The two key questions that need to be answered to enhance the chances of success are:

- Which of its product lines should an organisation sell in overseas markets?
- Does it need to adapt them for those markets?

## Product Line Choice

In all but the most exceptional cases, overseas markets will already have trade in similar or competing products to those a domestic supplier wishes to introduce. This implies that the overseas market will already support a distribution infrastructure with established trading practices, including exclusivity agreements and net-worked relationships. In addition, it will imply that there are existing consumer habits and preferences, competitor promotional activities and accepted pricing structures. Choosing a product line for such a market will require the identification of an opportunity derived from a good understanding of these market features. This should include:

- An analysis of potential competitor product performance.
- Market usage patterns and important application requirements.
- The composition of the market in terms of supply chain structures, the major determinants of price, communication channels and the major positioning variables.
- Customer expectations of a product.

The analysis should seek to highlight any trends in the market which will reduce the attractiveness of products currently available and to identify any products from existing suppliers which leave a gap between customer expectations and product performance. Where an organisation can identify a product line that has a cost or performance advantage which fits one of the gaps identified in an overseas market, it has an opportunity which it may be possible to exploit.

Before entering the market, however, the business must engage in product trials to ensure that the line has no fundamental weaknesses which will prohibit sales or which will be too costly to adapt. This, in turn, will be a function of market potential, market accessibility and the possible margins available.

## Product Adaptation

*Product applications are rarely universal and thus products must be adapted for different countries*

Unfortunately, it is rarely the case that a domestic product can be introduced into an overseas market without any form of adaptation. Research has shown that some of the biggest problems in product internationalisation have occurred when organisations have followed the rather naive belief that products are transferable from home to foreign markets without change of some kind. Thus, product application is hardly ever universal and even globally branded products such as Coca-Cola use different formulations for different parts of the world to accommodate taste variations between countries.

Apart from taste and cultural influences such as colour requirements, adaptations may be required by distribution complexities not encountered in home markets. Thus packaging and unitisation practices may differ by country and aspects such as product tracking mechanisms will often require modification once consignments enter a foreign land. Additionally, there are often legal or semi-legal requirements which must be satisfied. Thus, if a similar product or service already exists in a target country, there is likely to be a standard for it to which products will need to conform. Organisations must, therefore, have regard for:

- Legal requirements
  (such as environment/pollution legislation).
- Mandatory standards
  (such as electrical safety standards).
- Industry standards
  (such as light alloy wheels in Germany).
- Voluntary standards
  (such as paper size).

A further complication here is that, whereas standards are always well-defined, they tend to be:

- Different by country.
- Many in number as a result of covering measurement, quality, material, properties, performance and safety, etc.
- Different in legal backing/adherence and rationale.

As well as standards, products may also require adaptation as a consequence of the way in which they are used. Thus, other product characteristics that need to be most carefully researched in all foreign countries include:

- Physical properties, such as size, weight, materials, tolerances and instrumentation.
- Performance characteristics, such as mechanical, electrical and raw materials.
- Others, such as applications, symbols, codes, language, commissioning and service requirements.

As examples, in respect of physical characteristics, paper size is different in photocopiers in different markets and different flour quality affects the design of baking machinery. Similarly, with reference to performance, there are different generator-size requirements in different countries and in the case of application, tyre requirements differ significantly in hot countries, although the product is essentially the same. In addition, instruction and installation manuals will need to be rewritten and maintenance requirements may need to be altered to take account of service facilities in other countries.

*The financial risks involved in entering overseas markets must be carefully evaluated*

Whilst it is tempting to stop at product/market analysis, it is also prudent to consider product adaptation at a much broader or company level. Thus, it might be important for an organisation to consider whether it has: the design/technical capability; the raw material processing capability; the labour know-how; the equipment/technical know-how; the correct production processes, such as special assembly versus batch assembly; and so on. A good example is provided by power cables, where a European manufacturer had to switch machines and provide additional tooling in order to produce a product. In turn, this led to pressure on existing workflows, resulting in a production plan change, with consequent capacity constraints, slower throughputs, lower earnings for employees and, worst of all, increased production costs.

Overall, issues such as these lead to the conclusion that the financial risks involved in entering overseas markets need to be most carefully evaluated. In particular, an organisation is interested in the cost of adaptation, the resulting margins, the investment requirement and the likely return on investment (ROI), leading to a preliminary assessment of the volume required in any specific foreign market. In particular, the successful international company should be looking continuously for synergy and cost savings from any essential product adaptation. These are possible from:

- Economies of scale in production.
- Economies in product research and development.
- Economies in marketing as a result of consumer mobility.
- The impact of technology.

To plan satisfactorily for these circumstances, product managers thus have to be rigorous in their approach as summarised in Table 47.1.

**Table 47.1** Areas requiring attention in international product planning

| | |
|---|---|
| *The product functionality* | Standardisation<br>Adaptation |
| *Packaging and labelling* | Protection/security<br>Promotional/channel aspects<br>Cultural factors<br>Package size<br>Language |
| *Brands and trade markets* | Global or national<br>Legal<br>Cultural<br>Other marketing considerations |
| *Warranty and service* | Transferability of domestic terms and conditions<br>Safety<br>Varying quality control standards internationally<br>Varying use conditions<br>Service networks |

# TOPIC 48

# Organisational Structure and Marketing

One of the problems of managing marketing occurs when deciding exactly how marketing should fit within the existing, and developing, structure of the organisation. The first problem concerns whether or not to have a specific marketing department at all. If it is thought that this is the right option, the second decision is judging what scope, or range of activities, it should oversee. Once a department's overall responsibilities have been determined, the third step is to decide how it should be structured and who should do what job. If it is felt that a discrete marketing department is not appropriate, establishing and maintaining strong marketing leadership throughout the organisation becomes more than usually important.

*Structures provide evidence of how senior managers value an activity*

The significance of these problems is that organisations can only provide the environment within which people carry out their work; they cannot determine how the work is performed. However, structures, and the control systems associated with them, provide evidence of how senior managers value a particular activity and the role it plays in the organisation. In addition, it must be remembered that structure can also place hurdles in the way of people trying to get on with achieving their responsibilities by making communication, coordination and decision-making more difficult. It is, therefore, vital that organisations think carefully about the structures they create and how they are commensurate with the long-term objectives they are trying to achieve.

The typical evolutionary pattern for an organisation that has grown over time will lead it from a 'one-man-band' situation, where one person will perform all tasks and where sales essentially involve order-taking with small amounts of prospecting or advertising, to the multifunctioning super-department incorporating a

264

whole range of specialist activities as illustrated in Figure 48.1. As an organisation grows and becomes more sophisticated in its approach to marketing, it becomes faced with a number of options for structuring its range of marketing activities.

## Central and Decentralised Activities

For organisations which have expanded so that they operate in several regions, the first choice is between centralising or decentralising their marketing activities. Centralised operations make coordination much easier and are better at avoiding duplication. Decentralisation allows for more flexibility and better exploitation of local opportunities. In this respect, there are no 'right' or 'wrong' options. The choice will depend on the organisation's product diversity, the need for local variations and the management's ability to get a good balance between coordination and control. The latter is necessary to avoid fragmentation and to prevent managers feeling that they have no effective freedom of choice. Sadly, in many international organisations, it is not uncommon for local (i.e., decentralised) marketing personnel to find themselves with no influence over product decisions, price or delivery and who then become frustrated at having to manage a marketing mix over which they have little control.

An ideal arrangement, of course, is to organise around a combination of both in order to gain the benefits of each. This involves putting marketing as close to the customer as possible, whilst also having some kind of centralised marketing function. In this way, the potential for costly and unnecessary duplication is minimised and the possibility of achieving economies of scale and effective knowledge transfer is optimised.

*Ideally, marketing should sit close to the customer and there should be a centralised marketing function*

## Departmental Structures

For organisations with marketing departments, the second area of choice is the methodology for structuring the department's activities. The main decision is whether to organise around functions; products; markets; key accounts; geographical area; or some combination of two

**Typical Evolutionary Pattern of Marketing**

*One-man-band*
Basically an order-taker, probably
involved in technical side as well.

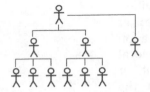

*Sales Team Marketing*
Sales people sent out to 'drum up
orders'. Self-generated sales support
materials.

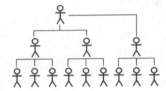

*Sales Force plus Marketing Sales Support*
Marketing provides materials and
information which support sales activities.

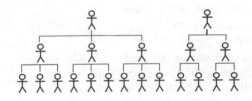

*Sales Force plus Ancillary Marketing*
Marketing expands activities and employs
specialists to prepare a range of
functions - still essentialy sales support.

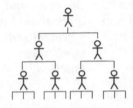

*Separate Sales and Marketing Departments*
Marketing takes on product or brand
management responsibilities and starts to
coordinate/influence sales strategies.

*Separate Sales and Marketing Departments*
A Sales and Marketing Director/VP
appointed to coordinate all activities.

**Figure 48.1**  Organisational structure and marketing

or more of these options. A functionally organised department would separate activities such as: new product management; market research; customer service; advertising; market analysis; public relations; sales promotions/special campaigns; and so on.

Alternatively, a department could be organised around a series of product managers who would be responsible for the whole range of activities associated with their products or brands. This would include stimulating activity within the sales force and third party re-sellers, as well as intra-company coordination. Organising around markets would involve the creation of market managers, whether geographically, by sector, or by segment. Variations on this theme have been referred to as vertical marketing, trade marketing and industry marketing.

In some cases, such as, for example, where there are very few customers, it is sensible to organise around key account management, whilst in others, it is appropriate to have marketing specialists with responsibility for all activities within a definable area. In many organisations, a combination of approaches is often in evidence. As examples, some businesses organise around brand managers, but separate the functions of public relations, customer service and planning, whilst others use both product and market managers in a matrix-type relationship.

*Many organisations use a combination of approaches to minimise the dangers inherent in any single approach*

The dangers inherent in any approach or methodology cover a number of areas. The first is that sometimes products or markets are lost from managers' perspectives. For instance, organising around markets would seem to be sensible for corporations which are interested in developing a marketing-orientated business. However, focusing on markets can lead to the neglect of smaller brands, the dilution or loss of functional skills or product knowledge, and excessive product customisation so that economies of scale are reduced. The second danger, therefore, is that focusing on functions, products and/or markets reduces the chances that all the tasks which need to be completed actually get done, and are performed in as professional or as effective a way as possible. The third is that responsibility and accountability become imbalanced, so that the objectives which people have to achieve are not commensurate with the areas over which they have control.

*Operationalising marketing involves achieving the correct balance between responsibility and accountability*

One of the key problems in operationalising marketing in organisations is achieving the correct balance between responsibility and accountability in the management of the marketing mix. Marketing managers are obviously concerned to manipulate the mix to create an offer irresistible to targeted customers. Many of the elements of the marketing mix, however, are quite rightly under the control of non-marketing managers, since they require specialist or technical skills to be managed well. Marketing managers are therefore in the position of being responsible for the profitable sales of the organisation's products, but without the authority to control the elements which will promote such sales. In many organisations, the conflict and poor relations which exist between sales and marketing personnel typifies this problem.

## Process Redesign

One attempt to overcome some of these difficulties has been to reorganise an organisation's activities around its core processes which either obtain value from suppliers or deliver value to customers. Instead of structuring a business around its functional activities such as operations, finance and human resources, etc., some organisations are looking at processes such as new product development, order fulfilment and cost reduction as the basis for managing operating units. Each process is managed by a team which has responsibility for delivering efficiency in that area and for meeting the objectives appropriate for competitive advantage. The teams may still be product or customer focused, depending on the nature of the business. The key difference between conventional structures and a core process, team-based approach, is that the team becomes multifunctional with responsibility for, say, inbound logistics, production, sales and supply, rather than each activity stage being a distinct and separate operation.

Under these circumstances, marketing functions would be provided by each of the teams, with ultimate marketing responsibility resting with the top team for each process. The organisation would also include a specialist marketing unit, which would provide information, advice or assistance on specialist topics such as conducting market research or designing a customer service strategy. Marketing would thus be brought closer to the areas it needs to influence, since a good part of all the elements of the marketing mix would be the responsibility of the cross-functional process team. Under this approach, marketing expertise would be injected into the team either through consultancy, training or 'contracting out'.

## Other Developments

In addition to the 'business process redesign' described above, there are a number of other developments which are likely to affect the position or structure of marketing within organisations.

The first of these is the decline of traditional brand management as retailers become more powerful and, in some cases, substitute brands. Rather than a brand's franchise in the market influencing the choice of supplier, retailers are now much more interested in costs, strategy alignment, and response to regional differences, as a basis for choosing suppliers.

The second development is the advancements being made in micro-marketing, which are encouraging marketing managers to look at differences between consumers in more elaborate ways and to use sales promotion activities and database marketing for more accurate targeting.

The third is the reduction in the effectiveness of mass advertising as media channels proliferate and as it becomes harder to reach mass markets. These trends will support moves away from national and international brand management as a basis for organising marketing, towards market-focused management structures, either as part of a process team, or as a framework based on relationships.

Fourth, the current popularity of category management as a basis for organising consumer goods marketing is also affecting how suppliers organise their marketing activities. To match their retail customers, suppliers are organising brand portfolios and appointing category managers, or 'champions', whose focus is on maximising profit from a category for the retailer rather than developing brand franchises.

*The position and structure of marketing is being challenged and impacted by developments throughout the supply chain*

*Structure is of only secondary importance in establishing effective marketing*

In the end, however, it must be remembered that structure is of only secondary importance in establishing marketing as an effective force within an organisation. Of greater significance is the attitude of the managers working within the structures and the ways in which they are able to influence other managers towards a market-orientated approach to their own responsibilities. If a market orientation is well embedded and stretches across its range of activities, it is almost possible to argue that structure is irrelevant to marketing effectiveness.

# TOPIC 49

# Budgeting for Marketing

One of the most vexing questions for any marketing manager, or indeed, any marketing organisation, is 'How much, and where, should we spend on marketing?' The question is difficult because it requires an understanding of what should be included in a marketing budget, the way in which costs are generated and the relationship between marketing expenditure and the results sought. Each of these areas is problematic and often requires sophisticated financial information and analytical tools for the development of effective programmes and budgets.

## Budgeting Practices

For many organisations, such information and tools are not readily available. In their absence, the most appealing approach is to use last year's figures as the base and to project forward. This, of course, takes into account inflation, prevailing market conditions and adds on an amount which senior controllers will deduct at the budget review!

### Zero-Based Budgeting

More preferable is an **iterative zero-based** approach which starts with marketing objectives and the programmes designed to achieve these objectives. Once activities have been identified, the incremental cost of these can be calculated and a budget can be established. If these are deemed to be too expensive, alternative activities or structures can be investigated. If these prove equally unacceptable, then a review of strategy is required, and so on. In this way, every item of expenditure can be traced back to specific objectives, and indeed, the overall corporate objectives of the organisation.

*Variable Cost Budgeting*

A less wide-ranging approach is to base the budget on
**variable costs**, particularly for short-term budgeting,
since certain costs, such as human resources and
physical facilities, can only be significantly altered in
the longer term. Periodically, however, this would
require a zero-based approach to be used to review all
products, markets and related activities. This would
enable organisations to abandon obsolete and unnecessary features and to make appropriate structural altera-
tions. Many of the moves away from brand management
towards category, or business process, management are
a result of such reviews.

*Life-Cycle Budgeting*

Budgeting for marketing can also incorporate **life-cycle
costing**. This involves assessments of the total costs
involved in managing products over their life in the
market. Such an approach requires marketing managers
to plan ahead in terms of product upgrades, changing
promotional activities, service and distribution support,
and the way price is likely to alter over the life of a
product. Long-term assessments of return on investment, payback and cash management can therefore be
made, which will help both short-term budgeting control
and organisational financial planning.

*Operating and Opportunity Budgeting*

A further approach to structuring a budget utilises the
notions of **operating budget**, versus **opportunity budgets**. Operating budgets cover those activities which are
a continuation of existing programmes. The key issues
here are in terms of efficiency and the maintenance of
expected performance levels. This highlights the fact that
marketing managers should be seeking constant cost-
reduction and better ways of managing the marketing
mix and obtaining marketing information, whilst at the
same time countering adverse developments. An opportunities budget should be developed for unexpected
circumstances which can yield financial and marketing

benefits for the organisation. One of the critical roles of marketing managers is to spot such opportunities and to feed them into the general management of their enterprise.

## Marketing Costs for Budgeting

Since marketing management requires the development of an offer, which consists of the various elements of the marketing mix, a marketing budget should, in theory, include all costs associated with operationalising this mix. In practice, marketing managers do not, of course, have control over all these elements. In addition, the activities over which they do have control will vary from one organisation to another.

For an organisation which buys-in products which are then sold via a direct sales force, some form of catalogue or a direct mail activity, the marketing budget may be comprehensive and include selling costs; order processing; stock-holding; merchandising; packaging; and credit. For a manufacturing concern with complex logistics, selling via distributors or retailers and utilising significant financial activities such as credit card or Electronic Data Interchange (EDI) facilities, marketing may be more focused on the generation of demand and market forecasting.

For budgeting purposes, the important factor here is to distinguish between **controllable** and **uncontrollable** costs. This is a particularly difficult problem when sales and marketing are organised as two separate activities. Whilst marketing managers may be held accountable for sales and profits, they may have no responsibility for selling, merchandising and discounts. Thus, the contents of marketing budgets need to be set in the context of specific organisational structures, the way in which senior management see the priorities of their business and the role of marketing within it.

*Marketing budgets need to be set in the context of organisation-specific factors*

## Costing Marketing Activities

Even where marketing responsibilities are clearly identifiable, budgeting problems can still arise as a result of the difficulties in allocating costs between different marketing activities. As an example, the ultimate profit centre for a business is each individual customer. For industrial companies with only a handful of customers, costs and profits may be easy to identify on a customer basis. Where larger numbers of customers exist, the allocation of expenditures such as advertising, sales and customer service between customers becomes confused. This is especially so since some customers can be easy to sell to whilst others may require much greater efforts. Similarly, some customers may place great demands on their suppliers, whilst others may be more self-sufficient. In addition, some customers may take a very profitable mix of products whilst others may only purchase those with low margin. Thus, establishing the profitability of a customer may be a very confusing process.

The problem for marketing managers lies in determining the most profitable courses of action and in targeting the organisation's activities in the best way possible. This requires good information about both customer profitability and product profitability, and as indicated, it may be hard to attribute costs in a way which will yield the appropriate information. In addition, the expected results of different types of campaign such as sales promotions, additional sales people, product upgrades and price adjustments may also be difficult to judge.

*Marketing managers must utilise both information and their professional judgement when setting budgets*

Some assistance can be gained from historical data which can be used to assess trends or to establish relationships between expenditure and results. Unfortunately, simple input/output relationships rarely exist in marketing, except at a very low level, since purchases are the result of a complex series of events which are unlikely to repeat themselves from one time-period to another. In the end, marketing managers must utilise both the information which does exist and their professional judgement, based on experience and sound marketing principles, to set their budgets.

Overall, then, budgeting for marketing is an imprecise science which will depend on an organisation's structure, its approach to marketing and the sophistication of its information systems for its quality. The process can be enhanced by focusing on the areas which are important to a business and ensuring that expenditure is related to specific marketing objectives. Distinguishing between order-filling activities and order-getting activities can help identify marketing responsibilities and a basis for analysing the effectiveness of marketing activities. Ultimately, however, the interweaving of a market orientation into all areas of operations, so that appropriate judgments can be made, will be most beneficial in directing and controlling marketing expenditure.

*A market orientation must be interwoven into all areas of operations*

# TOPIC 50

# World-class Marketing

Research conducted by Cranfield School of Management in the late 1990s with the assistance of some of Europe's best companies, large and small, has produced key indications of how successful companies use marketing to create sustainable competitive advantage.

The challenges such companies address to create this advantage include the pace of change; process thinking; market maturity; the expertise and power of customers; and the internationalisation of business. Studying the way these organisations have met these challenges has enabled the identification of 10 guidelines for world-class marketing.

## Marketing Orientation

*Market maturity is increasingly affecting activities and performance*

Market maturity has had a profound effect on most organisations during the past few years. Typical responses have been financial husbandry, ratio management and downsizing. In companies that are not market-driven this has led to *anorexia industrialosa* (an excessive desire to be leaner and fitter, leading to emaciation and eventually, death).

An alternative response has been attempts to introduce Total Quality Management (TQM) systems. In many cases, an over-focus on the systems aspect of this initiative has proved only a firm's ability to produce rubbish, perfectly and consistently. Quality can only ever be defined through the customer's eyes, so producing something perfectly that no one buys is a bit pointless. A similar situation can be found with efforts to re-engineer business processes or to implement a 'balanced score-card' approach to managing business; both of which have widely failed to live up to expectations.

Successful companies might have tried these initiatives but have always come back to the realisation that

276

- Develop customer orientation in all functions. Ensure that every function understands that they are there to serve the customer, not for their own narrow functional interests.
- This must be driven from the Board downwards.
- Where possible, organise in cross-functional teams around customer groups and core processes.
- Make customers the arbiter of quality.

**Figure 50.1**  Ensuring a market orientation

they have to lift their heads above the parapet and look at their markets and their customers rather than wasting their energy tinkering with their own internal workings. World-class companies believe passionately, from the Board downwards, that creating superior value for clearly defined groups of customers is the best way of creating wealth for all stakeholders. Only then do the superb initiatives referred to above work; otherwise they become fads. This leads to the first guideline as shown in Figure 50.1 – as far as possible, ensure that a strong market orientation exists within your organisation.

## Competitive Advantage

Successful organisations avoid offering an undifferentiated product or service in too broad a market, and they use any one or any combination of low costs, differentiation or protecting a niche to earn superior positions. Without something different to offer (provided the market requires it), companies will continue to struggle, relying on the inadequacies of their competitors rather than their own competitive strengths, for survival. Advantage within these approaches can come from any of a number of different sources including technological leadership, superior service, wide distribution coverage, strong positioning or any other value-creating proposition.

*Successful organisations seek competitive advantage through differentiation*

World leaders continuously strive to serve customer needs better and more cost-effectively, and work relentlessly towards the differential advantage that this brings. The foundations of this process are summarised in Figure 50.2.

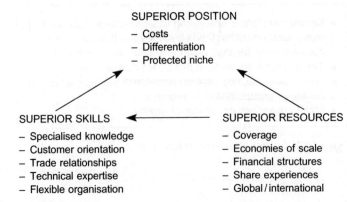

**Figure 50.2** Striving for competitive advantage

## Environmental Scanning

It goes without saying that failure to monitor hostile environmental changes is the most common reason for companies going to the wall. Had anyone at the end of the 1980s predicted that IBM would be losing billions of dollars by the mid-1990s, they would have been derided. But it was IBM's failure to respond to the changes taking place in their markets that caused just such problems.

Clearly, marketing plays a key role in this process. For successful organisations, this means devoting at least some of the time and resources of key executives to monitoring formally the changes taking place about them. The key areas requiring environmental scanning are summarised in Figure 50.3.

**Figure 50.3** Monitoring the environment: key areas

- Direct competitors
- Potential competitors
- Substitute products
- Forward integration by suppliers
- Backward integration by customers
- Competitors' profitability
- Competitors' strengths and weaknesses

**Figure 50.4**  Developing competitor profiles

## Competitor Surveillance

Excellent companies know as much about their close competitors as they know about themselves. This implies a structured competitor monitoring process covering the areas noted in Figure 50.4 in order to develop usable profiles. The results of this profiling exercise should be included in the marketing audit.

*Excellent companies know as much about their close competitors as they know about themselves*

## Market Segmentation

The ability to recognise groups of customers who share the same or similar needs and offer them appropriate value propositions has always been a major contributor to organisational success. However, the real secret, of course, is to change the offer in accordance with changing needs, and not to offer exactly the same product or service to everyone; the most frequent product-orientated mistake of unsuccessful organisations.

Steps in segmenting a market:

(a) Understand how your market works (market structure)
(b) List what is bought (including where, when, how, applications)
(c) List who buys (demographics, psychographics)
(d) List why they buy (needs, benefits sought)
(e) Search for groups with similar needs

The golden rule:
Select a segment and serve it.
Do not straddle segments and sit between them.

**Figure 50.5**  The process of market segmentation

*Market segmentation is the foundation of strategy*

This process of market segmentation is the basis for strategy formation and positioning. Without a good understanding of how needs within a market can vary, and how these variations can be used to identify different market segments, decisions about strategies and positioning become divorced from the markets in which they are supposed to secure competitive advantage. The process of segmentation is summarised in Figure 50.5.

### Strengths and Weaknesses Analysis

Market maturity, particularly in Western Europe, is a major challenge in most sectors. It is this, more than anything, which has led companies to pay greater attention to market segmentation as a source of continuing growth in profits.

Successful companies usually have a well-established and excellent grasp of the opportunities and threats facing them (derived from the previous three guidelines). The next step is to undertake a SWOT analysis to help understand their relative strengths and weaknesses in each of the segments resulting from the analysis outlined in the previous guideline. The process of identifying strengths and weaknesses is summarised in Figure 50.6.

---

For each segment in which an organisation competes, understand:

- What the 'qualifying' features and benefits are
- What the 'differential' features and benefits are
- How relatively important each of these are
- How well your product or service performs against your competitors' on each of these requirements

---

**Figure 50.6** Identifying strengths and weaknesses

### Mirroring Market Dynamics

Successful organisations use their understanding of their markets and their own positions within those markets to adapt their operations in line with changes as they occur.

| Key characteristics | | Product differentiation | Service differentiation | "Commodity" |
|---|---|---|---|---|
| Marketing message | Unique | Competitive | Brand values | Corporate |
| Sales | Explain | Relative benefits distribution support | Relationship-based | Availability-based |
| Distribution | Direct selling | Exclusive distribution | Mass distribution | 80:20 |
| Price | Very high | High | Medium | Low (Consumer Controlled) |
| Competitive intensity | None | Few | Many | Many |
| Costs | Very high | Medium | Medium/Low | Medium/Low |
| Profit | Medium/High | High | Medium/High | Medium/High cost |
| Management style | Visionary | Strategic | Operational | Cost management |

**Figure 50.7** The dynamics of product/market life-cycle

Some changes will result from the marketing activities of the firms themselves; others will be beyond their control being a consequence of predictable but inexorable trends or unforeseeable events. The combination of these factors creates the dynamics of a product-based market as it evolves from birth through growth and maturity to its eventual decline.

World-class businesses manage their way through this life-cycle so that they are in the best competitive position at each point in the evolutionary process. They build market share before maturity sets in; they try to ensure that they have a cost advantage when it does, and they recognise that different segments will have different life-cycles. Typical responses to the different dynamics of each life-cycle stage are illustrated in Figure 50.7.

### Adopt a Portfolio Management Approach

Successful companies recognise that they cannot be all things to all people and that they have greater or lesser strengths in serving each of their various markets. This recognition enables the development of a portfolio approach to determining appropriate objectives and the effective allocation of resources. The portfolio approach is most easily conceived as a matrix as illustrated in Figure 50.8.

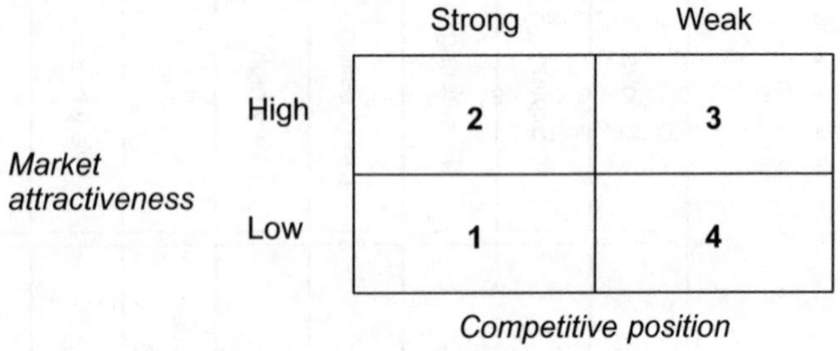

|  |  | Strong | Weak |
|---|---|:---:|:---:|
|  | High | 2 | 3 |
| *Market attractiveness* | Low | 1 | 4 |

*Competitive position*

Strategies for different boxes in the matrix:

- Box 1   Maintain and manage for sustained earnings
- Box 2   Invest and build for growth
- Box 3   Selectively invest
- Box 4   Manage for cash

**Figure 50.8**  Portfolio of products and markets

## Set Strategic Priorities

The previous six guidelines effectively comprise a marketing audit; the basis of a strategic marketing plan. World-class companies usually engage in some form of planning of this nature. However, the best also take great pains to avoid stifling creativity through excessively bureaucratic planning procedures. The strength of a good planning process is that it provides a sound and logical foundation for defining key target markets, sources of differential advantage and intended sources of revenue and profits.

This implies something more sophisticated than forecasts and budgets. Commercial history has demonstrated that any fool can spell out the financial results they wish to achieve. It takes intellect to spell out *how* they are to be achieved. This identification of what needs to be done to achieve logically derived objectives will then highlight the strategic imperatives for the business. Only when such priorities are clear can they be used to create key performance indicators and drive other business processes. The key contents of a good strategic marketing plan are listed in Figure 50.9.

*A good planning process identifies* **how** *objectives are to be achieved*

---

A written strategic marketing plan for 3 years usually contains:

- A mission statement
- A financial summary
- A market overview
- SWOT analyses on key segments
- A portfolio summary
- Assumptions
- Marketing objectives and strategies
- A budget

This strategic plan can then be converted into a detailed one-year plan.

---

**Figure 50.9** Contents of a strategic marketing plan

## Be Professional

Professional management skills, particularly in marketing, are the hallmark of commercial success. Leadership

*To be 'future robust' requires marketing professionalism*

and entrepreneurial skills, combined with hard-edged marketing skills, will see any company beyond the new millennium. Leading companies maintain a corporate optimism because they believe that what they are doing and what they have to offer is worthwhile.

They recognise, however, that the increasingly hostile and dynamic environments within which they work demands professionalism at a number of different levels. It requires the courage to question strategic priorities that do not appear to have been adequately defined or refined. It requires conventional wisdom to be challenged if it appears to be no longer relevant. It requires the discipline to follow the logical processes of strategic analysis and planning rather than jumping at the first good idea that comes along. But at its base, it also requires professional marketing skills and formal training in the underlying concepts, tools and techniques of marketing as management discipline. The core of this curriculum is outlined in Figure 50.10.

- Market research
- Gap analysis
- Market segmentation/positioning
- Product life cycle analysis
- Portfolio management
- The Four Ps
  - Product management
  - Pricing
  - Place (customer service, channel management)
  - Promotion (selling, sales force management, advertising, sales promotion)

**Figure 50.10**   Core professional curriculum

# Index